FIVE
SLAVE NARRATIVES

Selected from
THE AMERICAN NEGRO: HIS HISTORY AND LITERATURE
William Loren Katz
GENERAL EDITOR

FIVE
SLAVE NARRATIVES

Selected and edited by
William Loren Katz

ARNO PRESS and THE NEW YORK TIMES
NEW YORK 1969

SOUTHERN VIEWS
OF THE "PECULIAR INSTITUTION":
A Study in Black and White

> *The slaves are all well fed, well clad, have plenty of fuel, and are happy. They have no dread of the future—no fear of want. [The slaveholder] is the least selfish of men. . . . The institution of slavery gives full development and full play to the affections.*
>
> George Fitzhugh, Virginia planter, 1850[1]

> *So galling was our bondage, that to escape from it, we suffered the loss of all things, and braved every peril, and endured every hardship. Some of us left parents, some wives, some children. Some of us were wounded with guns and dogs, as we fled. Some of us secreted ourselves in the suffocating holds of ships. Nothing was so dreadful to us as slavery. . . .*
>
> New York Convention of fugitive slaves, 1850[2]

HISTORY HAS USUALLY CONSISTED OF TALES told by the victors. Dictated by conscience, and thus often displaying more self-justification than truth, for the original losers it has usually

iii

amounted to insult being heaped upon injury. Those who have been the victims of oppression have suffered again when their story is told by their oppressors. Perhaps the cruelest joke has been that the victims have been accused of lacking the detachment of those who have merely profited from their misery. This has long been the approach of historians to American Negro slavery.

Although the slave system in the United States has been studied as thoroughly as any institution of modern times, until recently few scholars have examined the testimony of its black victims. Presumably they were considered too unobservant, too subjective, and their views too poorly expressed to be of much value to the historian or sociologist. For the longest time the intellectual arbiters of the slave system were those who profited from it, their friends and relatives. The picture they painted was surrounded by nostalgia and based securely on myth: Negro slaves, brought from a savage land, achieved educational, religious and cultural advantages from their enslavement; therefore they cooperated with and remained loyal to their "white folks" and so found the slave experience suited to their mental capacities, limited skills and goals in life. The Southern white man's observations of life and truth have always been colored by this myth.

BLACK AND WHITE

Slavery afforded scant protection for the defenseless.

Thus the early accounts of Negro slavery sought to demonstrate the value of the institution to Negro and white, Northerner and Southerner. Senator John C. Calhoun maintained that slavery made Africans "so civilized and so improved, not only physically, but morally and intellectually."[3] Virginia planter and slavery apologist George Fitzhugh found that Negroes "love their master and his family, and the attachment is reciprocated. . . . Southern slavery has become a benign and protective institution, and our negroes are confessedly better off than any free laboring population in the world."[4] Inevitably, those who so arrogantly spoke for those they exploited soon recommended that Northern factory owners enslave their employees.

The pro-slavery argument rested on the basic assumption of Negro inferiority and to support this conclusion history was rewritten and science distorted. Dr. Samuel Cartwright of the University of Louisiana was one of many Southern medical men who discovered biological reasons for slavery's value to both master and slave. Negroes, noted Dr. Cartwright, "consume less oxygen than the white" and this fact "thus makes it a mercy and a blessing to negroes to have persons in authority set over them, to provide and take care of them." Among the eminent doctor's other con-

A PRIME AND ORDERLY GANG OF

68 Long Cotton Field Negroes,

Belonging to the Estate of the late Christopher J. Whaley.

WILBUR & SON

Will sell at PUBLIC AUCTION in Charleston,

At the Mart in Chalmers Street,

On Thursday, Feb. 2d, 1860,

COMMENCING AT ELEVEN O'CLOCK,

THE FOLLOWING GANG OF LONG COTTON NEGROES,

Who are said to be remarkably prime, and will be sold as per Catalogue.

NAMES.		AGES.	NAMES.		AGES.
Jimmy,	driver,	30	Carter,		36
Flora,	seamstress,	24	Taffy,		13
James,		5	Rachel, ($ 720,)		8
Charles, ($ 125,)		1	Jannett,		18
August,		52	Phebe, ($ 860,)		40
Mathias, ($ 1,220,)		18	Judy,		8
Sandy,		16	Major,		40
John,		13	Lavinia,		30
Tom,		70	Billy, ($ 550,)		10
Jack,		38	Tamor,		6
James,		6	Jimmy,		52
Leah,		5	Kate,		46
Flora,		2	Susan,		25
Andrew,		42	Thomas, ($ 380,)		6
Binah,		40	Kate,		1
Phillis,		20	Edward,	coachman,	49
Mary,		15	Amey,		22
Lymus,		10	Teneb,	washer,	30
Abram, ($ 275,)		2	Josephine,		9
Binah, ·		2 mos.	Sam,		11
Andrew,		29	Isaac,		5
Hagar,		25	William,		1
Dayman,		4	Amey,		27
Cuffy,		21	Louisa, ($ 750,)		8
Hagar, ($ 1,320,)		20	Joe,		3
Margaret,		85	Sam,	ruptured,	65
Lucy,	cripple,	60	Andrew,	dropsical,	61
John,		22	Daniel,		70
Ellick, ($ 1,160,)		18	Lymus,		30
Libby,		19	Lucy,	nurse,	58

TERMS.

One-third Cash; balance in one and two years, secured by bond, and mortgage of the negroes, with approved personal security. Purchasers to pay us for papers.

29

Announcement of slave sale in Charleston, in 1860.

clusions, widely-circulated and respected in the antebellum South, were the following:

> To expect to civilize or Christianize the negro without the intervention of slavery is to expect an impossibility.

* * *

> The plantation laws . . . are gradually and silently converting the African barbarian into a moral, rational and civilized being.

* * *

> The African will starve rather than engage in a regular system of agricultural labor, unless impelled by the stronger will of the white man.

* * *

> They [Negroes] are dishonest when in the abnormal condition without a master.

* * *

> . . . the obedience of the Nigritian to the Caucasian is *spontaneous* because it is normal for the weaker to yield obedience to the stronger.[5]

Dr. Cartwright further argued that since the Negro's natural condition was slavery, he never raised any opposition to this condition.

*Frederick Douglass is flogged by "slave-breaker"
Edward Covey.*

All forms of Negro resistance to bondage were classified as "Negro diseases." Thus, Dr. Cartwright found that Negroes who fled their masters suffered from "Draptomania, or the Disease Causing Negroes to Run Away;" those who sabotaged tools and crops or pitted masters against overseers suffered from "Dysthesia Aethiopica, or Herbitude of the Mind and Obtuse Sensibility of Body;"[6] when slaves carried out rebellions, such as the successful one in Haiti in the 1790's, Dr. Cartwright simply maintained:

> There never has been an insurrection of the prognathous [Negro] race against their masters; and from the nature of the ethnical elements of that race, there never can be. Hayti was no exception . . . when the true history of the so-called insurrection of that island is written.[7]

Out of such facts and documentation the theories of Negro inferiority and white racism were spun. Basic to the class of men who kept others in bondage, they were taught to white and black alike, and broadcast from pulpit, press, school room, lecture hall, and even the floor of Congress. They were the *sine qua non* of Southern society, "must" knowledge for the rest of the white community who assisted in

*A fugitive slave is seized in the North and re-
turned to bondage in the South.*

the enslavement of the Negro. Wrote ex-slave Frederick Douglass:

> The slaveholders are the South. . . . They are the only active power there. They rule the States entirely and tolerate no policy which in the least degree endangers their power. . . . The six millions of free non-slaveholding whites are but freight cars, full of cattle, attached to the three hundred and fifty thousand slaveholding locomotives. Where the locomotives go, the train must follow.[8]

The acceptance of racism had its impact on both Southern law and custom. Judge Ruffin of North Carolina ruled in an 1829 case: "The power of the master must be absolute to render the submission of the slave perfect. . . . The slave, to remain a slave, must be made sensible that there is no appeal from his master."[9] Non-slaveholding whites, forced to serve in the nightly slave patrols for six cents an hour, took out their fury on slaves caught without passes from their masters. Men such as John Long of Lexington, Missouri proudly advertised his special service for slave owners: "I would respectfully inform the citizens of Missouri that I still have my Nigger Dogs, and that they are in prime training, and ready to attend to all calls of Hunting and Catching runaway Niggers, at the following rates. . . ."[10] After the

Denmark Vesey slave plot of 1822 a Charleston pamphleteer emphasized that "The celebration of the Fourth of July belongs *exclusively* to the white population of the United States." He added:

It therefore seems to me improper to allow these people to be present on these occasions. In our speeches and orations, much, and sometimes more than is politically necessary, is said about personal liberty, which negro auditors know not how to apply, except by running the parallel with their own condition. They therefore imbibe false notions, and give reality in their minds to what has no real existence. The peculiar state of our community must be steadily kept in view.[11]

Individual slaveholders, of course, held widely divergent views of slavery's rationale. Untold numbers were deeply troubled by the moral questions raised by the sale and ownership of men, women and children. Patrick Henry was impaled on this dilemma:

Every thinking honest man rejects slavery in Speculation, how few in practice? Would anyone believe that I am Master of slaves of my own purchase? I am drawn along by the general inconvenience of living without them; I will not, I cannot justify it.[12]

Other American patriots and slaveholders, including George Washington, Thomas Jefferson and George Mason, father of the Bill of Rights, sought to appease their consciences by advocating a number of proposals other than outright abolition. Many slaveholders joined the American Colonization Society that linked manumission of slaves to their removal from America, an idea as impractical as it was grandiose.[13]

Those who ruled the lives of black men and women, whether convinced racists or not, became enmeshed in duplicity and contradictions when they discussed their slaves. British reporter William Howard Russell observed this Southern phenomenon when he toured a Louisiana plantation:

> The first place I visited with the overseer was a new sugar-house, which negro carpenters and masons were engaged in erecting. It would have been amusing had not the subject been so grave, to hear the overseer's praises of the intelligence and skill of these workmen, and his boast that they did all the work, of skilled labourers on the estate, and then listen to him, in a few minutes . . . on the utter helplessness and ignorance of the black race, their incapacity to do any good, or even to take care of themselves.

Later Russell generalized on his Southern tour in these words:

> I have seen, within the short time I have been in this part of the world, several dreadful accounts of murder and violence, in which masters suffered at the hands of their slaves. There is something suspicious in the constant never-ending statement that "we are not afraid of our slaves." The curfew and the night-patrol in the streets, the prisons and watch-houses, and the police regulations, prove that strict supervision, at all times, is needed and necessary.[14]

Both slaveholders and those who followed in their footsteps have endeavored to classify Negro resistance as crime, placing sabotage, rebellion and flight on a level with rape and murder.

Most slaveholders maintained that they "understood" their slaves and were expert at interpreting their behavior. One of the most consistent forms of slave resistance was the slow-down, accomplished through pretended sickness, infirmity, old age or mental disorder. During the Civil War Frederick A. Eustis returned to his plantation on the Sea Islands and hired his former slaves as free laborers. He found how distant had been the minds of masters and slaves. He told a Congressional committee:

> I never knew, during forty years of plantation life, so little sickness. Formerly, every man had a fever of some kind, and now the veriest old cripple, who did nothing under secesh rule, will row a boat three nights in succession to Edisto [island], or will pick up the corn about the corn house. There are twenty people whom I know who were considered worn out and too old to work under the slave system, who are now working cotton, as well as their two acres of provisions; and their crops look very well. I have an old woman who has taken six tasks (that is, an acre and a half), and last year [as a slave] she would do nothing.[15]

A most daring type of slave resistance—mass nonviolent resistance—took place during the Union capture of these Sea Islands and was described by Union General Rufus Saxton:

> They tried to take their negroes with them, but they would not go. They shot down their negroes in many instances because they would not go with them. They tied them behind their wagons, and tried to drag them off; but the negroes would not go. The great majority of negroes [eighty per cent] remained behind, and came into our lines.[16]

To protect themselves from the meaning of slave resistance, masters clamped a lid of secrecy on its existence. Reported a Charleston lady by private letter to a friend in 1822:

Last evening twenty-five hundred of our citizens were under arms to guard our property and lives. But it is a subject not to be mentioned; and unless you hear of it elsewhere, say nothing about it.[17]

Those Southerners who opposed slavery, particularly after the cotton gin made it so profitable, were forced into silence or exile. "I'll tell you why abolition is impossible," shouted a Carolina planter, "because every healthy negro can fetch a thousand dollars in the Charleston market at this moment." Thomas Jefferson began to confine his anti-slavery remarks to his private letters. Armed Viligance Committees terrorized those who favored abolition and in Texas and Mississippi put "suspects" to death. A Columbia, South Carolina editor told his readers "Let us declare, through the public journals of our country, that the question of slavery is not and shall not be open to discussion—that the very moment any private individual attempts to lecture us upon its evils and immorality, in the same moment his tongue shall be cut out

and cast upon the dunghill."[18] White Southerners who wished to examine slavery with any
degree of objectivity knew they were not welcome in their community. Hinton Helper, the
North Carolina poor white who thoroughly
documented his charge that slavery was in-
jurious to the entire South, had to publish his
best-seller, *The Impending Crisis*, after he
moved to the North. His book was proscribed
in the South.[19]

Frederick Law Olmstead, the Northern
traveller who was the most perceptive white
observer of the South's "peculiar institution,"
bemoaned the lack of reliable information
about the region:

> Of the masses of the South, black and white,
> it is more difficult for one to obtain informa-
> tion than of those of any country in Europe.
> I saw much more of what I had not antici-
> pated and less of what I had, in the Slave
> States, than with a somewhat extended trav-
> eling experience in any other country I ever
> visited.[20]

The "slave narrative," which first made its
appearance in 1705, was the Negro's answer
to his master's moonlight and magnolias por-
trait of slavery.[21] It was a dramatic, sometimes
starkly horrifying, and hard-hitting eyewitness

account of human bondage from the vantage point of one of its victims.

Many of these narratives were wholly written by white abolitionists who failed to preserve the flavor or the integrity of the black narrators; these read more like the evangelistic New England recorders than the Southern black men and women whose stories they were. Others were dictated to abolitionists who, while making literary, moral or sentimental additions, faithfully organized them into readable English. A large but undetermined number were written by the ex-slaves themselves with only a minimum of aid from outsiders. Readers have found little difficulty in separating the insights of the black narrator from the elaborations of the ghost-writer, editor or recorder.[22]

The hundreds of slave narratives produced during the Civil War era were designed to furnish the abolitionist forces with important intellectual weaponry for the assault on slavery. Both black authors and white ghost-writers were well aware that fraudulent claims and exaggerations would damage their cause and thus these autobiographies may often represent understatement.[23]

For many years the "slave narratives" were an important part of Americana and were highly popular reading in their own day. Most appeared in twenty-five cent editions and were hawked at anti-slavery meetings, often by the author and his friends. The narrators used their profits to buy the freedom of loved ones still in bondage or to begin a new life in the North or Canada. If there was any exploitation involved in the production and sale of these autobiographies, it benefited both black ex-slave authors and a reading public that was increasingly made aware of Southern slavery's inherent evils.

These popular eyewitness accounts of plantation life did include errors of fact, lapses of memory and judgment, and some fiction. But they projected deeply human sketches of Southern life as seen from its lowest social level. As might be expected from volumes written for propoganda value, they contain much that is morbid and shocking about the slave system; there is an understandable anger and bitterness toward many masters and overseers, but these narratives are surprisingly free of gross exaggeration, anti-white animosity or any desire for black vengeance. Almost always the enemy is the same—the slave system that imprisons both black and white.

These narratives provide much important information about the day-to-day workings of the "peculiar institution," its psychological and economic complexities, and the ever-so-human responses of its black victims. While they do not always make pleasant reading, they are necessary to an understanding of our common history. Though depicting an institution rooted in a by-gone era, they described patterns of thought and behavior that have a frightening relevance today.

The five narratives presented in this volume constitute a broad view of American Negro slavery. The narrators range from the famous Negro intellectual, William Wells Brown, to the unknown Moses Grandy; locales from the Maryland shore to the hills of Kentucky and south to Columbia, South Carolina; from the stories of blacksmiths and field hands to those of jockeys and small entrepreneurs; from slaves who fled to freedom to those who purchased their liberty or had it bestowed by Federal bayonets during the Civil War. Each has elements of typicality and atypicality, stories of good and bad whites, scenes of horror, humor and pathos.

Three were written by the men themselves shortly after their liberation during the slave era. Moses Grandy dictated his story to British abolitionist George Thompson, who preserved

Grandy's direct, factual style; Reverend Jacob Stroyer wrote his narrative many years after his emancipation.

The later history of each of these men, so far as it is known, is an instructive commentary on the slave system and its aftermath. Lunsford Lane was one of those rare products of the system who was able to utilize his inventive abilities to raise enough money to purchase the liberty of his large family—only to arouse the murderous wrath of poor whites. James W. C. Pennington escaped from bondage to become the first American Negro to graduate from a European university. After Heidelberg conferred a Doctor of Divinity Degee on Reverend Pennington, he returned to Brooklyn, New York where he led his congregation in some of our earliest nonviolent civil rights demonstrations; he also wrote the first textbook history of the Negro.[24] William Wells Brown escaped from bondage to become America's first black novelist (1853) and playwright (1858). A prolific writer and an indefatigable speaker, he lectured here and abroad for a wide range of reforms (antislavery, women's rights, world peace) and produced a number of travel, history and autobiographical books.[25] Reverend Jacob Stroyer later became a minister of a Salem, Massachusetts, Negro church. Moses Grandy, born in Camden County, North Carolina in the year that George Washington was elected President, has left no history other than his poignant narrative.

Each of these men lived under the oppressive slave system and lived to tell their tales in clear, readable prose. Their hatred of slavery grew out of their humanity; their stories represent a significant part of Americana that has too long been neglected as both history and literature.

William Loren Katz

NOTES

[1] George Fitzhugh, *Slavery Justified, By A Southerner* (Fredericksburg, 1850).

[2] "Letter to the American Slaves," *Anti-Slavery Bugle*, September 28, 1850, reprinted in *Common Ground*, VII (Spring, 1947) 22.

[3] *Congressional Globe,* 24th Congress, Second Session, P. 158.

[4] George Fitzhugh, *Cannibals All!* (Richmond, 1857) P. 200.

[5] E. N. Elliott, *Cotton is King, and Pro-Slavery Arguments* (Savannah, 1860) S. A. Cartwright, "Slavery in the Light of Ethnology," pp. 713–726.

[6] Dr. Cartwright of New Orleans, "1. Diseases and Peculiarities of the Negro Race," *De Bow's Review*, XII (September, 1851) 331–334.

[7] S. A. Cartwright, "Slavery in the Light of Ethnology," *Op. Cit.*

[8] *Frederick Douglass' Monthly*, April, 1861.

[9] William Goodell, *The American Slave Code* (New York, 1853) pp. 172–173. Similar decisions for Alabama, Virginia and Louisiana appear on pages 92–93 and 322–323.

[10] George W. Carlton (ed.), *The Suppressed Book About Slavery!* (New York, 1864) pp. 326–327. Another document, on pages 193–195, is the explanation of John Capehart, a slave-beater.

[11] Thomas Wentworth Higginson, "Denmark Vesey," *Atlantic Monthly* (June, 1861) 743.

[12] Lydia Maria Child, *The Evils of Slavery, and the Cure of Slavery* (Newburyport, 1836) P. 3.

[13] Dwight Lowell Dumond, *Antislavery: The Crusade for Freedom in America* (Ann Arbor, 1961) pp. 126–132 *et passim*; William Loren Katz, *Eyewitness: The Negro in American History* (New

York, 1967) pp. 145–147 depicts early interest in African colonization by significant Negro leadership and the total rejection of it by the Negro masses.

[14] William Howard Russell, *My Diary North and South* (New York, 1863) pp. 55, 105.

[15] Preliminary Report of the Freedmen's Inquiry Commission," June 30, 1863, *Official Records of the Union and Confederate Armies*, Series 3, III, P. 435.

[16] *Report of the Joint Committee on the Conduct of the War*, 37th Congress, Third Session (No. 108, Washington, D.C., 1863) P. 327.

[17] Harvey Wish, "American Slave Insurrections Before 1861," *Journal of Negro History* XXI (July, 1939) 239.

[18] Columbia (S. C.) *Telescope* cited in Ralph Korngold, *Two Friends of Man* (Boston, 1950) P. 90.

[19] Hinton Rowan Helper, *The Impending Crisis of the South* (New York, 1857) used statistics and documents to establish that slavery had ruined the Southern white as well as the Negro.

[20] Frederick Law Olmstead, *A Journey in the Seaboard Slave States* (New York, 1856) pp. 178–179; he was also convinced that the slave narratives had heavily influenced Northern opinion about slavery without shedding much light on the "peculiar institution."

[21] Charles H. Nichols, *Many Thousand Gone* (Leiden, Netherlands, 1963) P. xi.

[22] *Ibid.*, pp. xi-xiv; Sterling A. Brown, Arthur P. Davis, Ulysses Lee (Eds.) *The Negro Caravan* (New York, 1941) pp. 694–697. The Nichols volume and the editors of *The Negro Caravan* offer three categories similar to these.

[23] *Ibid.*

[24] *New-York Daily Tribune*, May 8, December 18, 19, 1855.

[25] Charles H. Nichols, *Op. Cit.*, pp. xii-xiii; Vernon Loggins, *The Negro Author* (New York, 1959) *passim*.

THE NARRATIVES

Romanticized abolitionist picture of slave run-aways reaching safety in Canada.

NARRATIVE

OF

LUNSFORD LANE.

The Slave Mother's Address

TO HER

INFANT CHILD.

I CANNOT tell how much I love
  To look on thee, my child ;
Nor how that looking rocks my soul
  As on a tempest wild ;
For I have borne thee to the world,
  And bid thee breathe its air,
But soon to see around thee drawn
  The curtains of despair.

Now thou art happy, child, I know,
  As little babe can be ;
Thou dost not fancy in thy dreams
  But thou art all as free
As birds upon the mountain winds,
  (If thou hast thought of bird,)
Or anything thou thinkest of,
  Or thy young ear has heard.

What are thy little thoughts about ?
  I cannot certain know,
Only there 's not a wing of them
  Upon a breath of woe,
For not a shadow 's on thy face,
  Nor billow heaves thy breast,—
All clear as any summer's lake
  With not a zephyr press'd.

But thou art born a slave, my child;
   Those little hands must toil,
That brow must sweat, that bosom ache
   Upon another's soil;
And if perchance some tender joy
   Should bloom upon thy heart,
Another's hand may enter there,
   And tear it soon apart.

Thou art a little joy to me,
   But soon thou may'st be sold,
Oh! lovelier to thy mother far
   Than any weight of gold;
Or I may see thee scourg'd and driv'n
   Hard on the cotton-field,
To fill a cruel master's store,
   With what thy blood may yield.

Should some fair maiden win thy heart,
   And thou should'st call her thine;
Should little ones around thee stand,
   Or round thy bosom twine,
Thou wilt not know how soon away
   These loves may all be riv'n,
Nor what a darkened troop of woe
   Through thy lone breast be driv'n.

Thy master may be kind, and give
   Thy every wish to thee,
Only deny that greatest wish,
   That longing to be free:
Still it will seem a comfort small
   That thou hast sweeter bread,
A better hut than other slaves,
   Or pillow for thy head.

What joys soe'er may gather round,
  What other comforts flow,—
That, like a mountain in the sea,
  O'ertops each wave below,
That ever-upward, firm desire
  To break the chains, and be
Free as the ocean is, or like
  The ocean-winds, be free.

Oh, child! thou art a little slave :
  And all of thee that grows,
Will be another's weight of flesh,—
  But thine the weight of woes
Thou art a little slave, my child,
  And much I grieve and mourn
That to so dark a destiny
  A lovely babe I've borne.

And gladly would I lay thee down
  To sleep beneath the sod,
And give thy gentle spirit back,
  Unmarr'd with grief, to God :
The tears I shed upon that turf
  Should whisper peace to me,
And tell me in the spirit land
  My lovely babe was free.

I then should know thy peace was sure,
  And only long to go
The road which thou had'st gone, and wipe
  Away these tears that flow.
Death to the slave has double power ;
  It breaks the earthly clod,
And breaks the tyrant's sway, that he
  May worship only God.   J. P. B.

TO THE READER.

I HAVE been solicited by very many friends, to give my narrative to the public. Whatever my own judgment might be, I should yield to theirs. In compliance, therefore, with this general request, and in the hope that these pages may produce an impression favorable to my countrymen in bondage ; also that I may realize something from the sale of my work towards the support of a numerous family, I have committed this publication to press. It might have been made two or three, or even six times larger, without diminishing from the interest of any one of its pages—*indeed with an increased interest*—but the want of the pecuniary means, and other considerations, have induced me to present it as here seen. Should another edition be called for, and should my friends advise, the work will then be extended to a greater length.

I have not, in this publication attempted or desired to argue anything. It is only a simple narration of such facts connected with my own case, as I thought would be most interesting and instructive to readers generally. The facts will, I think, cast some light upon the policy of a slaveholding community, and the effect on the minds of the more enlightened, the more humane, and the *Christian* portion of the southern people, of holding and trading in the bodies and souls of men.

I have said in the following pages, that my condition as a slave was comparatively a happy, indeed a highly favored one ; and to this circumstance is it owing that I have been able to come up from bondage and relate the story to the public ; and that my wife, my mother, and my seven children, are here with me this day. If for any thing this side the invisible world, I bless heaven, it is that I was not born a plantation slave, nor even a house servant under what is termed a hard and cruel master.

It has not been any part of my object to describe slavery generally, and in the narration of my own case I have dwelt as little as possible upon the dark side—have spoken mostly of the bright. In whatever I have been obliged to say unfavorable to others, I have endeavored not to overstate, but have chosen rather to come short of giving the full picture—omitting much which it did not seem important to my object to relate. And yet I would not venture to say that this publication does not contain a single period which might be twisted to convey an idea more than should be expressed.

Those of whom I have had occasion to speak, are regarded, where they are known, as among the most kind men to their slaves. Mr. Smith, some of whose conduct will doubtless seem strange to the reader, is sometimes taunted with being an abolitionist, in consequence of the interest he manifests towards the colored people. If to any his character appear like a riddle, they should remember that men, like other things, have "two sides," and often a top and a bottom in addition.

While in the South I succeeded by stealth in learning to read and write a little, and since I have been in the North I have learned more. But I need not say that I have been obliged to employ the services of a friend, in bringing this Narrative into shape for the public eye. And it should perhaps be said on the part of the writer, that it has been hastily compiled, with little regard to style, only to express the ideas accurately and in a manner to be understood.

LUNSFORD LANE.

Boston, July 4, 1842.

NARRATIVE.

The small city of Raleigh, North Carolina, it is known, is the capital of the State,
situated in the interior, and containing about
thirty six hundred inhabitants.* Here lived Mr. Sherwood Haywood, a man of considerable respectability, a planter, and the
cashier of a bank. He owned three plantations, at the distances respectively of
seventy-five, thirty, and three miles from
his residence in Raleigh. He owned in all
about two hundred and fifty slaves, among
the rest my mother, who was a house servant to her master, and of course a resident
in the city. My father was a slave to a
near neighbor. The apartment where I
was born and where I spent my childhood
and youth was called " the kitchen," situated
some fifteen or twenty rods from the " great
house." Here the house servants lodged and
lived, and here the meals were prepared for
the people in the mansion.

On the 30th of May, 1803, I was ushered
into the world; but I did not begin to see
the rising of its dark clouds, nor fancy how
they might be broken and dispersed, until

* 175 whites—207 free people of color—and 2,244
slaves. Total 3,626 ; according to the census of 1840.

some time afterwards. My infancy was
spent upon the floor, in a rough cradle, or
sometimes in my mother's arms. My early
boyhood in playing with the other boys and
girls, colored and white, in the yard, and
occasionally doing such little matters of
labor as one of so young years could. I
knew no difference between myself and the
white children ; nor did they seem to know
any in turn. Sometimes my master would
come out and give a biscuit to me, and
another to one of his own white boys; but
I did not perceive the difference between us.
I had no brothers or sisters, but there were
other colored families living in the same
kitchen, and the children playing in the
same yard, with me and my mother.

When I was ten or eleven years old, my
master set me regularly to cutting wood, in
the yard in the winter, and working in the
garden in the summer. And when I was
fifteen years of age, he gave me the care of
the pleasure horses, and made me his carriage driver; but this did not exempt me
from other labor, especially in the summer.
Early in the morning I used to take his three
horses to the plantation, and turn them into
the pasture to graze, and myself into the
cotton or cornfield, with a hoe in my hand,
to work through the day ; and after sunset
I would take these horses back to the city, a
distance of three miles, feed them, and then
attend to any other business my master or

any of his family had for me to do, until
bed time, when with my blanket in my
hand, I would go into the dining room to
rest through the night. The next day the
same round of labor would be repeated, unless some of the family wished to ride out,
in which case I must be on hand with the
horses to wait upon them, and in the meantime work about the yard. On Sunday I
had to drive to Church twice, which with
other things necessary to be done, took the
whole day. So my life went wearily on
from day to day, from night to night, and
from week to week.

When I began to work, I discovered the
difference between myself and my master's
white children. They began to order me
about, and were told to do so by my master
and mistress. I found, too, that they had
learned to read, while I was not permitted
to have a book in my hand. To be in the
possession of anything written or printed,
was regarded as an offence. And then there
was the fear that I might be sold away from
those who were dear to me, and conveyed
to the far South. I had learned that being
a slave I was subject to this worst (to us) of
all calamities; and I knew of others in similar situations to myself, thus sold away.
My friends were not numerous; but in pro-
portion as they were few they were dear;
and the thought that I might be separated
from them forever, was like that of having

the heart wrenched from its socket; while
the idea of being conveyed to the far South,
seemed infinitely worse than the terrors of
death. To know, also, that I was never to
consult my own will, but was, while I lived,
to be entirely under the control of another,
was another state of mind hard for me to
bear. Indeed all things now made me *feel*,
what I had before known only in words,
that *I was a slave*. Deep was this feeling,
and it preyed upon my heart like a never-
dying worm. I saw no prospect that my
condition would ever be changed. Yet I
used to plan in my mind from day to day,
and from night to night, how I might be
free.

One day, while I was in this state of
mind, my father gave me a small basket of
peaches. I sold them for thirty cents, which
was the first money I ever had in my life.
Afterwards I won some marbles, and sold
them for sixty cents, and some weeks after
Mr. Hog from Fayetteville, came to visit my
master, and on leaving gave me one dollar.
After that Mr. Bennahan from Orange
county gave me a dollar, and a son of my
master fifty cents. These sums, and the
hope that then entered my mind of purchasing at some future time my freedom, made
me long for money; and plans for money-
making took the principal possesssion of my
thoughts. At night I would steal away
with my axe, get a load of wood to cut for

twenty-five cents, and the next morning
hardly escape a whipping for the offence.
But I persevered until I had obtained twenty
dollars. Now I began to think seriously of
becoming able to buy myself; and cheered
by this hope, I went on from one thing to
another, laboring " at dead of night," after
the long weary day's toil for my master was
over, till I found I had collected one hundred
dollars. This sum I kept hid, first in one
place and then in another, as I dare not put
it out, for fear I should lose it.

After this I lit upon a plan which proved
of great advantage to me. My father sug-
gested a mode of preparing smoking tobacco,
different from any then or since employed.
It had the double advantage of giving the
tobacco a peculiarly pleasant flavor, and of
enabling me to manufacture a good article
out of a very indifferent material. I improved somewhat upon his suggestion, and
commenced the manufacture, doing as I have
before said, all my work in the night. The
tobacco I put up in papers of about a quarter of a pound each, and sold them at fifteen
cents. But the tobacco could not be smoked
without a pipe, and as I had given the
former a flavor peculiarly grateful, it occurred to me that I might so construct a pipe as
to cool the smoke in passing through it, and
thus meet the wishes of those who are more
fond of smoke than heat. This I effected by
means of a reed, which grows plentifully in

2 *

that region; I made a passage through the
reed with a hot wire, polished it, and attached a clay pipe to the end, so that the
smoke should be cooled in flowing through
the stem like whiskey or rum in passing
from the boiler through the worm of the
still.   These pipes I sold at ten cents apiece.
In the early part of the night I would sell
my tobacco and pipes, and manufacture
them in the latter part.   As the Legislature
sit in Raleigh every year, I sold these articles considerably to the members, so that I
became known not only in the city, but in
many parts of the State, as a *tobacconist*.

Perceiving that I was getting along so
well, I began, slave as I was, to think about
taking a wife.   So I fixed my mind upon
Miss Lucy Williams, a slave of Thomas
Devereaux, Esq., an eminent lawyer in the
place; but failed in my undertaking.   Then
I thought I never would marry; but at the
end of two or three years my resolution began to slide away, till finding I could not
keep it longer I set out once more in pursuit
of a wife.   So I fell in with her to whom I
am now united, Miss MARTHA CURTIS, and
the bargain between *us* was completed.   I
next went to her master, Mr. Boylan, and
asked him, according to the custom, if I
might " marry his woman."   His reply was,
" Yes, if you will behave yourself."   I told
him I would.   " And make her behave herself?"   To this I also assented; and then

proceeded to ask the approbation of my master, which was granted. So in May, 1828, I was bound as fast in wedlock as a slave can be. God may at any time sunder that band in a freeman; either master may do the same at pleasure in a slave. The bond is not recognized in law. But in my case it has never been broken; and now it cannot be, except by a higher power.

When we had been married nine months and one day, we were blessed with a son, and two years afterwards with a daughter. My wife also passed from the hands of Mr. Boylan into those of Mr. BENJAMIN B. SMITH, a merchant, a member and class-leader in the Methodist church, and in much repute for his deep piety and devotion to religion. But grace (of course) had not wrought in the same *manner* upon the heart of Mr. Smith, as nature had done upon that of Mr. Boylan, who made no religious profession. This latter gentleman used to give my wife, who was a favorite slave, (her mother nursed every one of his own children,) sufficient food and clothing to render her comfortable, so that I had to spend for her but little, except to procure such small articles of extra comfort as I was prompted to from time to time. Indeed Mr. Boylan was regarded as a very kind master to all the slaves about him; that is, to his house servants; nor did he inflict much cruelty upon his field hands, except by proxy. The overseer on his nearest plantation (I know but little about the rest) was a very cruel man ; in one instance, as it was said among the slaves, he whipped a man *to death ;* but of course denied that the man died in consequence of the whipping. Still it was the choice of my wife to pass into the hands of Mr. Smith, as she had become attached to him in consequence of belonging to the same church, and receiving his religious instruction and counsel as her class-leader, and in consequence of the peculiar devotedness to the cause of religion for which he was noted, and which he always seemed to manifest.— But when she became his slave, he withheld both from her and her children, the needful food and clothing, while he exacted from them to the uttermost all the labor they were able to perform. Almost every article of clothing worn either by my wife or children, especially every article of much value, I had to purchase ; while the food he furnished the family amounted to less than a meal a day, and that of the coarser kind. I have no remembrance that he ever gave us a blanket or any other article of bedding, although it is considered a rule at the South that the master shall furnish each of his slaves with one blanket a year. So that, both as to food and clothing, I had in fact to support both my wife and the children, while he claimed them as his property, and received all their labor. She was house ser-

vant to **Mr.** Smith, sometimes cooked the
food for his family, and usually took it from
the table, but her mistress was so particular
in giving it out to be cooked, or so watched
it, that she always knew whether it was all
returned ; and when the table was cleared
away, the stern old lady would sit by and
see that every dish (except the very little
she would send into the kitchen) was put
away, and then she would turn the key upon
it, so as to be sure her slaves should not die
of gluttony.   This practice is common with
some families in that region ; but with others
it is not.   It was not so in that of her less
pious master, Mr. Boylan, nor was it pre-
cisely so at my master's.   We used to have
corn bread enough, and some meat.   When
I was a boy, the pot-liquor, in which the
meat was boiled for the "great house," together with some little corn-meal balls that
had been thrown in just before the meat was
done, was poured into a tray and set in the
middle of the yard, and a clam shell or pew-
ter spoon given to each of us children, who
would fall upon the delicious fare as greedi-
ly as pigs.   It was not generally so much as
we wanted, consequently it was customary
for some of the white persons who saw us
from the piazza of the house where they
were sitting, to order the more stout and
greedy ones to eat slower, that those more
young and feeble might have a chance. But
it was not so with Mr. Smith : such luxu-

ries were more than he could afford, kind
and Christian man as he was considered to
be. So that by the expense of providing for
my wife and children, all the money I had
earned and could earn by my night labor
was consumed, till I found myself reduced
to five dollars, and this I lost one day in going to the plantation. My light of hope now
went out. My prop seemed to have given
way from under me. Sunk in the very
night of despair respecting my freedom, I
discovered myself, as though I had never
known it before, a husband, the father of
two children, a family looking up to me for
bread, and I a slave, penniless, and well
watched by my master, his wife and his
children, lest I should, perchance, catch the
friendly light of the stars to make something in order to supply the cravings of nature in those with whom my soul was bound
up; or lest some plan of freedom might lead
me to trim the light of diligence after the
day's labor was over, while the rest of the
world were enjoying the hours in pleasure or
sleep.

At this time an event occurred, which,
while it cast a cloud over the prospects of
some of my fellow slaves, was a rainbow
over mine. My master died, and his widow,
by the will, became sole executrix of his
property. To the surprize of all, the bank
of which he had been cashier presented a claim against the estate for forty thou-

sand dollars. By a compromise, this sum was reduced to twenty thousand dollars; and my mistress, to meet the amount, sold some of her slaves, and hired out others. I hired my time of her,* for which I paid her a price varying from one hundred dollars to one hundred and twenty dollars per year. This was a privilege which comparatively few slaves at the South enjoy; and in this I felt truly blessed.

I commenced the manufacture of pipes and tobacco on an enlarged scale. I opened a regular place of business, labelled my tobacco in a conspicuous manner with the names of "*Edward and Lunsford Lane*," and of some of the persons who sold it for me,—established agencies for the sale in various parts of the State, one at Fayetteville, one at Salisbury, one at Chapel Hill, and so on,—sold my articles from my place of business, and about town, also deposited them in stores on commission, and thus, after paying my mistress for my time, and rendering such support as necessary to my family,

---

* It is contrary to the laws of the State for a slave to have command of his own time in this way, but in Raleigh it is sometimes winked at. I knew one slave-man who was *doing well for himself*, taken up by the public authorities and hired out for the public good, three times in succession for this offence. The time of hiring in such a case is one year. The master is subject to a fine. But generally, as I have said, if the slave is *orderly* and appears to be *making nothing*, neither he nor the master is interfered with.

I found in the space of some six or eight years, that I had collected the sum of one thousand dollars. During this time I had found it politic to go shabbily dressed, and to appear to be very poor, but to pay my mistress for my services promptly. I kept my money hid, never venturing to put out a penny, nor to let any body but my wife know that I was making any. The thousand dollars was what I supposed my mistress would ask for me, and so I determined now what I would do.

I went to my mistress and inquired what was her price for me. She said a thousand dollars. I then told her that I wanted to be free, and asked her if she would sell me to be made free. She said she would; and accordingly I arranged with her, and with the master of my wife, Mr. Smith, already spoken of, for the latter to take my money * and buy of her my freedom, as I could not legally purchase it, and as the laws forbid emancipation except for "meritorious services." This done, Mr. Smith endeavored to emancipate me formally, and to get my manumission recorded; I tried also; but the court judged that I had done nothing "meri-

---

* _Legally_, my money belonged to my mistress; and she could have taken it and refused to grant me my freedom. But she was a very kind woman for a slave owner; and she would under the circumstances, scorn to do such a thing. I have known of slaves, however, served in this way.

torious," and so I remained, nominally only,
the slave of Mr. Smith for a year; when,
feeling unsafe in that relation, I accompanied him to New York whither he was
going to purchase goods, and was there regularly and formally made a freeman, and
there my manumission was recorded. I returned to my family in Raleigh and endeavored to do by them as a freeman should. I
had known what it was to be a slave, and I
knew what it was to be free.

But I am going too rapidly over my story.
When the money was paid to my mistress
and the conveyance fairly made to Mr.
Smith, I felt that I was free. And a queer
and a joyous feeling it is to one who has
been a slave. I cannot describe it, only it
seemed as though I was in heaven. I used
to lie awake whole nights thinking of it.
And oh, the strange thoughts that passed
through my soul, like so many rivers of
light; deep and rich were their waves as
they rolled;—these were more to me than
sleep, more than soft slumber after long
months of watching over the decaying,
fading frame of a friend, and the loved one
laid to rest in the dust. But I cannot describe my feelings to those who have never
been slaves; then why should I attempt it?
He who has passed from spiritual death to
life, and received the witness within his soul
that his sins are forgiven, may possibly form
some distant idea, like the ray of the setting

3

sun from the far off mountain top, of the emotions of an emancipated slave. That opens heaven. To break the bonds of slavery, opens up at once both earth and heaven. Neither can be truly seen by us while we are slaves.

And now will the reader take with me a brief review of the road I had trodden. I cannot here dwell upon its dark shades, though some of these were black as the pencillings of midnight, but upon the light that had followed my path from my infancy up, and had at length conducted me quite out of the deep abyss of bondage. There is a hymn opening with the following stanza, which very much expresses my feelings :

" When all thy mercies, Oh my God,
    My rising soul surveys,
    Transported with the view, I'm lost
    ' In wonder, love, and praise."

I had endured what a freeman would indeed call hard fare; but my lot, on the whole, had been a favored one for a slave. It is known that there is a wide difference in the situations of what are termed house servants, and plantation hands. I, though sometimes employed upon the plantation, belonged to the former, which is the favored class. My master, too, was esteemed a kind and humane man; and altogether I fared quite differently from many poor fel-

lows whom it makes my blood run chill to
think of, confined to the plantation, with not
enough of food and that little of the coarsest
kind, to satisfy the gnawings of hunger,—
compelled oftentimes, to hie away in the
night-time, when worn down with work,
and *steal*, (if it be stealing,) and privately
devour such things as they can lay their
hands upon,—made to feel the rigors of
bondage with no cessation,—torn away
sometimes from the few friends they love,
friends doubly dear because they are few,
and transported to a climate where in a few
hard years they die,—or at best conducted
heavily and sadly to their resting place under the sod, upon their old master's plantation,—sometimes, perhaps, enlivening the
air with merriment, but a forced merriment,
that comes from a stagnant or a stupified
heart. Such as this is the fate of the plantation slaves generally, but such was not my
lot. My way was comparatively light, and
what is better, it conducted to freedom.
And my wife and children were with me.
After my master died, my mistress sold a
number of her slaves from their families
and friends—but not me. She sold several
children from their parents—but my children
were with me still. She sold two husbands
from their wives—but I was still with mine.
She sold one wife from her husband—but
mine had not been sold from me. The master of my wife, Mr. Smith, had separated

members of families by sale—but not of
mine. With me and my house, the tenderer
tendrils of the heart still clung to where the
vine had entwined; pleasant was its shade
and delicious its fruit to our taste, though
we knew, and what is more, we *felt* that we
were slaves. But all around I could see
where the vine had been torn down, and its
bleeding branches told of vanished joys, and
of new wrought sorrows, such as, slave
though I was, had never entered into my
practical experience.

I had never been permitted to learn to
read; but I used to attend church, and there
I received instruction which I trust was of
some benefit to me. I trusted, too, that I
had experienced the renewing influences of
the gospel; and after obtaining from my
mistress a written *permit*, (a thing *always*
required in such a case,) I had been bap-
tised and received into fellowship with the
Baptist denomination. So that in religious
matters, I had been indulged in the exercise
of my own conscience—a favor not always
granted to slaves. Indeed I, with others,
was often told by the minister how good
God was in bringing us over to this country
from dark and benighted Africa, and per-
mitting us to listen to the sound of the gospel. To me, God also granted temporal
freedom, which *man* without God's consent,
had stolen away.

I often heard select portions of the scriptures read. And on the Sabbath there was one sermon preached expressly for the colored people which it was generally my privilege to hear. I became quite familiar with the texts, "Servants be obedient to your masters."—"Not with eye service as men pleasers."—"He that knoweth his master's will and doeth it not, shall be beaten with many stripes," and others of this class : for they formed the basis of most of these public instructions to us. The first commandment impressed upon our minds was to obey our masters, and the second was like unto it, namely, to do as much work when they or the overseers were not watching us as when they were. But connected with these instructions there was more or less that was truly excellent; though mixed up with much that would sound strangely in the ears of freedom. There was one very kind hearted Episcopal minister whom I often used to hear; he was very popular with the colored people. But after he had preached a sermon to us in which he argued from the Bible that it was the will of heaven from all eternity we should be slaves, and our masters be our owners, most of us left him ; for like some of the faint hearted disciples in early times we said,—"This is a hard saying, who can bear it ? "

My manumission, as I shall call it; that is, the bill of sale conveying me to Mr. Smith, was dated Sept. 9th, 1835. I contin-

3 *

ued in the tobacco and pipe business as already described, to which I added a small trade in a variety of articles; and some two years before I left Raleigh, I entered also into a considerable business in wood, which I used to purchase by the acre standing, cut it, haul it into the city, deposit it in a yard and sell it out as I advantageously could. Also I was employed about the office of the Governor as I shall hereafter relate. I used to keep one or two horses, and various vehicles, by which I did a variety of work at hauling about town. Of course I had to hire more or less help, to carry on my business.

In the manufacture of tobacco I met with considerable competition, but none that materially injured me. The method of preparing it having originated with me and my father, we found it necessary, in order to secure the advantage of the invention, to keep it to ourselves, and decline, though often solicited, going into partnership with others. Those who undertook the manufacture could neither give the article a flavor so pleasant as ours, nor manufacture it so cheaply, so they either failed in it, or succeeded but poorly.

Not long after obtaining my own freedom, I began seriously to think about purchasing the freedom of my family. The first proposition was that I should buy my wife, and that we should jointly labor to obtain the

freedom of the children afterwards as we
were able. But that idea was abandoned,
when her master, Mr. Smith, refused to sell
her to me for less than one thousand dollars,
a sum which then appeared too much for me
to raise.

Afterwards, however, I conceived the idea
of purchasing at once the entire family. I
went to Mr. Smith to learn his price, which
he put at *three thousand dollars* for my wife
and six children, the number we then had.
This seemed a large sum, both because it
was a great deal for me to raise; and also
because Mr. Smith, when he bought my wife
and *two* children, had actually paid but five
hundred and sixty dollars for them, and had
received, ever since, their labor, while I had
almost entirely supported them, both as to
food and clothing. Altogether, therefore,
the case seemed a hard one, but as I was
entirely in his power I must do the best I
could. At length he concluded, perhaps
partly of his own motion, and partly through
the persuasion of a friend, to sell the family
for $2,500, as I wished to free them, though
he contended still that they were worth
three thousand dollars. Perhaps they would
at that time have brought this larger sum,
if sold for the Southern market. The arrangement with Mr. Smith was made in
December, 1838. I gave him five notes of
five hundred dollars each, the first due in
January, 1840, and one in January each

succeeding year ; for which he transferred my family into my own possession, with a *bond* to give me a bill of sale when I should pay the notes. With this arrangement, we found ourselves living in our own house—a house which I had previously purchased—in January, 1839.

After moving my family, my wife was for a short time sick, in consequence of her labor and the excitement in moving, and her excessive joy. I told her that it reminded me of a poor shoemaker in the neighborhood who purchased a ticket in a lottery; but not expecting to draw, the fact of his purchasing it had passed out of his mind. But one day as he was at work on his last, he was informed that his ticket had drawn the liberal prize of ten thousand dollars; and the poor man was so overjoyed, that he fell back on his seat, and immediately expired.

In this new and joyful situation, we found ourselves getting along very well, until September, 1840, when to my surprise, as I was passing the street one day, engaged in my business, the following note was handed me. " Read it," said the officer, " or if you cannot read, get some white man to read it to you." Here it is, *verbatim:*

> *To Lunsford Lane, a free man of Colour*
>
> Take notice that whereas complaint has been made to us two Justices of the Peace for the county of Wake and state of North Carolina that you are a free negro from another state who has migrated into this state contrary to

the provisions of the act of assembly concerning free ne-
gros and mulattoes now notice is given you that unless you
leave and remove out of this state within twenty days that
you will be proceeded against for the penalty porscribed by
said act of assembly and be otherwise dealt with as the law
directs given under our hands and seals this the 5th Sept
1840   WILLIS SCOTT JP (Seal)
               JORDAN WOMBLE JP (Seal)

This was a terrible blow to me; for it
prostrated at once all my hopes in my cherished object of obtaining the freedom of my
family, and led me to expect nothing but a
separation from them forever.

In order that the reader may understand
the full force of the foregoing notice, I will
copy the Law of the State under which it
was issued :

Sec. 65.   It shall not be lawful for any free negro or
mulatto to migrate into this State : and if he or she shall
do so, contrary to the provisions of this act, and being
thereof informed, shall not, within twenty days thereafter,
remove out of the State, he or she being thereof convicted
in the manner hereafter directed, shall be liable to a penalty of five hundred dollars; and upon failure to pay the
same, within the time prescribed in the judgment awarded
against such person or persons, he or she shall be liable to
be held in servitude and at labor for a term of time not ex-
ceeding ten years, in such manner and upon such terms
as may be provided by the court awarding such sentence,
and the proceeds arising therefrom shall be paid over to
the county trustee for county purposes :   Provided, that
in case any free negro or mulatto shall pay the penalty of
five hundred dollars, according to the provisions of this act,
it shall be the duty of such free negro or mulatto to remove him or herself out of this State within twenty days
thereafter, and for every such failure, he or she shall be

subject to the like penalty, as is prescribed for a failure to remove in the first instance.—*Revised Statutes North Carolina, chap.* 111.

The next section provides that if the free person of color so notified, does not leave within the twenty days after receiving the notice, he may be arrested on a warrant from any Justice, and be held to bail for his appearance at the next county court, when he will be subject to the penalties specified above; or in case of his failure to give bonds, he may be sent to jail.

I made known my situation to my friends, and after taking legal counsel it was determined to endeavor to induce, if possible, the complainants to prosecute no farther at present, and then as the Legislature of the State was to sit in about two months, to petition that body for permission to remain in the State until I could complete the purchase of my family; after which I was willing, if necessary, to leave.

From January 1st, 1837, I had been employed as I have mentioned, in the office of the Governor of the State, principally under the direction of his private Secretary, in keeping the office in order, taking the letters to the Post Office, and doing such other duties of the sort as occurred from time to time. This circumstance, with the fact of the high standing in the city of the family of my former master, and of the former masters of my wife, had given me the friendship of the first people in the place generally, who from that time forward acted towards me the friendly part.

Mr. BATTLE, then private Secretary to Governor Dudley, addressed the following letter to the prosecuting attorney in my behalf:

RALEIGH, Nov. 3, 1840.

DEAR SIR :—Lunsford Lane, a free man of color, has been in the employ of the State under me since my entering on my present situation. I understand that under a law of the State, he has been notified to leave, and that the time is now at hand.

In the discharge of the duties I had from him, I have found him prompt, obedient, and faithful. At this particular time, his absence to me would be much regretted, as I am now just fixing up my books and other papers in the new office, and I shall not have time to learn another what he can already do so well. With me the period of the Legislature is a very busy one, and I am compelled to have a servant who understands the business I want done, and one I can trust. I would not wish to be an obstacle in the execution of any law, but the enforcing of the one against him, will be doing me a serious inconvenience, and the object of this letter is to ascertain whether I could not procure a suspension of the sentence till after the adjournment of the Legislature, say about 1st January, 1841.

I should feel no hesitation in giving my word that he will conduct himself orderly and obediently.

I am most respectfully,
Your obedient servant,
C. C. BATTLE.

G. W. HAYWOOD, ESQ.
    Attorney at Law, Raleigh, N. C.

To the above letter the following reply was made :

RALEIGH, Nov. 3, 1840.

My DEAR SIR :—I have no objection so far as I am concerned, that all further proceedings against Lunsford should be postponed until after the adjournment of the Legislature.

The process now out against him is one issued by two magistrates, Messrs. Willis Scott and Jordan Womble, over which I have no control. You had better see them to-day, and perhaps, at your request, they will delay further action on the subject. Respectfully yours,

GEO. W. HAYWOOD.

Mr. Battle then enclosed the foregoing correspondence to Messrs. Scott and Womble, requesting their "favorable consideration." They returned the correspondence, but neglected to make any reply.

In consequence, however, of this action on the part of my friends, I was permitted to remain without further interruption, until the day the Legislature commenced its session. On that day a warrant was served upon me, to appear before the county court, to answer for the sin of having remained in the place of my birth for the space of twenty days and more after being warned out. I escaped going to jail through the kindness of Mr. Haywood, a son of my former master, and Mr. Smith, who jointly became security for my appearance at court.

This was on Monday ; and on Wednesday I appeared before the court ; but as my prosecutors were not ready for the trial, the case was laid over three months, to the next term.

I then proceeded to get up a petition to the Legislature. It required much hard labor and persuasion on my part to start it; but after that, I readily obtained the signatures of the principal men in the place.— Then I went round to the members, many of whom were known to me, calling upon them at their rooms, and urging them for my sake, for humanity's sake, for the sake of my wife and little ones, whose hopes had been excited by the idea that they were even now free; I appealed to them as husbands, fathers, brothers, sons, to vote in favor of my petition, and allow me to remain in the State long enough to purchase my family. I was doing well in business, and it would be but a short time before I could accomplish the object. Then, if it was desired, I and my wife and children, redeemed from bondage, would together seek a more friendly home, beyond the dominion of slavery. The following is the petition presented, endorsed as the reader will see:

To the Hon. General Assembly of the State of North Carolina.

GENTLEMEN:—The petition of Lunsford Lane humbly shews—That about five years ago, he purchased his freedom from his mistress, Mrs. Sherwood Haywood, and by great economy and industry has paid the purchase money; that he has a wife and seven children whom he has agreed to purchase, and for whom he has paid a part of the purchase money; but not having paid in full, is not yet able to leave the State, without parting with his wife and children.

Your petitioner prays your Honorable Body to pass a law, allowing him to remain a limited time within the State, until

4

he can remove his family also. Your petitioner will give bond
and good security for his good behaviour while he remains.
Your petitioner will ever pray, &c.

LUNSFORD LANE.

———

The undersigned are well acquainted with Lunsford Lane,
the petitioner, and join in his petition to the Assembly for relief.

Charles Manly,	Drury Lacy,
R. W. Haywood,	Will. Peck,
Eleanor Haywood,	W. A. Stith,
Wm. Hill,	A. B. Stith,
R. Smith,	J. Brown,
Wm. Peace,	William White,
Jos. Peace,	Geo. Simpson,
Wm. M'Pheeters,	Jno. I. Christophers,
Wm. Boylan,	John Primrose,
Fabius J. Haywood,	Hugh M'Queen,
D. W. Stone,	Alex. J. Lawrence,
T. Meredith,	C. L. Hinton.
A. J. Battle,	

———

Lunsford Lane, the petitioner herein, has been servant to the
Executive Office since the 1st of January, 1837, and it gives
me pleasure to state that, during the whole time, without exception, I have found him faithful and obedient, in keeping
every thing committed to his care in good condition. From
what I have seen of his conduct and demeanor, I cheerfully join
in the petition for his relief.   C. C. BATTLE,

P. Secretary to Gov. Dudley.

Raleigh, Nov. 20, 1840.

The foregoing petition was presented to
the Senate. It was there referred to a committee. I knew when the committee was
to report, and watched about the State
House that I might receive the earliest news
of the fate of my petition. I should have
gone within the senate chamber, but no colored man has that permission. I do not
know why, unless for fear he may hear the
name of *Liberty*. By and by a member

came out, and as he passed me, said, " *Well,
Lunsford, they have laid you out ; the nigger
bill is killed.*" I need not tell the reader
that my feelings did not enter into the merriment of this honorable senator. To me,
the fate of my petition was the last blow to
my hopes. I had done all I could do, had
said all I could say, laboring night and day,
to obtain a favorable reception to my petition ; but all in vain. Nothing appeared
before me but I must leave the State, and
leave my wife and my children never to see
them more. My friends had also done all
they could for me.

And why must I be banished ? Ever after I entertained the first idea of being free,
I had endeavored so to conduct myself as
not to become obnoxious to the white inhabitants, knowing as I did their power, and
their hostility to the colored people. The
two points necessary in such a case I had
kept constantly in mind. First, I had made
no display of the little property or money I
possessed, but in every way I wore as much
as possible the aspect of poverty. Second,
I had never appeared to be even so intelligent as I really was. This all colored people at the south, free and slaves, find it peculiarly necessary to their own comfort and
safety to observe.

I should, perhaps, have mentioned that
on the same day I received the notice to
leave Raleigh, similar notices were present-

ed to two other free colored people, who had
been slaves; were trying to purchase their
families; and were otherwise in a like situation to myself. And they took the same
course I did to endeavor to remain a limited
time. Isaac Hunter, who had a family with
five children, was one; and Waller Freeman, who had six children, was the other.
Mr. Hunter's petition went before mine; and
a bill of some sort passed the Senate, which
was so cut down in the Commons, as to allow him only *twenty days* to remain in the
State. He has since, however, obtained the
freedom of his family, who are living with
him in Philadelphia.

Mr. Freeman's petition received no better
fate than mine. His family were the property of Judge Badger, who was afterwards
made a member of Mr. Harrison's cabinet.
When Mr. Badger removed to Washington,
he took with him among other slaves this
family; and Freeman removed also to that
city. After this, when Mr. B. resigned his
office, with the other members of the cabinet under President Tyler, he entered into
some sort of contract with Freeman, to sell
him this family, which he left at Washington, while he took the rest of his slaves
back to Raleigh. Freeman is now endeavoring to raise money to make the purchase.

It was now between two and three months
to the next session of the court; and I knew
that before or at that time I must leave the

State. I was bound to appear before the court; but it had been arranged between my lawyer and the prosecuting attorney, that if I would leave the State, and pay the costs of court, the case should be dropped, so that my bondsmen should not be involved. I therefore concluded to stay as long as I possibly could, and then leave. I also determined to appeal to the kindness of the friends of the colored man in the North, for assistance, though I had but little hope of succeeding in this way. Yet it was the only course I could think of, by which I could see any possible hope of accomplishing the object.

I had paid Mr. Smith six hundred and twenty dollars; and had a house and lot worth $500, which he had promised to take when I should raise the balance. He gave me also a bill of sale of one of my children, Laura, in consideration of two hundred and fifty dollars of the money already paid; and her I determined to take with me to the North. The costs of court which I had to meet, amounted to between thirty and forty dollars, besides the fee of my lawyer.

On the 18th of May, 1841, three days after the court commenced its session, I bid adieu to my friends in Raleigh, and set out for the city of New York. I took with me a letter of introduction and recommendation from Mr. John Primrose, a very estimable man, a recommendatory certificate from Mr.

4*

Battle, and a letter from the church of which I was a member, together with such papers relating to the affair as I had in my possession. Also I received the following :

RALEIGH, N. C. May, 1841.

The bearer, Lunsford Lane, a free man of color, for some time a resident in this place, being about to leave North Carolina in search of a more favorable location to pursue his trade, has desired us to give him a certificate of his good conduct heretofore.

We take pleasure in saying that his habits are temperate and industrious, that his conduct has been orderly and proper. and that he has for these qualities been distinguished among his caste.

Wm. Hill,	R. Smith,
Weston R. Gales,	C. Dewey.
C. L. Hinton,	

The above was certified to officially in the usual form by the clerk of the court of Common Pleas and Quarter Sessions.

My success in New York was at first small; but at length I fell in with two friends who engaged to raise for me three hundred dollars, provided I should first obtain from other sources the balance of the sum required, which balance would be one thousand and eighty dollars. Thus encouraged, I proceeded to Boston; and in the city and vicinity the needful sum was contributed by about the 1st of April, 1842. My thanks I have endeavored to express in my poor way to the many friends who so kindly and liberally assisted me. I cannot reward them; I hope they will receive their reward in another world. If the limits of this publication would permit, I should like to record the names of many to whom I am very especially indebted for their kindness and aid, not only in contributing, but by introducing me and opening various ways of access to others.

On the 5th of February, 1842, finding that I should soon have in my possession the sum necessary to procure my family, and fearing that there might be danger in visiting Raleigh for that purpose, in consequence of the strong opposition of many of the citizens against colored people, their opposition to me, and their previously persecuting me from the city, I wrote to Mr. Smith, requesting him to see the Governor and obtain under his hand a permit to visit the State for a sufficient time to accomplish this business. I requested Mr. Smith to publish the permit in one or two of the city papers, and then to enclose the original to me. This letter he answered, under date of Raleigh, 19th Feb. 1842, as follows:

LUNSFORD :—Your letter of the 5th inst. came duly to hand, and in reply I have to inform you, that owing to the absence of Gov. Morehead, I cannot send you the permit you requested, but this will make no difference, for you can come home, and after your arrival you may obtain one to remain long enough to settle up your affairs. You ought of course to apply to the Governor immediately on your arrival, before any malicious person would have time to inform against you; I don't think by pursuing this course you need apprehend any danger.

    *   *   *   *   *   *

We are all alive at present in Raleigh on the subjects of temperance and religion. We have taken into the temperance societies, about five hundred members, and about fifty persons

have been happily converted.   * * *   The work seems still
to be spreading, and such a time I have never seen before in
my life.   Glorious times truly.

Do try and get all the religion in your heart you possibly can,
for it is the only thing worth having after all.

Your, &c.   B. B. SMITH.

The way now appeared to be in a measure
open ; also I thought that the religious and
temperance interest mentioned in the latter
portion of Mr. Smith's letter, augured a state
of feeling which would be a protection to me.
But fearing still that there might be danger
in visiting Raleigh without the permit from
the Governor, or at least wishing to take
every possible precaution, I addressed another letter to Mr. Smith, and received under
date of March 12th, a reply, from which I
copy as follows :

"The Governor has just returned, and I called upon him to
get the permit as you requested, but he said he had no authority
by law to grant one ; and he told me to say to you, that you
might in perfect safety come ho ne in a quiet manner, and remain twenty days without being interrupted.   I also consulted
Mr. Manly [a lawyer] and he told me the same thing. * * *
*Surely you need not fear any thing under these circumstances.
You had therefore better come on just as soon as possible.*"

I need not say, what the reader has already seen, that my life so far had been one
of joy succeeding sorrow, and sorrow following joy ; of hope, of despair ; of bright
prospects, of gloom ; and of as many hues
as ever appear on the varied sky, from the
black of midnight, or the deep brown of a

tempest, to the bright warm glow of a clear
noon day.   On the 11th of April it was noon
with me; I left Boston on my way for Raleigh with high hopes, intending to pay over
the money for my family and return with
them to Boston, which I intended should be
my future home; for there I had found
friends and there I would find a grave. The
visit I was making to the South was to be a
farewell one; and I did not dream that my
old cradle, hard as it once had jostled me,
would refuse to rock me a pleasant, or even
an affectionate good bye.   I thought, too,
that the assurances I had received from the
Governor, through Mr. Smith, and the assurances of other friends, were a sufficient
guaranty that I might visit the home of my
boyhood, of my youth, of my manhood, in
peace, especially as I was to stay but for a
few days and then to return.   With these
thoughts, and with the thoughts of my family and freedom, I pursued my way to Raleigh, and arrived there on the 23d of the
month.   It was Saturday about four o'clock,
P. M. when I found myself once more in the
midst of my family.   With them I remained over the Sabbath, as it was sweet to spend
a little time with them after so long an absence, an absence filled with so much of interest to us, and as I could not do any business until the beginning of the week.   On
Monday morning between eight and nine
o'clock, while I was making ready to leave

the house for the first time after my arrival,
to go to the store of Mr. Smith, where I was
to transact my business with him, two con-
stables, Messrs. Murray and Scott, entered,
accompanied by two other men, and summoned me to appear immediately before the
police. I accordingly accompanied them to
the City Hall, but as it was locked and the
officers could not at once find the key, we
were told that the court would be held in
Mr. Smith's store, a large and commodious
room. This was what is termed in common
phrase in Raleigh a "call court." The
Mayor, Mr. Loring, presided, assisted by
William Boylan and Jonathan Busbye, Esqs.
Justices of the Peace. There was a large
number of people together—more than could
obtain admission to the room, and a large
company of mobocratic spirits crowded a-
round the door. Mr. Loring read the writ,
setting forth that I had been guilty of *deliv-*
ering abolition lectures in the State of Massa-
chusetts. He asked me whether I was guilty
or not guilty. I told him I did not know
whether I had given abolition lectures or
not, but if it pleased the court, I would relate the course I had pursued during my absence from Raleigh. He then said that I
was at liberty to speak.

The circumstances under which I left
Raleigh, said I, are perfectly familiar to you.
It is known that I had no disposition to re-
move from this city, but resorted to every

lawful means to remain. After I found that I could not be permitted to stay, I went away leaving behind everything I held dear with the exception of one child, whom I took with me, after paying two hundred and fifty dollars for her. It is also known to you and to many other persons here present, that I had engaged to purchase my wife and children of her master, Mr. Smith, for the sum of twenty-five hundred dollars, and that I had paid of this sum (including my house and lot) eleven hundred and twenty dollars, leaving a balance to be made up of thirteen hundred and eighty dollars. I had previously to that lived in Raleigh, a slave, the property of Mr. Sherwood Haywood, and had purchased my freedom by paying the sum of one thousand dollars. But being driven away, no longer permitted to live in this city, to raise the balance of the money due on my family, my last resort was to call upon the friends of humanity in other places, to assist me.

I went to the city of Boston, and there I related the story of my persecutions here, the same as I have now stated to you. The people gave ear to my statements; and one of them, Rev. Mr. Neale, wrote back, unknown to me, to Mr. Smith, inquiring of him whether the statements made by me were correct. After Mr. Neale received the answer he sent for me, informed me of his having written, and read to me the reply.

The letter fully satisfied Mr. Neale and his friends. He placed it in my hands, remarking that it would, in a great measure, do away the necessity of using the other documents in my possession. I then with that letter in my hands went out from house to house, from place of business to place of business, and from church to church, relating (where I could gain an ear) the same heart-rending and soul-trying story which I am now repeating to you. In pursuing that course, the people, first one and then another contributed, until I had succeeded in raising the amount alluded to, namely, thirteen hundred and eighty dollars. I may have had contributions from abolitionists; but I did not stop to ask those who assisted me whether they were anti-slavery or pro-slavery, for I considered that the money coming from either, would accomplish the object I had in view. These are the facts; and now, sir, it remains for you to say, whether I have been giving abolition lectures or not.

In the course of my remarks I presented the letter of Mr. Smith to Mr. Neale, showing that I had acted the open part while in Massachusetts; also I referred to my having written to Mr. Smith requesting him to obtain for me the permit of the Governor; and I showed to the court, Mr. Smith's letters in reply, in order to satisfy them that I had reason to believe I should be unmolested in my return.

Mr. Loring then whispered to some of the leading men; after which he remarked that he saw nothing in what I had done, according to my statements, implicating me in a manner worthy of notice. He called upon any present who might be in possession of information tending to disprove what I had said, or to show any wrong on my part, to produce it, otherwise I should be set at liberty. No person appeared against me; so I was discharged.

I started to leave the house; but just before I got to the door I met Mr. James Litchford, who touched me on the shoulder, and I followed him back. He observed to me that if I went out of that room I should in less than five minutes be a dead man; for there was a mob outside waiting to drink my life. Mr. Loring then spoke to me again and said that notwithstanding I had been found guilty of nothing, yet public opinion was law; and he advised me to leave the place the next day, otherwise he was convinced I should have to suffer death. I replied, " not to-morrow, but to-day." He answered that I could not go that day, because I had not done my business. I told him that I would leave my business in his hands and in those of other such gentlemen as himself, who might settle it for me and send my family to meet me at Philadelphia. This was concluded upon, and a guard appointed to conduct me to the depot. I took

5

my seat in the cars, when the mob that had
followed us surrounded me, and declared
that the cars should not go, if I were permitted to go in them.   Mr. Loring inquired
what they wanted of me ; he told them that
there had been an examination, and nothing
had been found against me; that they were
at the examination invited to speak if they
knew of aught to condemn me, but they
had remained silent, and that now it was
but right I should be permitted to leave in
peace.   They replied that they wanted a
more thorough investigation, that they wished to search my trunks (I had but one trunk)
and see if I was not in possession of abolition papers.   It now became evident that
I should be unable to get off in the cars ;
and my friends advised me to go the short-
est way possible to jail, for my safety.
They said they were persuaded that what
the rabble wanted was to get me into their
possession, and then to murder me.   The
mob looked dreadfully enraged, and seemed
to lap for blood.   The whole city was in an
uproar.   But the first men and the more
wealthy were my friends : and they did
everything in their power to protect me.
Mr. Boylan, whose name has repeatedly
occurred in this publication, was more than
a father to me ; and Mr. Smith and Mr.
Loring, and many other gentlemen, whose
names it would give me pleasure to mention,
were exceedingly kind.

The guard then conducted me through the mob to the prison; and I felt joyful that even a prison could protect me. Looking out from the prison window, I saw my trunk in the hands of Messrs. Johnson, Scott, and others, who were taking it to the City Hall for examination. I understood afterwards that they opened my trunk; and as the lid flew up, Lo! a paper! a paper!! Those about seized it, three or four at once, as hungry dogs would a piece of meat after forty days famine. But the meat quickly turned to a stone; for the paper it happened, was one *printed in Raleigh*, and edited by WESTON R. GALES, a nice man to be sure, but no abolitionist. The only other printed or written things in the trunk were some business cards of a firm in Raleigh—not incendiary.

Afterwards I saw from the window **Mr.** Scott, accompanied by Mr. Johnson, lugging my carpet-bag in the same direction my trunk had gone. It was opened at the City Hall, and found actually to contain a pair of old shoes, and a pair of old boots!—but they did not conclude that these were incendiary.

Mr. Smith now came to the prison and told me that the examination had been completed, and nothing found against me; but that it would not be safe for me to leave the prison immediately. It was agreed that I should remain in prison until after night-fall,

and then steal secretly away, being let
out by the keeper, and pass unnoticed to the
house of my old and tried friend Mr. Boylan. Accordingly I was discharged between
nine and ten o'clock. I went by the back
way leading to Mr. Boylan's; but soon and
suddenly a large company of men sprang
upon me, and instantly I found myself in
their possession. They conducted me sometimes high above ground and sometimes
dragging me along, but as silently as possible, in the direction of the gallows, which is
always kept standing upon the Common, or
as it is called "the pines," or "piny old
field." I now expected to pass speedily into
the world of spirits; I thought of that un-
seen region to which I seemed to be hastening; and then my mind would return to my
wife and children, and the labors I had made
to redeem them from bondage. Although I
had the money to pay for them according to
a bargain already made, it seemed to me
some white man would get it, and they
would die in slavery, without benefit from
my exertions and the contributions of my
friends. Then the thought of my own
death, to occur in a few brief moments,
would rush over me, and I seemed to bid
adieu in spirit to all earthly things, and to
hold communion already with eternity. But
at length I observed those who were carrying me away, changed their course a little
from the direct line to the gallows, and hope,

a faint beaming, sprung up within me; but then as they were taking me to the woods, I thought they intended to murder me there, in a place where they would be less likely to be interrupted than in so public a spot as where the gallows stood. They conducted me to a rising ground among the trees, and set me down. "Now," said they, "tell us the truth about those abolition lectures you have been giving at the North." I replied that I had related the circumstances before the court in the morning; and could only repeat what I had then said. "But that was not the truth—tell us the truth." I again said that any different story would be false, and as I supposed I was in a few minutes to die, I would not, whatever they might think I would say under other circumstances, pass into the other world with a lie upon my lips. Said one, "you were always, Lunsford, when you were here, a clever fellow, and I did not think you would be engaged in such business as giving abolition lectures." To this and similar remarks, I replied that the people of Raleigh had always said the abolitionists did not believe in buying slaves, but contended that their masters ought to free them without pay. I had been laboring to buy my family; and how then could they suppose me to be in league with the abolitionists?

After other conversation of this kind, and after they seemed to have become tired of questioning me, they held a consultation in a low whisper among themselves.   Then a bucket was brought and set down by my side ; but what it contained or for what it was intended, I could not divine.   But soon, one of the number came forward with a pillow, and then hope sprung up, a flood of light and joy within me.   The heavy weight on my heart rolled off ; death had passed by and I unharmed.   They commenced stripping me till every rag of clothes was removed ; and then the bucket was set near, and I discovered it to contain tar.   One man, I will do him the honor to record his name, Mr. WILLIAM ANDRES, a journeyman printer, when he is any thing, except a tar-and-featherer, put his hands the first into the bucket, and was about passing them to my face.   " Don't put any in his face or eyes," said one.*   So he desisted ; but he, with three other "gentlemen," whose names I should be happy to record if I could recall them, gave me as nice a coat of tar all over, face only excepted, as any one would wish to see.   Then they took the pillow and ripped it open at one end, and with the open end commenced the operation at the head and so worked downwards, of putting a coat

* I think this was Mr. Burns, a blacksmith in the place, but I am not certain.   At any rate, this man was my *friend* (if so he may be called) on this occasion ; and it was fortunate for me that the company generally seemed to look up to him for wisdom.

of its contents over that of the contents of the bucket. A fine escape from the hanging this will be, thought I, provided they do not with a match set fire to the feathers. I had some fear they would. But when the work was completed they gave me my clothes, and one of them handed me my watch which he had carefully kept in his hands; they all expressed great interest in my welfare, advised me how to proceed with my business the next day, told me to stay in the place as long as I wished, and with other such words of consolation they bid me good night.

After I had returned to my family, to their inexpressible joy, as they had become greatly alarmed for my safety, some of the persons who had participated in this outrage, came in (probably influenced by a curiosity to see how the tar and feathers would be got off) and expressed great sympathy for me. They said they regretted that the affair had happened—that they had no objections to my living in Raleigh—I might feel perfectly safe to go out and transact my business preparatory to leaving—I should not be molested.

Meanwhile, my friends understanding that I had been discharged from prison, and perceiving I did not come to them, had commenced a regular search for me, on foot and on horseback, every where; and Mr. Smith called upon the Governor to obtain his official interference; and after my return, a

guard came to protect me; but I chose not
to risk myself at my own house, and so
went to Mr. Smith's, where this guard kept
me safely until morning. They seemed
friendly indeed, and were regaled with a
supper during the night by Mr. Smith. My
friend, Mr. Battle, (late private secretary to
the Governor,) was with them; and he made
a speech to them setting forth the good qualities I had exhibited in my past life, particularly in my connection with the Governor's
office.

In the morning Mr. Boylan, true as ever,
and unflinching in his friendship, assisted
me in arranging my business,* so that I
should start with my family *that day* for the
north. He furnished us with provisions
more than sufficient to sustain the family to
Philadelphia, where we intended to make a
halt; and sent his own baggage wagon to
convey our baggage to the depot, offering
also to send his carriage for my family. But
my friend, Mr. Malone, had been before him
in this kind offer, which I had agreed to
accept.

Brief and sorrowful was the parting from

---

* Of course I was obliged to sacrifice much on my property, leaving in this hurried manner. And while I was in
the North, a kind *friend* had removed from the wood-lot,
wood that I had cut and corded, for which I expected to
receive over one hundred dollars; thus saving me the
trouble of making sale of it, or of being burdened with
the money it would bring. I suppose I have no redress.
I might add other things as bad.

my kind friends; but the worst was the
thought of leaving my mother. The cars
were to start at ten o'clock in the morning.
I called upon my old mistress, Mrs. Haywood, who was affected to weeping by the
considerations that naturally came to her
mind. She had been kind to me; the day
before she and her daughter, Mrs. Hogg,
now present, had jointly transmitted a communication to the court representing that in
consequence of my good conduct from my
youth, I could not be supposed to be guilty
of any offence. And now, " with tears that
ceased not flowing," they gave me their
parting blessing. My mother was still Mrs.
Haywood's slave, and I her only child. Our
old mistress could not witness the sorrow
that would attend the parting with my
mother. She told her to go with me; and
said that if I ever became able to pay two
hundred dollars for her, I might; otherwise
it should be her loss. She gave her the following paper, which is in the ordinary form
of a *pass :*

RALEIGH, N. C. April 26, 1842.
Know all persons by these presents, that the bearer of this,
Clarissa, a slave, belonging to me, hath my permission to visit
the city of New York with her relations, who are in company
with her ; and it is my desire that she may be protected and
permitted to pass without molestation or hindrance, on good
behavior. Witness my hand this 26th April, 1842.
ELEANOR HAYWOOD.
Witness—J. A. Campbell.

On leaving Mrs. Haywood's, I called upon
Mrs. Badger, another daughter, and wife of
6

Judge Badger, previously mentioned. She
seemed equally affected; she wept as she
gave me her parting counsel. She and Mrs.
Hogg and I had been children together, playing in the same yard, while yet none of us
had learned that they were of a superior and
I of a subject race. And in those infant years
there were pencillings made upon the heart,
which time and opposite fortunes could not
all efface.—May these friends never be slaves
as I have been; nor their bosom companions and their little ones be slaves like mine.

When the cars were about to start, the
whole city seemed to be gathered at the depot; and among the rest the mobocratic portion, who appeared to be determined still
that I should not go peaceably away. Ap-
prehending this, it had been arranged with
my friends and the conductor, that my family should be put in the cars and that I
should go a distance from the city on foot,
and be taken up as they passed. The mob,
therefore, supposing that I was left behind,
allowed the cars to start.

Mr. Whiting, known as the agent of the
rail road company, was going as far as Pe-
tersburg, Va.; and he kindly assisted in purchasing our tickets, and enabling us to pass
on unmolested. After he left, Capt. Guyan,
of Raleigh, performed the same kind office
as far as Alexandria, D. C., and then he
placed us in the care of a citizen of Philadelphia, whose name I regret to have for-

gotten, who protected us quite out of the
land of slavery. But for this we should
have been liable to be detained at several
places on our way, much to our embarrassment, at least, if nothing had occurred of a
more serious nature.

One accident only had happened: we lost
at Washington a trunk containing most of
our valuable clothing. This we have not
recovered; but our lives have been spared
to bless the day that conferred freedom upon
us. I felt when my feet struck the pave-
ments in Philadelphia, as though I had
passed into another world. I could draw in
a full long breath, with no one to say to the
ribs, " why do ye so ?"

On reaching Philadelphia we found that
our money had all been expended, but kind
friends furnished us with the means of proceeding as far as New-York ; and thence we
were with equal kindness aided on to Boston.

In Boston and in the vicinity, are persons
almost without number, who have done me
favors more than I can express. The
thought that I was now in my new, though
recently acquired home—that my family
were with me where the stern, cruel, hated
hand of slavery could never reach us more—
the greetings of friends—the interchange of
feeling and sympathy — the kindness bestowed upon us, more grateful than rain to
the thirsty earth,—the reflections of the past
that would rush into my mind,—these and

more almost overwhelmed me with emotion, and I had deep and strange communion with my own soul.   Next to God from whom every good gift proceeds, I feel under the greatest obligations to my kind friends in Massachusetts.   To be rocked in their cradle of Liberty,—Oh, how unlike being stretched on the pillory of slavery !   May that cradle rock forever ; may many a poor care-worn child of sorrow, many a spirit-bruised (worse than lash-mangled) victim of oppression, there sweetly sleep to the lullaby of Freedom, sung by Massachusetts sons and daughters.

A number of meetings have been held at which friends have contributed to our temporal wants, and individuals have sent us various articles of provision and furniture and apparel, so that our souls have been truly made glad.   There are now ten of us in the family, my wife, my mother, and myself, with seven children, and we expect soon to be joined by my father, who several years ago received his freedom by legacy.   The wine fresh from the clustering grapes never filled so sweet a cup as mine.   May I and my family be permitted to drink it, remembering whence it came !

I suppose such of my readers as are not accustomed to trade in human beings, may be curious to see the Bills of Sale, by which I have obtained the right to my wife and children. They are both in the hand writing of Mr. Smith. The first—that for Laura is as follows:

State of North Carolina, Wake County.

Know all men by these presents, that for and in consideration of the sum of two hundred and fifty dollars, to me in hand paid, I have this day bargained and sold; and do hereby bargain, sell and deliver unto Lunsford Lane, a free man of color, a certain negro girl by the name of Laura, aged about seven years, and hereby warrant and defend the right and title of the said girl to the said Lunsford and his heirs forever, free from the claims of all persons whatsoever.

In witness whereof, I have hereunto set my hand and seal at Raleigh, this 17th May, 1841.

B. B. SMITH, [seal.]

Witness—Robt. W. Haywood.

—

Below is the Bill of Sale for my wife and other six children, to which the papers that follow are attached.

State of North Carolina, Wake County.

Know all men by these presents, that for and in consideration of the sum of eighteen hundred and eighty dollars to me in hand paid, the receipt of which is hereby acknowledged, I have this day bargained, sold and delivered unto Lunsford Lane, a free man of color, one dark mulatto woman named Patsy, one boy named Edward, one boy also named William, one boy also named Lunsford, one girl named Maria, one boy also named Ellick, and one girl named Lucy, to have and to

7

hold the said negroes free from the claims of all persons whatsoever.

In witness whereof, I have hereunto affixed my hand and
seal this 25th day of April, 1842.

B. B. SMITH, [seal.]

Witness—Th. L. West.

State of North Carolina, Wake County.
Office of Court of Pleas and Quarter Sessions, April 26, 1842.
The execution of the within bill of sale was this day duly
acknowledged before me by B. B. Smith, the executor of the
same.

In testimony whereof, I have hereunto affixed the seal of
[L. S.] said Court, and subscribed my name at office in
Raleigh, the date above.

JAS. T. MARRIOTT, Clerk.

State of North Carolina, Wake County.
I, Wm. Boylan, presiding magistrate of the Court of Pleas
and Quarter Sessions for the county aforesaid, certify that
James T. Marriott, who has written and signed the above certificate, is Clerk of the Court aforesaid,—that the same is in due
form, and full faith and credit are due to such his official acts.

Given under my hand and private seal (having no seal of
office) this 26th day of April, 1842.

WM. BOYLAN, P. M. [seal.]

The State of North Carolina.
To all to whom these presents shall come, Greeting :
Be it known, that William Boylan, whose signature appears
in his own proper hand writing to the annexed certificate, was
at the time of signing the same and now is a Justice of the
Peace and the Presiding Magistrate for the county of Wake,
in the State aforesaid, and as such he is duly qualified and empowered to give said certificate, which is here done in the
usual and proper manner ; and full faith and credit are due to
the same, and ought to be given to all the official acts of the
said William Boylan as Presiding Magistrate aforesaid.

In testimony whereof, I, J. M. Morehead, Governor, Captain
General and Commander in Chief, have caused
the Great Seal of the State to be hereunto affixed,
and signed the same at the city of Raleigh, on the
[L. S.] 26th day of April, in the year of our Lord one
thousand eight hundred and forty-two, and in the
sixty-sixth year of the Independence of the United
States.   J. M. MOREHEAD.
By the Governor.
P. Reynolds, Private Secretary.

THE
FUGITIVE BLACKSMITH;

Mr. CHARLES GILPIN,

My Dear Sir,

The information just communicated to me by you, that another edition of my little book, " The Fugitive Blacksmith," is called for, has agreeably surprised me.   The British public has laid me under renewed obligations by this mark of liberality, which I hasten to acknowledge.   I would avail myself of this moment also, to acknowledge the kindness of the gentlemen of the newspaper press for the many favourable reviews which my little book has received.   It is to them I am indebted, in no small degree, for the success with which I have been favoured in getting the book before the notice of the public.

Yours truly,

J. W. C. PENNINGTON.

Hoxton, Oct. 15th, 1849.

PREFACE.

THE brief narrative I here introduce to the public, consists of outline notes originally thrown together to guide my memory when lecturing on this part of the subject of slavery. This will account for its style, and will also show that the work is not full.

The question may be asked, Why I have published anything so long after my escape from slavery? I answer I have been induced to do so on account of the increasing disposition to overlook the fact, that THE SIN of slavery lies in the chattel principle, or relation. Especially have I felt anxious to save professing Christians, and my brethren in the ministry, from falling into a great mistake. My feelings are always outraged when I hear them speak of " kind masters,"—" Christian masters,"—" the mildest form of slavery,"—" well fed and clothed slaves," as extenuations of slavery ; I am satisfied they either mean to pervert the truth, or they do not know what they say. The being of slavery, its soul and body, lives and moves in the chattel principle, the property principle, the bill of sale principle ; the cart-whip, starvation, and nakedness, are its inevitable consequences to a greater or less extent, warring with the dispositions of men.

There lies a skein of silk upon a lady's work-table. How smooth and handsome are the threads. But while that lady goes out to make a call, a party of children enter the apartment, and in amusing themselves, tangle the skein of silk, and now who can untangle it? The relation between master and slave is even as delicate as a skein of silk: it is liable to be entangled at any moment.

The mildest form of slavery, if there be such a form, looking at the chattel principle as the definition of slavery, is comparatively the worst form. For it not only keeps the slave in the most unpleasant apprehension, like a prisoner in chains awaiting his trial; but it actually, in a great majority of cases, where kind masters do exist, trains him under the most favourable circumstances the system admits of, and then plunges him into the worst of which it is capable.

It is under the mildest form of slavery, as it exists in Maryland, Virginia, and Kentucky, that the finest specimens of coloured females are reared. There are no mothers who rear, and educate in the natural graces, finer daughters than the Ethiopian women, who have the least chance to give scope to their maternal affections. But what is generally the fate of such female slaves? When they are not raised for the express purpose of supplying the market of a class of economical Louisian and Mississippi gentlemen, who do not wish to incur the expense of rearing legitimate families, they are, nevertheless, on account of their attractions, exposed to the most shameful degradation, by the young masters in the families where it is claimed they are so well off. My master once owned a beautiful girl about twenty-four. She had been raised in a family where her mother was a great favourite. She was her mother's darling child. Her master was a lawyer of eminent abilities and great fame, but owing to habits of intemperance, he failed in business, and my master purchased this girl for a nurse. After he had owned her about a year, one of his sons became attached to her, for no honourable purposes; a fact which was not only well-known among all of the slaves, but which became a source of unhappiness to his mother and sisters.

The result was, that poor Rachel had to be sold to "Georgia." Never shall I forget the heart-rending scene, when one day one of the men was ordered to get "the one-horse cart ready to go into town;" Rachel, with her few articles of clothing, was placed in it, and taken into the very town where her parents lived, and there sold to the traders before their weeping eyes. That same son who had degraded her, and who was the cause of her being sold, acted as salesman, and bill of saleman. While this cruel business was being transacted, my master stood aside, and the girl's father, a pious member and exhorter in the Methodist Church, a venerable grey-headed man, with his hat off, besought that he might be allowed to get some one in the place to purchase his child. But no; my master was invincible. His reply was, " She has offended in my family, and I can only restore confidence by sending her out of hearing." After lying in prison a short time, her new owner took her with others to the far South, where her parents heard no more of her.

Here was a girl born and reared under the mildest form of slavery. Her original master was reputed to be even indulgent. He lived in a town, and was a high-bred gentleman, and a lawyer. He had but a few slaves, and had no occasion for an overseer, those negro leeches, to watch and drive them; but when he became embarrassed by his own folly, the chattel principle doomed this girl to be sold at the same sale with his books, house, and horses. With my master she found herself under far more stringent discipline than she had been accustomed to, and finally degraded, and sold where her condition could not be worse, and where she had not the least hope of ever bettering it.

This case presents the legitimate working of the great chattel principle. It is no accidental result—it is the fruit of the tree. You cannot constitute slavery without the chattel principle—and with the chattel principle you cannot save it from these results. Talk not then about kind and christian masters. They are not masters of the system. The system is master of them; and the slaves are their vassals.

These storms rise on the bosom of the calmed waters of the system. You are a slave, a being in whom another owns property. Then you may rise with his pride, but remember the day is at hand when you must also fall with his folly. To-day you may be pampered by his meekness; but to-morrow you will suffer in the storm of his passions.

In the month of September, 1848, there appeared in my study, one morning, in New York City, an aged coloured man of tall and slender form. I saw depicted on his countenance anxiety bordering on despair, still I was confident that he was a man whose mind was accustomed to faith. When I learned that he was a native of my own state, Maryland, having been born in the county of Montgomery, I at once became much interested in him. He had been sent to me by my friend, William Harned, Esq., of the Anti-Slavery Office, 61, John Street. He put into my hand the following bill of distress :—

" Alexander, Virginia, *September 5th,* 1848.

" The bearer, Paul Edmondson, is the father of two girls, Mary Jane and Emily Catherine Edmondson. These girls have been purchased by us, and once sent to the South ; and upon the positive assurance that the money for them would be raised if they were brought back, they were returned. Nothing, it appears, has as yet been done in this respect by those who promised, and we are on the very eve of sending them south a second time ; and we are candid in saying, that if they go again, we will not regard any promises made in relation to them.

" The father wishes to raise money to pay for them, and intends to appeal to the liberality of the humane and the good to aid him, and has requested us to state

in writing *the conditions upon which we will sell his
daughters.*

"We expect to start our servants to the South in a
few days; if the sum of twelve hundred dollars be
raised and paid us in fifteen days, or we be assured of
that sum, then we will retain them for twenty-five
days more, to give an opportunity for raising the
other thousand and fifty dollars, otherwise we shall
be compelled to send them along with our other
servants.

(Signed)   "Bruin and Hill."

The old man also showed me letters from other
individuals, and one from the Rev. Matthew A.
Turner, pastor of Asbury Chapel, where himself and
his daughters were members. He was himself free,
but his wife was a slave. Those two daughters were
two out of fifteen children he had raised for the owner
of his wife. These two girls had been sold, along
with four brothers, to the traders, for an attempt to
escape to the North, and gain their freedom.

On the next Sabbath evening, I threw the case
before my people, and the first fifty dollars of the
sum was raised to restore the old man his daughters.
Subsequently the case was taken up under the manage-
ment of a committee of ministers of the Methodist
Episcopal Church, consisting of the Rev. G. Peck, D.D.,
Rev. E. E. Griswold, and Rev. D. Curry, and the
entire sum of 2,250 dollars, (£450.) was raised for
two girls, fourteen and sixteen years of age!

But why this enormous sum for two mere children ?   Ah, reader, they were reared under the mildest form of slavery known to the laws of Maryland !   The mother is an invalid, and allowed to live with her free husband ; but she is a woman of excellent mind, and has bestowed great pains upon her daughters.   If you would know, then, why these girls were held at such a price, even to their own father, read the following extract of a letter from one who was actively engaged in behalf of them, and who had several interviews with the traders to induce them to reduce the price, but without success. Writing from Washington, D. C., September 12th, 1848, this gentleman says to William Harned, " The truth is, *and is confessed to be, that their destination is prostitution ;* of this you would be satisfied on seeing them : they are of elegant form, and fine faces."

And such, dear reader, is the sad fate of hundreds of my young countrywomen, natives of my native state.   Such is the fate of many who are not only reared under the mildest form of slavery, but of those who have been made acquainted with the milder system of the Prince of Peace.

When Christians, and Christian ministers, then, talk about the "mildest form of slavery,"—"Christian masters," &c., I say my feelings are outraged.   It is a great mistake to offer these as an extenuation of the system.   It is calculated to mislead the public mind. The opinion seems to prevail, that the negro, after having toiled as a slave for centuries to enrich his white brother, to lay the foundation of his proud institutions, after having been sunk as low as slavery can sink him, needs now only a second-rate civilization, a lower standard of civil and religious privileges than the whites claim for themselves.

During the last year or two, we have heard of nothing but revolutions, and the enlargements of the eras of freedom, on both sides of the Atlantic. Our white brethren everywhere are reaching out their hands to grasp more freedom. In the place of absolute monarchies they have limited monarchies, and in the place of limited monarchies they have republics : so tenacious are they of their own liberties.

But when we speak of slavery, and complain of the wrong it is doing us, and ask to have the yoke removed, we are told, "O, you must not be impatient, you must not create undue excitement. You are not so badly off, for many of your masters are kind Christian masters." Yes, sirs, many of our masters are professed Christians ; and what advantage is that to us ? The grey heads of our fathers are brought down by scores to the grave in sorrow, on account of their young and tender sons, who are sold to the far South, where they have to toil without requite to supply the world's market with *cotton, sugar, rice, tobacco, &c.* Our venerable mothers are borne down with poignant grief at the fate of their children. Our sisters, if not by the law, are by common consent made the prey of vile men, who can bid the highest.

In all the bright achievements we have obtained in the great work of emancipation, if we have not settled the fact that the chattel principle is wrong, and cannot be maintained upon Christian ground, then

we have wrought and triumphed to little purpose,
and we shall have to do our first work over again.

It is this that has done all the mischief connected
with slavery; it is this that threatens still further
mischief. Whatever may be the ill or favoured condition of the slave in the matter of mere personal
treatment, it is the chattel relation that robs him of
his manhood, and transfers his ownership in himself
to another. It is this that transfers the proprietor-
ship of his wife and children to another. It is this
that throws his family history into utter confusion,
and leaves him without a single record to which he
may appeal in vindication of his character, or honour.
And has a man no sense of honour because he was
born a slave? Has he no need of character?

Suppose insult, reproach, or slander, should render
it necessary for him to appeal to the history of his
family in vindication of his character, where will he
find that history? He goes to his native state, to his
native county, to his native town; but no where does
he find any record of himself *as a man*. On looking
at the family record of his old, kind, Christian, master,
there he finds his name on a catalogue with the horses,
cows, hogs and dogs. However humiliating and de-
grading it may be to his feelings to find his name
written down among the beasts of the field, *that* is
just the place, and the *only* place assigned to it by the
chattel relation. I beg our Anglo-Saxon brethren to
accustom themselves to think that we need something
more than mere kindness. We ask for justice, truth
and honour as other men do.

My coloured brethren are now widely awake to the degradation which they suffer in having property vested in their persons, and they are also conscious of the deep and corrupting disgrace of having our wives and children owned by other men—men, who have shown to the world that their own virtue is not infallible, and who have given us no flattering encouragement to entrust that of our wives and daughters to them.

I have great pleasure in stating that my dear friend W. W., spoken of in this narrative, to whom I am so deeply indebted, is still living. I have been twice to see him within four years, and have regular correspondence with him. In one of the last letters I had from him, he authorises me to use his name in connection with this narrative in these words,—"As for using my name, by reference or otherwise, in thy narrative, it is at thy service. I know thee so well James, that I am not afraid of thy making a bad use of it, nor am I afraid or ashamed to have it known that I took thee in and gave thee aid, when I found thee travelling alone and in want.—W. W."

On the second page of the same sheet I have a few lines from his excellent lady, in which she says, " James, I hope thee will not attribute my long silence in writing to indifference. No such feeling can ever exist towards thee in our family. Thy name is mentioned almost every day. Each of the children claims the next letter from thee. It will be for thee to decide which shall have it.—P. W."

In a postscript following this, W. W. says again :—

"Understand me, James, that thee is at full liberty to use my name in any way thee wishes in thy narrative. We have a man here from the eastern shore of thy state. He is trying to learn as fast as thee did when here.—W. W."

I hope the reader will pardon me for introducing these extracts. My only apology is, the high gratification I feel in knowing that this family has not only been greatly prospered in health and happiness, but that I am upon the most intimate and pleasant terms with all its members, and that they all still feel a deep and cordial interest in my welfare.

There is another distinguished individual whose sympathy has proved very gratifying to me in my situation—I mean that true friend of the negro, *Gerrit Smith, Esq.* I was well acquainted with the family in which Mr. Smith married in Maryland. My attention has been fixed upon him for the last ten years, for I have felt confident that God had set him apart for some great good to the negro. In a letter dated Peterborough, November 7th, 1848, he says:—

"J. W. C. PENNINGTON,

"Slight as is my *personal* acquaintance with you, I nevertheless am well acquainted with you. I am familiar with many passages in your history—all that part of your history extending from the time when, a sturdy blacksmith, you were running away from Maryland oppression, down to the present, when you are the successor of my lamented friend, Theodore S. Wright. Let me add that my acquaintance with you has inspired me with a high regard for your wisdom and integrity."

Give us a few more such men in America, and slavery will soon be numbered among the things that were. A few men who will not only have the moral courage to aim the severing blow at the chattel relation between master and slave, without parley, palliation or compromise ; but who have also the christian fidelity to brave public scorn and contumely, to seize a coloured man by the hand, and elevate him to the position from whence the avarice and oppression of the whites have degraded him. These men have the right view of the subject. They see that in every case where the relation between master and slave is broken, slavery is weakened, and that every coloured man elevated, becomes a step in the ladder upon which his whole people are to ascend. They would not have us accept of some modified form of liberty, while the old mischief working chattel relation remains unbroken, untouched and unabrogated.

J. W. C. PENNINGTON.

13, *Princes Square, London,*
    August 15th, 1849.

CONTENTS.

THE FUGITIVE BLACKSMITH.

CHAPTER I.

MY BIRTH AND PARENTAGE.——THE TREATMENT OF
SLAVES GENERALLY IN MARYLAND.

I was born in the state of Maryland, which is one
of the smallest and most northern of the slave-
holding states; the products of this state are wheat,
rye, Indian corn, tobacco, with some hemp, flax, &c.
By looking at the map, it will be seen that Maryland, like Virginia her neighbour, is divided by the
Chesapeake Bay into eastern and western shores. My
birthplace was on the eastern shore, where there are
seven or eight small counties; the farms are small,
and tobacco is mostly raised.

At an early period in the history of Maryland, her
lands began to be exhausted by the bad cultivation
peculiar to slave states; and hence she soon commenced the business of breeding slaves for the more
southern states. This has given an enormity to
slavery, in Maryland, differing from that which attaches to the system in Louisiana, and equalled by
none of the kind, except Virginia and Kentucky, and
not by either of these in extent.

My parents did not both belong to the same owner:
my father belonged to a man named ——— ; my
mother belonged to a man named ———. This not
only made me a slave, but made me the slave of him

B

to whom my mother belonged ; as the primary law of slavery is, that the child shall follow the condition of the mother.

When I was about four years of age, my mother, an older brother and myself, were given to a son of my master, who had studied for the medical profession, but who had now married wealthy, and was about to settle as a wheat planter in Washington County, on the western shore. This began the first of our family troubles that I knew anything about, as it occasioned a separation between my mother and the only two children she then had, and my father, to a distance of about two hundred miles. But this separation did not continue long ; my father being a valuable slave, my master was glad to purchase him.

About this time, I began to feel another evil of slavery—I mean the want of parental care and attention. My parents were not able to give any attention to their children during the day. I often suffered much from *hunger* and other similar causes. To estimate the sad state of a slave child, you must look at it as a helpless human being thrown upon the world without the benefit of its natural guardians. It is thrown into the world without a social circle to flee to for hope, shelter, comfort, or instruction. The social circle, with all its heaven-ordained blessings, is of the utmost importance to the *tender child ;* but of this, the slave child, however tender and delicate, is robbed.

There is another source of evil to slave children, which I cannot forbear to mention here, as one which early embittered my life,—I mean the tyranny of the master's children. My master had two sons, about the ages and sizes of my older brother and myself. We were not only required to recognise these young sirs as our young masters, but *they* felt themselves to be such; and, in consequence of this feeling, they sought to treat us with the same air of authority that their father did the older slaves.

Another evil of slavery that I felt severely about this time, was the tyranny and abuse of the over- seers. These men seem to look with an evil eye upon children. I was once visiting a menagerie, and being struck with the fact, that the lion was comparatively indifferent to every one around his cage, while he eyed with peculiar keenness a little boy I had; the keeper informed me that such was always the case. Such is true of those human beings in the slave states, called overseers. They seem to take pleasure in torturing the children of slaves, long before they are large enough to be put at the hoe, and consequently under the whip.

We had an overseer, named Blackstone; he was an extremely cruel man to the working hands. He always carried a long hickory whip, a kind of pole. He kept three or four of these in order, that he might not at any time be without one.

I once found one of these hickories lying in the yard, and supposing that he had thrown it away, I picked it up, and boy-like, was using it for a horse; he came along from the field, and seeing me with it, fell upon me with the one he then had in his hand, and flogged me most cruelly. From that, I lived in constant dread of that man; and he would show how much he delighted in cruelty by chasing me from my play with threats and imprecations. I have lain for hours in a wood, or behind a fence, to hide from his eye.

At this time my days were extremely dreary. When I was nine years of age, myself and my brother were hired out from home ; my brother was placed with a pump-maker, and I was placed with a stone-mason.   We were both in a town some six miles from home.   As the men with whom we lived were not slaveholders, we enjoyed some relief from the peculiar evils of slavery.   Each of us lived in a family where there was no other negro.

The slaveholders in that state often hire the children of their slaves out to non-slaveholders, not only because they save themselves the expense of taking care of them, but in this way they get among their slaves useful trades.   They put a bright slave-boy with a tradesman, until he gets such a knowledge of the trade as to be able to do his own work, and then he takes him home.   I remained with the stonemason until I was eleven years of age : at this time I was taken home.   This was another serious period in my childhood ; I was separated from my older brother, to whom I was much attached ; he continued at his place, and not only learned the trade to great perfection, but finally became the property of the man with whom he lived, so that our separation was permanent, as we never lived nearer after, than six miles.   My master owned an excellent blacksmith, who had obtained his trade in the way I have mentioned above. When I returned home at the age of eleven, I was set about assisting to do the mason-work of a new smith's shop.   This being done, I was placed at the business, which I soon learned, so as to be called a "first-rate blacksmith."   I continued to work at this business for nine years, or until I was twenty-one, with the exception of the last seven months.

In the spring of 1828, my master sold me to a Methodist man, named ———, for the sum of seven hundred dollars. It soon proved that he had not work enough to keep me employed as a smith, and he offered me for sale again. On hearing of this, my old master re-purchased me, and proposed to me to undertake the carpentering business. I had been working at this trade six months with a white work-man, who was building a large barn when I left. I will now relate the abuses which occasioned me to fly.

Three or four of our farm hands had their wives and families on other plantations. In such cases, it is the custom in Maryland to allow the men to go on Satur-day evening to see their families, stay over the Sab-bath, and return on Monday morning, not later than "half-an-hour by sun." To overstay their time is a grave fault, for which, especially at busy seasons, they are punished.

One Monday morning, two of these men had not been so fortunate as to get home at the required time : one of them was an uncle of mine. Besides these, two young men who had no families, and for whom no such provision of time was made, having gone somewhere to spend the Sabbath, were absent. My master was greatly irritated, and had resolved to have, as he said, " a general whipping-match among them."

Preparatory to this, he had a rope in his pocket, and a cowhide in his hand, walking about the pre-mises, and speaking to every one he met in a very insolent manner, and finding fault with some without just cause. My father, among other numerous and responsible duties, discharged that of shepherd to a large and valuable flock of Merino sheep. This

morning he was engaged in the tenderest of a shepherd's duties ;—a little lamb, not able to go alone, lost
its mother ; he was feeding it by hand. He had been
keeping it in the house for several days. As he stooped
over it in the yard, with a vessel of new milk he had
obtained, with which to feed it, my master came
along, and without the least provocation, began by
asking, "Bazil, have you fed the flock ?"

"Yes, sir."

"Were you away yesterday ?"

"No, sir."

"Do you know why these boys have not got home
this morning yet ?"

"No, sir, I have not seen any of them since Saturday
night."

"By the Eternal, I'll make them know their hour.
The fact is, I have too many of you ; my people are
getting to be the most careless, lazy, and worthless in
the country."

"Master," said my father, "I am always at my
post ; Monday morning never finds me off the plantation."

"Hush, Bazil! I shall have to sell some of you ; and
then the rest will have enough to do ; I have not work
enough to keep you all tightly employed ; I have too
many of you."

All this was said in an angry, threatening, and
exceedingly insulting tone. My father was a high-
spirited man, and feeling deeply the insult, replied to
the last expression,—"If I am one too many, sir, give
me a chance to get a purchaser, and I am willing to
be sold when it may suit you."

"Bazil, I told you to hush !" and suiting the action
to the word, he drew forth the "cowhide" from under

his arm, fell upon him with most savage cruelty, and inflicted fifteen or twenty severe stripes with all his strength, over his shoulders and the small of his back. As he raised himself upon his toes, and gave the last stripe, he said, "By the * * * I will make you know that I am master of your tongue as well as of your time !"

Being a tradesman, and just at that time getting my breakfast, I was near enough to hear the insolent words that were spoken to my father, and to hear, see, and even count the savage stripes inflicted upon him.

Let me ask any one of Anglo-Saxon blood and spirit, how would you expect a *son* to feel at such a sight ?

This act created an open rupture with our family —each member felt the deep insult that had been inflicted upon our head ; the spirit of the whole family was roused ; we talked of it in our nightly gatherings, and showed it in our daily melancholy aspect. The oppressor saw this, and with the heartlessness that was in perfect keeping with the first insult, commenced a series of tauntings, threatenings, and insinuations, with a view to crush the spirit of the whole family.

Although it was sometime after this event before I took the decisive step, yet in my mind and spirit, I never was a *Slave* after it.

Whenever I thought of the great contrast between my father's employment on that memorable Monday morning, (feeding the little lamb,) and the barbarous conduct of my master, I could not help cordially despising the proud abuser of my sire ; and I believe he discovered it, for he seemed to have diligently sought an occasion against me. Many incidents occurred to

convince me of this, too tedious to mention ; but there
is one I will mention, because it will serve to show the
state of feeling that existed between us, and how it
served to widen the already open breach.

I was one day shoeing a horse in the shop yard.   I
had been stooping for some time under the weight of
the horse, which was large, and was very tired ; meanwhile, my master had taken his position on a little
hill just in front of me, and stood leaning back on his
cane, with his hat drawn over his eyes.   I put down
the horse's foot, and straightened myself up to rest
a moment, and without knowing that he was there,
my eye caught his.   This threw him into a panic of
rage ; he would have it that I was watching him.
" What are you rolling your white eyes at me for,
you lazy rascal ?"   He came down upon me with his
cane, and laid on over my shoulders, arms, and legs,
about a dozen severe blows, so that my limbs and flesh
were sore for several weeks ; and then after several
other offensive epithets, left me.

This affair my mother saw from her cottage,
which was near ; I being one of the oldest sons of my
parents, our family was now mortified to the lowest
degree.   I had always aimed to be trustworthy ;
and feeling a high degree of mechanical pride, I had
aimed to do my work with dispatch and skill, my
blacksmith's pride and taste was one thing that had
reconciled me so long to remain a slave.   I sought
to distinguish myself in the finer branches of the
business by invention and finish ; I frequently tried
my hand at making guns and pistols, putting blades
in penknives, making fancy hammers, hatchets, sword-
canes, &c., &c.   Besides I used to assist my father at
night in making straw-hats and willow-baskets, by

which means we supplied our family with little articles
of food, clothing and luxury, which slaves in the
mildest form of the system never get from the master;
but after this, I found that my mechanic's pleasure
and pride were gone. I thought of nothing but the
family disgrace under which we were smarting, and
how to get out of it.

Perhaps I may as well extend this note a little.
The reader will observe that I have not said much
about my master's cruel treatment; I have aimed
rather to shew the cruelties incident to the system.
I have no disposition to attempt to convict him of
having been one of the most cruel masters—that
would not be true—his prevailing temper was kind,
but he was a perpetualist. He was opposed to emancipation; thought free negroes a great nuisance, and
was, as respects discipline, a thorough slaveholder. He
would not tolerate a look or a word from a slave like
insubordination. He would suppress it at once, and
at any risk. When he thought it necessary to secure
unqualified obedience, he would strike a slave with
any weapon, flog him on the bare back, and sell.
And this was the kind of discipline he also empowered
his overseers and sons to use.

I have seen children go from our plantations to
join the chained-gang on its way from Washington
to Louisiana; and I have seen men and women flogged
—I have seen the overseers strike a man with a hay-
fork—nay more, men have been maimed by shooting!
Some dispute arose one morning between the overseer
and one of the farm hands, when the former made
at the slave with a hickory club; the slave taking to
his heels, started for the woods; as he was crossing
the yard, the overseer turned, snatched his gun which

was near, and fired at the flying slave, lodging several shots in the calf of one leg. The poor fellow continued his flight, and got into the woods; but he was in so much pain that he was compelled to come out in the evening, and give himself up to his master, thinking he would not allow him to be punished as he had been shot. He was locked up that night; the next morning the overseer was allowed to tie him up and flog him; his master then took his instruments and picked the shot out of his leg, and told him, it served him just right.

My master had a deeply pious and exemplary slave, an elderly man, who one day had a misunderstanding with the overseer, when the latter attempted to flog him. He fled to the woods; it was noon; at evening he came home orderly. The next morning, my master, taking one of his sons with him, a rope and cowhide in his hand, led the poor old man away into the stable; tied him up, and ordered the son to lay on thirty-nine lashes, which he did, making the keen end of the cowhide lap around and strike him in the tenderest part of his side, till the blood sped out, as if a lance had been used.

While my master's son was thus engaged, the sufferer's little daughter, a child six years of age, stood at the door, weeping in agony for the fate of her father. I heard the old man articulating in a low tone of voice; I listened at the intervals between the stripes, and lo! he was praying!

When the last lash was laid on, he was let down; and leaving him to put on his clothes, they passed out of the door, and drove the man's weeping child away! I was mending a hinge to one of the barn doors; I saw and heard what I have stated. Six months after, this same man's eldest daughter, a girl fifteen years old, was sold to slave-traders, where he never saw her more.

This poor slave and his wife were both Methodists, so was the wife of the young master who flogged him. My old master was an Episcopalian.

These are only a few of the instances which came under my own notice during my childhood and youth on our plantations; as to those which occurred on other plantations in the neighbourhood, I could state any number.

I have stated that my master was watching the movements of our family very closely. Sometime after the difficulties began, we found that he also had a confidential slave assisting him in the business. This wretched fellow, who was nearly white, and of Irish descent, informed our master of the movements of each member of the family by day and by night, and on Sundays. This stirred the spirit of my mother, who spoke to our fellow-slave, and told him he ought to be ashamed to be engaged in such low business.

Master hearing of this, called my father, mother, and myself before him, and accused us of an attempt to resist and intimidate his "confidential servant." Finding that only my mother had spoken to him, he swore that if she ever spoke another word to him, he would flog her.

I knew my mother's spirit and my master's temper as well. Our social state was now perfectly intolerable. We were on the eve of a general fracas. This last scene occurred on Tuesday; and on Saturday evening following, without counsel or advice from any one, I determined to fly.

CHAPTER II.

It was the Sabbath : the holy day which God in his infinite wisdom gave for the rest of both man and beast. In the state of Maryland, the slaves generally have the Sabbath, except in those districts where the evil weed, tobacco, is cultivated ; and then, when it is the season for setting the plant, they are liable to be robbed of this only rest.

It was in the month of November, somewhat past the middle of the month. It was a bright day, and all was quiet. Most of the slaves were resting about their quarters ; others had leave to visit their friends on other plantations, and were absent. The evening previous I had arranged my little bundle of clothing, and had secreted it at some distance from the house. I had spent most of the forenoon in my workshop, engaged in deep and solemn thought.

It is impossible for me now to recollect all the perplexing thoughts that passed through my mind during that forenoon ; it was a day of heartaching to me. But I distinctly remember the two great difficulties that stood in the way of my flight : I had a father and mother whom I dearly loved,—I had also six sisters and four brothers on the plantation. The question was, shall I hide my purpose from them? moreover, how will my flight affect them when I am gone? Will they not be suspected? Will not the whole family be sold off as a disaffected family, as is generally the case when one of its members flies? But a still more trying question was, how can I expect to succeed, I have no knowledge of distance or direction. I know that Pennsylvania is a free state, but I know not where its soil begins, or where that of Maryland ends? Indeed, at this time there was no safety in Pennsylvania, New Jersey, or New York, for a fugitive, except in lurking-places, or under the care of judicious friends, who could be entrusted not only with liberty, but also with life itself.

With such difficulties before my mind, the day had rapidly worn away; and it was just past noon. One of my perplexing questions I had settled—I had resolved to let no one into my secret; but the other difficulty was now to be met. It was to be met without the least knowledge of its magnitude, except by imagination. Yet of one thing there could be no mistake, that the consequences of a failure would be most serious. Within my recollection no one had attempted to escape from my master; but I had many cases in my mind's eye, of slaves of other planters who had failed, and who had been made examples of the most cruel treatment, by flogging and selling to the far South, where they were never to see their friends more. I was not without serious apprehension that such would be my fate. The bare possibility was impressively solemn; but the hour was now come, and the man must act and be free, or remain a slave for ever. How the impression came to be upon my mind I cannot tell; but there was a strange and horrifying belief, that if I did not meet the crisis that day, I should be self-doomed—that my ear would be nailed to the door-post for ever. The emotions of that moment I cannot fully depict.

Hope, fear, dread, terror, love, sorrow, and deep melancholy were mingled in my mind together ; my mental state was one of most painful distraction.   When I looked at my numerous family—a beloved father and mother, eleven brothers and sisters, &c. ; but when I looked at slavery as such ; when I looked at it in its mildest form, with all its annoyances ; and above all, when I remembered that one of the chief annoyances of slavery, in the most mild form, is the liability of being at any moment sold into the worst form ; it seemed that no consideration, not even that of life itself, could tempt me to give up the thought of flight.   And then when I considered the difficulties of the way—the reward that would be offered—the human blood-hounds that would be set upon my track —the weariness—the hunger—the gloomy thought, of not only losing all one's friends in one day, but of having to seek and to make new friends in a strange world.   But, as I have said, the hour was come, and the man must act, or for ever be a slave.

It was now two o'clock.   I stepped into the quarter ; there was a strange and melancholy silence mingled with the destitution that was apparent in every part of the house.   The only morsel I could see in the shape of food, was a piece of Indian flour bread, it might be half-a-pound in weight.   This I placed in my pocket, and giving a last look at the aspect of the house, and at a few small children who were playing at the door, I sallied forth thoughtfully and melancholy, and after crossing the barn-yard, a few moments' walk brought me to a small cave, near the mouth of which lay a pile of stones, and into which I had deposited my clothes.   From this, my course lay through thick and heavy woods and back lands to —— town, where my brother lived. This town was six miles distance. It was now near three o'clock, but my object was neither to be seen on the road, or to approach the town by daylight, as I was well-known there, and as any intelligence of my having been seen there would at once put the pursuers on my track. This first six miles of my flight, I not only travelled very slowly, therefore, so as to avoid carrying any daylight to this town ; but during this walk another very perplexing question was agitating my mind. Shall I call on my brother as I pass through, and shew him what I am about ? My brother was older than I, we were much attached ; I had been in the habit of looking to him for counsel.

I entered the town about dark, resolved, all things in view, *not* to shew myself to my brother. Having passed through the town without being recognised, I now found myself under cover of night, a solitary wanderer from home and friends; my only guide was the *north star*, by this I knew my general course north-ward, but at what point I should strike Penn, or when and where I should find a friend, I knew not. Another feeling now occupied my mind,—I felt like a mariner who has gotten his ship outside of the har-bour and has spread his sails to the breeze. The cargo is on board—the ship is cleared—and the voyage I must make; besides, this being my first night, almost every thing will depend upon my clearing the coast before the day dawns. In order to do this my flight must be rapid. I therefore set forth in sorrowful earnest, only now and then I was cheered by the *wild* hope, that I should somewhere and at sometime be free.

The night was fine for the season, and passed on

with little interruption for want of strength, until, about three o'clock in the morning, I began to feel the chilling effects of the dew.

At this moment, gloom and melancholy again spread through my whole soul. The prospect of utter destitution which threatened me was more than I could bear, and my heart began to melt. What substance is there in a piece of dry Indian bread ; what nourishment is there in it to warm the nerves of one already chilled to the heart ? Will this afford a sufficient sustenance after the toil of the night ? But while these thoughts were agitating my mind, the day dawned upon me, in the midst of an open extent of country, where the only shelter I could find, without risking my travel by daylight, was a corn shock, but a few hundred yards from the road, and here I must pass my first day out. The day was an unhappy one ; my hiding-place was extremely precarious. I had to sit in a squatting position the whole day, without the least chance to rest. But, besides this, my scanty pittance did not afford me that nourishment which my hard night's travel needed. Night came again to my relief, and I sallied forth to pursue my journey. By this time, not a crumb of my crust remained, and I was hungry and began to feel the desperation of distress.

As I travelled I felt my strength failing and my spirits wavered ; my mind was in a deep and melancholy dream. It was cloudy ; I could not see my star, and had serious misgivings about my course.

In this way the night passed away, and just at the dawn of day I found a few sour apples, and took my shelter under the arch of a small bridge that crossed the road. Here I passed the second day in ambush.

This day would have been more pleasant than the previous, but the sour apples, and a draught of cold water, had produced anything but a favourable effect; indeed, I suffered most of the day with severe symptoms of cramp. The day passed away again without any further incident, and as I set out at nightfall, I felt quite satisfied that I could not pass another twenty-four hours without nourishment. I made but little progress during the night, and often sat down, and slept frequently fifteen or twenty minutes. At the dawn of the third day I continued my travel. As I had found my way to a public turnpike road during the night, I came very early in the morning to a toll-gate, where the only person I saw, was a lad about twelve years of age. I inquired of him where the road led to. He informed me it led to Baltimore. I asked him the distance, he said it was eighteen miles.

This intelligence was perfectly astounding to me. My master lived eighty miles from Baltimore. I was now sixty-two miles from home. That distance in the right direction, would have placed me several miles across Mason and Dixon's line, but I was evidently yet in the state of Maryland.

I ventured to ask the lad at the gate another question—Which is the best way to Philadelphia? Said he, you can take a road which turns off about half-a-mile below this, and goes to Getsburgh, or you can go on to Baltimore and take the packet.

I made no reply, but my thought was, that I was as near Baltimore and Baltimore-packets as would answer my purpose.

In a few moments I came to the road to which the lad had referred, and felt some relief when I had gotten

c

out of that great public highway, "The National Turnpike," which I found it to be.

When I had walked a mile on this road, and when it had now gotten to be about nine o'clock, I met a young man with a load of hay.   He drew up his horses, and addressed me in a very kind tone, when the following dialogue took place between us.

"Are you travelling any distance, my friend?"

"I am on my way to Philadelphia."

"Are you free?"

"Yes, sir."

"I suppose, then, you are provided with free papers?"

"No, sir.   I have no papers."

"Well, my friend, you should not travel on this road : you will be taken up before you have gone three miles.   There are men living on this road who are constantly on the look-out for your people ; and it is seldom that one escapes them who attempts to pass by day."

He then very kindly gave me advice where to turn off the road at a certain point, and how to find my way to a certain house, where I would meet with an old gentleman who would further advise me whether I had better remain till night, or go on.

I left this interesting young man ; and such was my surprise and chagrin at the thought of having so widely missed my way, and my alarm at being in such a dangerous position, that in ten minutes I had so far forgotten his directions as to deem it unwise to attempt to follow them, lest I should miss my way, and get into evil hands.

I, however, left the road, and went into a small piece of wood, but not finding a sufficient hiding-place, and it being a busy part of the day, when persons were at work about the fields, I thought I should excite less suspicion by keeping in the road, so I returned to the road; but the events of the next few moments proved that I committed a serious mistake.

I went about a mile, making in all two miles from the spot where I met my young friend, and about five miles from the toll-gate to which I have referred, and I found myself at the twenty-four miles' stone from Baltimore. It was now about ten o'clock in the forenoon; my strength was greatly exhausted by reason of the want of suitable food; but the excitement that was then going on in my mind, left me little time to think of my *need* of food. Under ordinary circumstances as a traveller, I should have been glad to see the "Tavern," which was near the mile-stone; but as the case stood with me, I deemed it a dangerous place to pass, much less to stop at. I was therefore passing it as quietly and as rapidly as possible, when from the lot just opposite the house, or sign-post, I heard a coarse stern voice cry, "Halloo!"

I turned my face to the left, the direction from which the voice came, and observed that it proceeded from a man who was digging potatoes. I answered him politely; when the following occurred :—

"Who do *you* belong to?"

"I am free, sir."

"Have you got papers?"

"No, sir."

"Well, you must stop here."

By this time he had got astride the fence, making his way into the road. I said,

"My business is onward, sir, and I do not wish to stop."

c 2

" I will see then if you don't stop, you black rascal."

He was now in the middle of the road, making after me in a brisk walk.

I saw that a crisis was at hand; I had no weapons of any kind, not even a pocket-knife ; but I asked myself, shall I surrender without a struggle.   The instinctive answer was " No."   What will you do ? continue to walk ; if he runs after you, run ; get him as far from the house as you can, then turn suddenly and smite him on the knee with a stone ; that will render him, at least, unable to pursue you.

This was a desperate scheme, but I could think of no other, and my habits as a blacksmith had given my eye and hand such mechanical skill, that I felt quite sure that if I could only get a stone in my hand, and have time to wield it, I should not miss his knee-pan.

He began to breathe short.   He was evidently vexed because I did not halt, and I felt more and more provoked at the idea of being thus pursued by a man to whom I had not done the least injury.   I had just began to glance my eye about for a stone to grasp, when he made a tiger-like leap at me. This of course brought us to running.   At this moment he yelled out " Jake Shouster !" and at the next moment the door of a small house standing to the left was opened, and out jumped a shoemaker girded up in his leather apron, with his knife in hand. He sprang forward and seized me by the collar, while the other seized my arms behind.   I was now in the grasp of two men, either of whom were larger bodied than myself, and one of whom was armed with a dangerous weapon.

Standing in the door of the shoemaker's shop, was a third man ; and in the potatoe lot I had passed, was still a fourth man. Thus surrounded by superior physical force, the fortune of the day it seemed to me was gone.

My heart melted away, I sunk resistlessly into the hands of my captors, who dragged me immediately into the tavern which was near. I ask my reader to go in with me, and see how the case goes.

GREAT MORAL DILEMMA.

A few moments after I was taken into the bar-room, the news having gone as by electricity, the house and yard were crowded with gossippers, who had left their business to come and see " the runaway nigger." This hastily assembled congregation consisted of men, women, and children, each one had a look to give at, and a word to say about, the " nigger."

But among the whole, there stood one whose name I have never known, but who evidently wore the garb of a man whose profession bound him to speak for the dumb, but he, standing head and shoulders above all that were round about, spoke the first hard sentence against me. Said he, " That fellow is a runaway I know ; put him in jail a few days, and you will soon hear where he came from." And then fixing a fiend-like gaze upon me, he continued, " if I lived on this road, *you* fellows would not find such clear running as you do, I'd trap more of you."

But now comes the pinch of the case, the case of conscience to me even at this moment. Emboldened by the cruel speech just recited, my captors enclosed me, and said, " Come now, this matter may easily be settled without you going to jail ; who do you belong to, and where did you come from ?"

The facts here demanded were in my breast. I knew according to the law of slavery, who I belonged to and where I came from, and I must now do one of three things—I must refuse to speak at all, or I must communicate the fact, or I must tell an untruth. How would an untutored slave, who had never heard of such a writer as Archdeacon Paley, be likely to act in such a dilemma? The first point decided, was, the facts in this case are my private property. These men have no more right to them than a highway robber has to my purse. What will be the consequence if I put them in possession of the facts. In forty-eight hours, I shall have received perhaps one hundred lashes, and be on my way to the Louisiana cotton fields. Of what service will it be to them. They will get a paltry sum of two hundred dollars. Is not my liberty worth more to me than two hundred dollars are to them?

I resolved therefore, to insist that I was free. This not being satisfactory without other evidence, they tied my hands and set out, and went to a magistrate who lived about half a mile distant. It so happened, that when we arrived at his house he was not at home. This was to them a disappointment, but to me it was a relief; but I soon learned by their conversation, that there was still another magistrate in the neighbourhood, and that they would go to him. In about twenty minutes, and after climbing fences and jumping ditches, we, captors and captive, stood before his door, but it was after the same manner as before—he was not at home. By this time the day had worn away to one or two o'clock, and my captors evidently began to feel somewhat impatient of the loss of time. We were about a mile and a quarter from the tavern.

As we set out on our return, they began to parley. Finding it was difficult for me to get over fences with my hands tied, they untied me, and said, "Now John," that being the name they had given me, "if you have run away from any one, it would be much better for you to tell us!" but I continued to affirm that I was free. I knew, however, that my situation was very critical, owing to the shortness of the distance I must be from home : my advertisement might overtake me at any moment.

On our way back to the tavern, we passed through a small skirt of wood, where I resolved to make an effort to escape again. One of my captors was walking on either side of me ; I made a sudden turn, with my left arm sweeping the legs of one of my captors from under him ; I left him nearly standing on his head, and took to my heels. As soon as they could recover they both took after me. We had to mount a fence. This I did most successfully, and making across an open field towards another wood ; one of my captors being a long-legged man, was in advance of the other, and consequently nearing me. We had a hill to rise, and during the ascent he gained on me. Once more I thought of self-defence. I am trying to escape peaceably, but this man is determined that I shall not.

My case was now desperate ; and I took this desperate thought : "I will run him a little farther from his coadjutor ; I will then suddenly catch a stone, and wound him in the breast." This was my fixed purpose, and I had arrived near the point on the top of the hill, where I expected to do the act, when to my surprise and dismay, I saw the other side of the hill was not only all ploughed up, but we came suddenly upon a man ploughing, who as suddenly left his plough and cut off my flight, by seizing me by the collar, when at the same moment my pursuer seized my arms behind. Here I was again in a sad fix. By this time the other pursuer had come up ; I was most savagely thrown down on the ploughed ground with my face downward, the ploughman placed his knee upon my shoulders, one of my captors put his upon my legs, while the other tied my arms behind me. I was then dragged up, and marched off with kicks, punches and imprecations.

We got to the tavern at three o'clock. Here they again cooled down, and made an appeal to me to make a disclosure. I saw that my attempt to escape strengthened their belief that I was a fugitive. I said to them, " If you will not put me in jail, I will now tell you where I am from." They promised. " Well," said I, " a few weeks ago, I was sold from the eastern shore to a slave-trader, who had a large gang, and set out for Georgia, but when he got to a town in Virginia, he was taken sick, and died with the small-pox. Several of his gang also died with it, so that the people in the town became alarmed, and did not wish the gang to remain among them. No one claimed us, or wished to have anything to do with us ; I left the rest, and thought I would go somewhere and get work."

When I said this, it was evidently believed by those who were present, and notwithstanding the unkind feeling that had existed, there was a murmur of approbation. At the same time I perceived that a panic began to seize some, at the idea that I was one of a small-pox gang. Several who had clustered near me, moved off to a respectful distance. One or two left the bar-room, and murmured, "better let the small-pox nigger go."

I was then asked what was the name of the slave-trader. Without premeditation, I said, "John Henderson."

"John Henderson!" said one of my captors, "I knew him; I took up a yaller boy for him about two years ago, and got fifty dollars. He passed out with a gang about that time, and the boy ran away from him at Frederickstown. What kind of a man was he?"

At a venture, I gave a description of him. "Yes," said he, "that is the man." By this time, all the gossippers had cleared the coast; our friend, "Jake Shouster," had also gone back to his bench to finish his custom work, after having "lost nearly the whole day, trotting about with a nigger tied," as I heard his wife say as she called him home to his dinner. I was now left alone with the man who first called to me in the morning. In a sober manner, he made this proposal to me: "John, I have a brother living in Risterstown, four miles off, who keeps a tavern; I think you had better go and live with him, till we see what will turn up. He wants an ostler." I at once assented to this. "Well," said he, "take something to eat, and I will go with you."

Although I had so completely frustrated their designs for the moment, I knew that it would by no means answer for me to go into that town, where there were prisons, handbills, newspapers, and travellers. My intention was, to start with him, but not to enter the town alive.

I sat down to eat; it was Wednesday, four o'clock, and this was the first regular meal I had since Sunday

morning. This over, we set out, and to my surprise,
he proposed to walk. We had gone about a mile
and a-half, and were approaching a wood through
which the road passed with a bend. I fixed upon
that as the spot where I would either free myself from
this man, or die in his arms. I had resolved upon a
plan of operation—it was this: to stop short, face
about, and commence action; and neither ask or
give quarters, until I was free or dead !

We had got within six rods of the spot, when a
gentleman turned the corner, meeting us on horseback. He came up, and entered into conversation
with my captor, both of them speaking in Dutch, so
that I knew not what they said. After a few moments, this gentleman addressed himself to me in
English, and I then learned that he was one of the
magistrates on whom we had called in the morning.;
I felt that another crisis was at hand. Using his
saddle as his bench, he put on an extremely stern
and magisterial-like face, holding up his horse not
unlike a field-marshal in the act of reviewing troops,
and carried me through a most rigid examination in
reference to the statement I had made. I repeated
carefully all I had said; at the close, he said, " Well,
you had better stay among us a few months, until
we see what is to be done with you." It was then
agreed that we should go back to the tavern, and
there settle upon some further plan. When we
arrived at the tavern, the magistrate alighted from
his horse, and went into the bar-room. He took
another close glance at me, and went over some points
of the former examination. He seemed quite satisfied of the correctness of my statement, and made the
following proposition : that I should go and live with

him for a short time, stating that he had a few acres of corn and potatoes to get in, and that he would give me twenty-five cents per day. I most cheerfully assented to this proposal. It was also agreed that I should remain at the tavern with my captor that night, and that he would accompany me in the morning. This part of the arrangement I did not like, but of course I could not say so. Things being thus arranged, the magistrate mounted his horse, and went on his way home.

It had been cloudy and rainy during the afternoon, but the western sky having partially cleared at this moment, I perceived that it was near the setting of the sun.

My captor had left his hired man most of the day to dig potatoes alone; but the waggon being now loaded, it being time to convey the potatoes into the barn, and the horses being all ready for that purpose, he was obliged to go into the potatoe field and give assistance.

I should say here, that his wife had been driven away by the small-pox panic about three o'clock, and had not yet returned; this left no one in the house, but a boy, about nine years of age.

As he went out, he spoke to the boy in Dutch, which I supposed, from the little fellow's conduct, to be instructions to watch me closely, which he certainly did.

The potatoe lot was across the public road, directly in front of the house; at the back of the house, and about 300 yards distant, there was a thick wood. The circumstances of the case would not allow me to think for one moment of remaining there for the night—the time had come for another effort—but there were two serious difficulties. One was, that I must either deceive or dispatch this boy who is watching me with intense vigilance. I am glad to say, that the latter did not for a moment seriously enter my mind. To deceive him effectually, I left my coat and went to the back door, from which my course would be direct to the wood. When I got to the door, I found that the barn, to which the waggon must soon come, lay just to the right, and overlooking the path I must take to the wood. In front of me lay a garden surrounded by a picket fence, to the left of me was a small gate, and that by passing through that gate would throw me into an open field, and give me clear running to the wood; but on looking through the gate, I saw that my captor, being with the team, would see me if I attempted to start before he moved from the position he then occupied. To add to my difficulty the horses had baulked; while waiting for the decisive moment, the boy came to the door and asked me why I did not come in. I told him I felt unwell, and wished him to be so kind as to hand me a glass of water; expecting while he was gone to get it, the team would clear, so that I could start. While he was gone, another attempt was made to start the team but failed; he came with the water and I quickly used it up by gargling my throat and by drinking a part. I asked him to serve me by giving me another glass: he gave me a look of close scrutiny, but went in for the water. I heard him fill the glass, and start to return with it; when the hind end of the waggon cleared the corner of the house, which stood in a range with the fence along which I was to pass in getting to the wood. As I passed out the gate, I "squared my main yard,"

and laid my course up the line of fence, I cast a last
glance over my right shoulder, and saw the boy just
perch his head above the garden picket to look after
me ; I heard at the same time great confusion with
the team, the rain having made the ground slippery,
and the horses having to cross the road with a slant
and rise to get into the barn, it required great effort
after they started to prevent their baulking. I felt
some assurance that although the boy might give
the alarm, my captor could not leave the team until
it was in the barn. I heard the horses' feet on the
barn-floor, just as I leaped the fence, and darted into
the wood.

The sun was now quite down behind the western
horizon, and just at this time a heavy dark curtain of
clouds was let down, which seemed to usher in haste
the night shade. I have never before or since seen
anything which seemed to me to compare in sublimity
with the spreading of the night shades at the close of
that day. My reflections upon the events of that day,
and upon the close of it, since I became acquainted
with the Bible, have frequently brought to my mind
that beautiful passage in the Book of Job, "He
holdeth back the face of His throne, and spreadeth a
cloud before it."

Before I proceed to the critical events and final
deliverance of the next chapter, I cannot forbear to
pause a moment here for reflection. The reader may
well imagine how the events of the past day affected my
mind. You have seen what was done to me ; you have
heard what was said to me—you have also seen what
I have done, and heard what I have said. If you
ask me whether I had expected before I left home, to
gain my liberty by shedding men's blood, or breaking

their limbs? I answer, no! and as evidence of this, I
had provided no weapon whatever; not so much as a
penknife—it never once entered my mind.   I cannot
say that I expected to have the ill fortune of meeting
with any human being who would attempt to impede
my flight.

If you ask me if I expected when I left home to gain
my liberty by fabrications and untruths? I answer,
no! my parents, slaves as they were, had always taught
me, when they could, that "truth may be blamed but
cannot be shamed;" so far as their example was concerned, I had no habits of untruth.   I was arrested, and
the demand made upon me, "Who do you belong to?"
knowing the fatal use these men would make of *my*
truth, I at once concluded that they had no more right
to it than a highwayman has to a traveller's purse.

If you ask me whether I now really believe that I
gained my liberty by those lies? I answer, no!   I
now believe that I should be free, had I told the truth;
but, at that moment, I could not see any other way to
baffle my enemies, and escape their clutches.

The history of that day has never ceased to inspire
me with a deeper hatred of slavery; I never recur to
it but with the most intense horror at a system which
can put a man not only in peril of liberty, limb, and
life itself, but which may even send him in haste to
the bar of God with a lie upon his lips.

Whatever my readers may think, therefore, of the
history of events of the day, do not admire in it
the fabrications; but *see* in it the impediments that
often fall into the pathway of the flying bondman.
See how human bloodhounds gratuitously chase, catch,
and tempt him to shed blood and lie; how, when he
would do good, evil is thrust upon him.

CHAPTER III.

ALMOST immediately on entering the wood, I not only found myself embosomed in the darkness of the night, but I also found myself entangled in a thick forest of undergrowth, which had been quite thoroughly wetted by the afternoon rain.

I penetrated through the wood, thick and thin, and more or less wet, to the distance I should think of three miles. By this time my clothes were all thoroughly soaked through, and I felt once more a glôom and wretchedness; the recollection of which makes me shudder at this distant day. My young friends in this highly favoured Christian country, surrounded with all the comforts of home and parental care, visited by pastors and Sabbath-school teachers, think of the dreary condition of the blacksmith boy in the dark wood that night; and then consider that thousands of his brethren have had to undergo much greater hardships in their flight from slavery.

I was now out of the hands of those who had so cruelly teased me during the day; but a number of fearful thoughts rushed into my mind to alarm me. It was dark and cloudy, so that I could not see the *north star*. How do I know what ravenous beasts are in this wood? How do I know what precipices may be within its bounds? I cannot rest in this wood to-morrow, for it will be searched by those men from whom I have escaped; but how shall I regain the road? How shall I know when I am on the right road again?

These are some of the thoughts that filled my mind with gloom and alarm.

At a venture I struck an angle northward in search of the road. After several hours of zigzag and laborious travel, dragging through briars, thorns and running vines, I emerged from the wood and found myself wading marshy ground and over ditches.

I can form no correct idea of the distance I travelled, but I came to a road, I should think about three o'clock in the morning. It so happened that I came out near where there was a fork in the road of three prongs.

Now arose a serious query—which is the right prong for me? I was reminded by the circumstance of a superstitious proverb among the slaves, that " the left-hand turning was unlucky," but as I had never been in the habit of placing faith in this or any similar superstition, I am not aware that it had the least weight upon my mind, as I had the same difficulty with reference to the right-hand turning. After a few moments parley with myself, I took the central prong of the road and pushed on with all my speed.

It had not cleared off, but a fresh wind had sprung up; it was chilly and searching. This with my wet clothing made me very uncomfortable; my nerves began to quiver before the searching wind. The barking of mastiffs, the crowing of fowls, and the

distant rattling of market waggons, warned me that
the day was approaching.

My British reader must remember that in the
region where I was, we know nothing of the long
hours of twilight you enjoy here. With us the day
is measured more by the immediate presence of the
sun, and the night by the prevalence of actual
darkness.

The day dawned upon me when I was near a small
house and barn, situate close to the road side. The
barn was too near the road, and too small to afford
secure shelter for the day; but as I cast my eye
around by the dim light, I could see no wood, and no
larger barn. It seemed to be an open country to a
wide extent. The sun was travelling so rapidly from
his eastern chamber, that ten or fifteen minutes would
spread broad daylight over my track. Whether *my*
deed was evil, *you* may judge, but I freely confess
that I did *then* prefer darkness rather than light; I
therefore took to the mow of the little barn at a great
risk, as the events of the day will show. It so happened that the barn was filled with corn fodder, newly
cured and lately gotten in. You are aware that
however quietly one may crawl into such a bed, he is
compelled to make much more noise than if it were
a feather-bed; and also considerably more than if it
were hay or straw. Besides inflicting upon my own
excited imagination the belief that I made noise
enough to be heard by the inmates of the house who
were likely to be rising at the time, I had the mis-
fortune to attract the notice of a little house-dog,
such as we call in that part of the world a " fice,'
on account of its being not only the smallest species
of the canine race, but also, because it is the most

D

saucy, noisy, and teasing of all dogs. This little
creature commenced a fierce barking. I had at once
great fears that the mischievous little thing would
betray me ; I fully apprehended that as soon as the
man of the house arose, he would come and make
search in the barn. It now being entirely daylight,
it was too late to retreat from this shelter, even if I
could have found another ; I, therefore, bedded myself
down into the fodder as best I could, and entered
upon the annoyances of the day, with the frail hope
to sustain my mind.

It was Thursday morning ; the clouds that had
veiled the sky during the latter part of the previous
day and the previous night were gone. It was not
until about an hour after the sun rose that I heard
any out-door movements about the house. As soon
as I heard those movements, I was satisfied there
was but one man about the house, and that he
was preparing to go some distance to work for the
day. This was fortunate for me ; the busy movements about the yard, and especially the active preparations in the house for breakfast, silenced my
unwelcome little annoyer, the fice, until after the man
had gone, when he commenced afresh, and continued
with occasional intermissions through the day. He
made regular sallies from the house to the barn, and
after smelling about, would fly back to the house,
barking furiously ; thus he strove most skilfully
throughout the entire day to raise an alarm. There
seemed to be no one about the house but one or two
small children and the mother, after the man was
gone. About ten o'clock my attention was gravely
directed to another trial : how I could pass the day
without food. The reader will remember it is Thurs-

day, and the only regular meal I have taken since
Sunday, was yesterday, in the midst of great agitation, about four o'clock ; that since that I have performed my arduous night's travel.   At one moment,
I had nearly concluded to go and present myself at
the door, and ask·the woman of the house to have
compassion and give me food ; but then I feared the
consequences might be fatal, and I resolved to suffer
the day out.   The wind sprang up fresh and cool ;
the barn being small and the crevices large, my wet
clothes were dried by it, and chilled me through and
through.

I cannot now, with pen or tongue, give a correct
idea of the feeling of wretchedness I experienced ;
every nerve in my system quivered, so that not a
particle of my flesh was at rest.   In this way I passed
the day till about the middle of the afternoon, when
there seemed to be an unusual stir about the public
road, which passed close by the barn.   Men seemed
to be passing in parties on horseback, and talking
anxiously.   From a word which I now and then
overheard, I had not a shadow of doubt that they
were in search of me.   One I heard say, " I ought to
catch such a fellow, the only liberty he should have
for one fortnight, would be ten feet of rope."   Another
I heard say, " I reckon he is in that wood now."
Another said, " Who would have thought that rascal
was so 'cute ?"   All this while the little fice was ming-
ling his voice with those of the horsemen, and the
noise of the horses' feet.   I listened and trembled.

Just before the setting·of the sun, the labouring man
of the house returned, and commenced his evening
duties about the house and barn ; chopping wood, getting up his cow, feeding his pigs, &c., attended by the

D 2

little brute, who continued barking at short intervals. He came several times into the barn below. While matters were passing thus, I heard the approach of horses again, and as they came up nearer, I was led to believe that all I had heard pass, were returning in one party. They passed the barn and halted at the house, when I recognised the voice of my old captor; addressing the labourer, he asked, "Have you seen a runaway nigger pass here to-day?"

LABOURER.—"No; I have not been at home since early this morning. Where did he come from?"

CAPTOR.—"I caught him down below here yesterday morning. I had him all day, and just at night he fooled me and got away. A party of us have been after him all day; we have been up to the line, but can't hear or see anything of him. I heard this morning where he came from. He is a blacksmith, and a stiff reward is out for him, two hundred dollars."

LAB.—"He is worth looking for."

CAP.—"I reckon so. If I get my clutches on him again, I'll mosey* him down to —— before I eat or sleep."

Reader, you may if you can, imagine what the state of my mind was at this moment. I shall make no attempt to describe it to you; to my great relief, however, the party rode off, and the labourer after finishing his work went into the house. Hope seemed now to dawn for me once more; darkness was rapidly approaching, but the moments of twilight seemed much longer than they did the evening before. At length the sable covering had spread itself over the earth. About eight o'clock, I ventured to descend from the mow of the barn into the road. The little

---

* An expression which signifies to drive in a hurry.

dog the while began a furious fit of barking, so much so, that I was sure that with what his master had learned about me, he could not fail to believe I was about his premises. I quickly crossed the road, and got into an open field opposite. After stepping lightly about two hundred yards, I halted, and on listening, I heard the door open. Feeling about on the ground, I picked up two stones, and one in each hand I made off as fast as I could, but I heard nothing more that indicated pursuit, and after going some distance I discharged my encumbrance, as from the reduced state of my bodily strength, I could not afford to carry ballast.

This incident had the effect to start me under great disadvantage to make a good night's journey, as it threw me at once off the road, and compelled me to encounter at once the tedious and laborious task of beating my way across marshy fields, and to drag through woods and thickets where there were no paths.

After several hours I found my way back to the road, but the hope of making anything like clever speed was out of the question. All I could do was to keep my legs in motion, and this I continued to do with the utmost difficulty. The latter part of the night I suffered extremely from cold. There came a heavy frost; I expected at every moment to fall on the road and perish. I came to a corn-field covered with heavy shocks of Indian corn that had been cut; I went into this and got an ear, and then crept into one of the shocks; eat as much of it as I could, and thought I would rest a little and start again, but weary nature could not sustain the operation of grinding hard corn for its own nourishment, and I sunk to sleep.

When I awoke, the sun was shining around; I
started with alarm, but it was too late to think of
seeking any other shelter; I therefore nestled myself
down, and concealed myself as best I could from
the light of day. After recovering a little from my
fright, I commenced again eating my whole corn.
Grain by grain I worked away at it; when my jaws
grew tired, as they often did, I would rest, and then
begin afresh. Thus, although I began an early breakfast, I was nearly the whole of the forenoon before I
had done.

Nothing of importance occurred during the day,
until about the middle of the afternoon, when I was
thrown into a panic by the appearance of a party
of gunners, who passed near me with their dogs.
After shooting one or two birds, however, and passing
within a few rods of my frail covering, they went on,
and left me once more in hope. Friday night came
without any other incident worth naming. As I
sallied out, I felt evident benefit from the ear of corn
I had nibbled away. My strength was considerably
renewed; though I was far from being nourished, I
felt that my life was at least safe from death by
hunger. Thus encouraged, I set out with better
speed than I had made since Sunday and Monday
night. I had a presentiment, too, that I must be
near free soil. I had not yet the least idea where I
should find a home or a friend, still my spirits were
so highly elated, that I took the whole of the road
to myself; I ran, hopped, skipped, jumped, clapped
my hands, and talked to myself. But to the old slaveholder I had left, I said, "Ah! ha! old fellow, I
told you I'd fix you."

After an hour or two of such freaks of joy, a gloom

would come over me in connexion with these questions, "But where are you going? What are you going to do? What will you do with freedom without father, mother, sisters, and brothers? What will you say when you are asked where you were born? You know nothing of the world; how will you explain the fact of your ignorance?"

These questions made me feel deeply the magnitude of the difficulties yet before me.

Saturday morning dawned upon me; and although my strength seemed yet considerably fresh, I began to feel a hunger somewhat more destructive and pinching, if possible, than I had before. I resolved, at all risk, to continue my travel by day-light, and to ask information of the first person I met.

The events of the next chapter will shew what fortune followed this resolve.

CHAPTER IV.

THE resolution of which I informed the reader at
the close of the last chapter, being put into practice,
I continued my flight on the public road; and a
little after the sun rose, I came in sight of a toll-gate
again. For a moment all the events which followed
my passing a toll-gate on Wednesday morning, came
fresh to my recollection, and produced some hesitation; but at all events, said I, I will try again.

On arriving at the gate, I found it attended by an
elderly woman, whom I afterwards learned was a
widow, and an excellent Christian woman. I asked
her if I was in Pennsylvania. On being informed
that I was, I asked her if she knew where I could
get employ? She said she did not; but advised me
to go to W. W., a Quaker, who lived about three miles
from her, whom I would find to take an interest in
me. She gave me directions which way to take; I
thanked her, and bade her good morning, and was
very careful to follow her directions.

In about half an hour I stood trembling at the
door of W. W. After knocking, the door opened
upon a comfortably spread table; the sight of which
seemed at once to increase my hunger sevenfold. Not
daring to enter, I said I had been sent to him in
search of employ. "Well," said he, "Come in and

take thy breakfast, and get warm, and we will talk about it ; thee must be cold without any coat." *"Come in and take thy breakfast, and get warm !"* These words spoken by a stranger, but with such an air of simple sincerity and fatherly kindness, made an overwhelming impression upon my mind. They made me feel, spite of all my fear and timidity, that I had, in the providence of God, found a friend and a home. He at once gained my confidence ; and I felt that I might confide to him a fact which I had, as yet, confided to no one.

From that day to this, whenever I discover the least disposition in my heart to disregard the wretched condition of any poor or distressed persons with whom I meet, I call to mind these words—*"Come in and take thy breakfast, and get warm."* They invariably remind me of what I was at that time ; my condition was as wretched as that of any human being can possibly be, with the exception of the loss of health or reason. I had but four pieces of clothing about my person, having left all the rest in the hands of my captors. I was a starving fugitive, without home or friends—a reward offered for my person in the public papers—pursued by cruel manhunters, and no claim upon him to whose door I went. Had he turned me away, I must have perished. Nay, he took me in, and gave me of his food, and shared with me his own garments. Such treatment I had never before received at the hands of any white man.

A few such men in slaveholding America, have stood, and even now stand, like Abrahams and Lots, to stay its forthcoming and well-earned and just judgment.

The limits of this work compel me to pass over many interesting incidents which occurred during my six months' concealment in that family. I must confine myself only to those which will show the striking providence of God, in directing my steps to the door of W. W., and how great an influence the incidents of that six months has had upon all my subsequent history. My friend kindly gave me employ to saw and split a number of cords of wood, then lying in his yard, for which he agreed with me for liberal pay and board. This inspired me with great encouragement. The idea of beginning to earn something was very pleasant. Next; we confidentially agreed upon the way and means of avoiding surprise, in case any one should come to the house as a spy, or with intention to arrest me. This afforded still further relief, as it convinced me that the whole family would now be on the look out for such persons.

The next theme of conversation was with reference to my education.

"Can thee read or write any, James?" was the question put to me the morning after my arrival, by W. W.

"No, sir, I cannot; my duties as a blacksmith have made me acquainted with the figures on the common mechanics' square. There was a day-book kept in the shop, in which the overseer usually charged the smithwork we did for the neighbours. I have spent entire Sabbaths looking over the pages of that book; knowing the names of persons to whom certain pieces of work were charged, together with their prices, I strove anxiously to learn to write in this way. I got paper, and picked up feathers about the yard, and made ink of —— berries. My quills being too soft, and my skill in making a pen so poor, that

I undertook some years ago to make a steel pen.* In this way I have learnt to make a few of the letters, but I cannot write my own name, nor do I know the letters of the alphabet."

W. W., (handing a slate and pencil.)—" Let me see how thee makes letters ; try such as thou hast been able to make easily."

A. B. C. L. G.

P. W., (wife of W. W.)—" Why, those are better than I can make."

W. W.—" Oh, we can soon get thee in the way, James."

Arithmetic and astronomy became my favourite studies. W. W. was an accomplished scholar ; he had been a teacher for some years, and was cultivating a small farm on account of ill-health, which had compelled him to leave teaching. He is one of the most far-sighted and practical men I ever met with. He taught me by familiar conversations, illustrating his themes by diagrams on the slate, so that I caught his ideas with ease and rapidity.

I now began to see, for the first time, the extent of the mischief slavery had done to me. Twenty-one years of my life were gone, never again to return, and I was as profoundly ignorant, comparatively, as a child five years old. This was painful, annoying, and humiliating in the extreme. Up to this time, I recollected to have seen one copy of the New Testament, but the entire Bible I had never seen, and had never heard of the Patriarchs, or of the Lord Jesus Christ. I recollected to have heard two sermons, but had heard no mention in them of Christ, or the way

* This attempt was as early as 1822.

of life by Him. It is quite easy to imagine, then, what was the state of my mind, having been reared in total moral midnight; it was a sad picture of mental and spiritual darkness.

As my friend poured light into my mind, I saw the darkness; it amazed and grieved me beyond description. Sometimes I sank down under the load, and became discouraged, and dared not hope that I could ever succeed in acquiring knowledge enough to make me happy, or useful to my fellow-beings.

My dear friend, W. W., however, had a happy tact to inspire me with confidence; and he, perceiving my state of mind, exerted himself, not without success, to encourage me. He cited to me various instances of coloured persons, of whom I had not heard before, and who had distinguished themselves for learning, such as Bannicker, Wheatley, and Francis Williams.

How often have I regretted that the six months I spent in the family of W. W., could not have been six years. The danger of recapture, however, rendered it utterly imprudent that I should remain longer; and early in the month of March, while the ground was covered with the winter's snow, I left the bosom of this excellent family, and went forth once more to try my fortune among strangers.

My dear reader, if I could describe to you the emotions I felt when I left the threshold of W. W.'s door, you could not fail to see how deplorable is the condition of the fugitive slave, often for months and years after he has escaped the immediate grasp of the tyrant. When I left my parents, the trial was great, but I had now to leave a friend who had done more for me than parents could have done as slaves ; and hence I felt an endearment to that friend which was heightened by a sense of the important relief he had afforded me in the greatest need, and hours of pleasant and highly profitable intercourse.

About a month previous to leaving the house of W. W., a small circumstance occurred one evening, which I only name to shew the harassing fears and dread in which I lived during most of the time I was there. He had a brother-in-law living some ten miles distant—he was a friend to the slave ; he often came unexpectedly and spent a few hours—sometimes a day and a night. I had not, however, ever known him to come at night. One night about nine o'clock, after I had gone to bed, (my lodging being just over the room in which W. W. and his wife were sitting,) I heard the door open and a voice ask, " Where is the boy ?" The voice sounded to me like the voice of my master ; I was sure it must be his. I sprang and listened for a moment—it seemed to be silent ; I heard nothing, and then it seemed to me there was a confusion. There was a window at the head of my bed, which I could reach without getting upon the floor : it was a single sash and opened upon hinges. I quickly opened this window and waited in a perfect tremour of dread for further development. There was a door at the foot of the stairs ; as I heard that door open, I sprang for the window, and my head was just out, when the gentle voice of my friend W. W. said, " James ?" * " Here," said I, " ——— has come, and he would like to have thee put up his horse." I drew a breath of relief, but my strength and presence

---

* If W. W. had ascended the stairs without calling, I should certainly have jumped out of the window.

of mind did not return for some hours.   I slept none that night ; for a moment I could doze away, but the voice would sound in my ears, " Where is that boy ?" and it would seem to me it must be the tyrant in quest of his weary prey, and would find myself starting again.

From that time the agitation of my mind became so great that I could not feel myself safe.   Every day seemed to increase my fear, till I was unfit for work, study or rest.   My friend endeavoured, but in vain, to get me to stay a week longer.

The events of the spring proved that I had not left too soon.   As soon as the season for travelling fairly opened, active search was made, and my master was seen in a town, twenty miles in advance of where I had spent my six months.

The following curious fact also came out.   That same brother-in-law who frightened me, was putting up one evening at a hotel some miles off, and while sitting quietly by himself in one part of the room, he overheard a conversation between a travelling pedler and several gossippers of the neighbourhood, who were lounging away the evening at the hotel.

PEDLER.—" Do you know one W. W. somewhere about here ?"

GOSSIPER.—" Yes, he lives ―― miles off."

PED.—" I understand he had a black boy with him last winter, I wonder if he is there yet ? "

GOS.—" I don't know, he most always has a run-away nigger with him."

PED.—" I should like to find out whether that fellow is there yet."

BROTHER-IN-LAW, (turning about.)—" What does thee know about that boy ?"

PED.—" Well he is a runaway."

BROTHER - IN - LAW. — " Who did he run away from ? "

PED.—" From Col—— in ——."

BROTHER-IN-LAW.—" How did thee find out that fact ?"

PED.—" Well, I have been over there peddling."

BROTHER-IN-LAW.—" Where art thou from ? "

PED.—" I belong in Conn."

BROTHER-IN-LAW.—" Did thee see the boy's master ?"

PED.—" Yes."

BROTHER-IN-LAW.—" What did he offer thee to find the boy ?"

PED.—" I agreed to find out where he was, and let him know, and if he got him, I was to receive ——."

BROTHER-IN-LAW.—" How didst thou hear the boy had been with W. W."

PED.—" Oh, he is known to be a notorious rascal for enticing away, and concealing slaves ; he'll get himself into trouble yet, the slaveholders are on the look out for him."

BROTHER-IN-LAW.—" W. W. is my brother-in-law ; the boy of whom thou speakest is not with him, and to save thee the trouble of abusing him, I can moreover say, he is no rascal."

PED.—" He may not be there now, but it is because he has sent him off. His master heard of him, and from the description, he is sure it must have been his boy. He could tell me pretty nigh where he was ; he said he was a fine healthy boy, twenty-one, a first-rate blacksmith ; he would not have taken a thousand dollars for him."

BROTHER-IN-LAW.—" I know not where the boy is, but I have no doubt he is worth more to himself than he ever was to his master, high as he fixes the price on him ; and I have no doubt thee will do better to pursue thy peddling honestly, than to neglect it for the sake of serving negro-hunters at a venture."

All this happened within a month or two after I left my friend. One fact which makes this part of the story deeply interesting to my own mind, is, that some years elapsed before it came to my knowledge.

CHAPTER V.

On leaving W. W., I wended my way in deep
sorrow and melancholy, onward towards Philadelphia,
and after travelling two days and a night, I found
shelter and employ in the family of J. K., another
member of the Society of Friends, a farmer.

The religious atmosphere in this family was excellent. Mrs. K. gave me the first copy of the Holy
Scriptures I ever possessed, she also gave me much
excellent counsel. She was a preacher in the Society
of Friends ; this occasioned her with her husband to
be much of their time from home. This left the
charge of the farm upon me, and besides put it out of
their power to render me that aid in my studies which
my former friend had. I, however, kept myself closely
concealed, by confining myself to the limits of the
farm, and using all my leisure time in study. This
place was more secluded, and I felt less of dread and
fear of discovery than I had before, and although
seriously embarrassed for want of an instructor, I
realized some pleasure and profit in my studies. I
often employed myself in drawing rude maps of the
solar system, and diagrams illustrating the theory of
solar eclipses. I felt also a fondness for reading the

Bible, and committing chapters, and verses of hymns to memory. Often on the Sabbath when alone in the barn, I would break the monotony of the hours by endeavouring to speak, as if I was addressing an audience. My mind was constantly struggling for thoughts, and I was still more grieved and alarmed at its barrenness ; I found it gradually freed from the darkness entailed by slavery, but I was deeply and anxiously concerned how I should fill it with useful knowledge. I had a few books, and no tutor.

In this way I spent seven months with J. K., and should have continued longer, agreeably to his urgent solicitation, but I felt that life was fast wearing, and that as I was now free, I must adventure in search of knowledge. On leaving J. K., he kindly gave me the following certificate,—

" East Nautmeal, Chester County, Pennsylvania,
Tenth Month 5th, 1828.

" I hereby certify, that the bearer, J. W. C. Pennington, has been in my employ seven months, during most of which time I have been from home, leaving my entire business in his trust, and that he has proved a highly trustworthy and industrious young man. He leaves with the sincere regret of myself and family ; but as he feels it to be his duty to go where he can obtain education, so as to fit him to be more useful, I cordially commend him to the warm sympathy of the friends of humanity wherever a wise providence may appoint him a home.
          Signed,   "J. K."

Passing through Philadelphia, I went to New York, and in a short time found employ on Long Island, near the city. At this time, the state of things was extremely critical in New York. It was just two years after the general emancipation in that state. In the city it was a daily occurrence for slaveholders from the southern states to catch their slaves, and by certificate from Recorder Riker take them back. I often felt serious apprehensions of danger, and yet I felt also that I must begin the world somewhere.

I was earning respectable wages, and by means of evening schools and private tuition, was making encouraging progress in my studies.

Up to this time, it had never occurred to me that I was a slave in another and a more serious sense. All my serious impressions of mind had been with reference to the slavery from which I had escaped. Slavery had been my theme of thought day and night.

In the spring of 1829, I found my mind unusually perplexed about the state of the slave. I was enjoying rare privileges in attending a Sabbath school; the great value of Christian knowledge began to be impressed upon my mind to an extent I had not been conscious of before. I began to contrast my condition with that of ten brothers and sisters I had left in slavery, and the condition of children I saw sitting around me on the Sabbath, with their pious teachers, with that of 700,000, now 800,440 slave children, who had no means of Christian instruction.

The theme was more powerful than any my mind had ever encountered before. It entered into the deep chambers of my soul, and stirred the most agitating emotions I had ever felt. The question was, what can I do for that vast body of suffering brotherhood I have left behind. To add to the weight and magnitude of the theme, I learnt for the first time, how many slaves there were. The question completely staggered my mind; and finding myself more and more borne down with it, until I was in an agony; I thought I would make it a subject of prayer to God, although prayer had not been my habit, having never attempted it but once.

I not only prayed, but also fasted. It was while engaged thus, that my attention was seriously drawn to the fact that I was a lost sinner, and a slave to Satan; and soon I saw that I must make another escape from another tyrant. I did not by any means forget my fellow-bondmen, of whom I had been sorrowing so deeply, and travailing in spirit so earnestly; but I now saw that while man had been injuring me, I had been offending God; and that unless I ceased to offend him, I could not expect to have his sympathy in my wrongs; and moreover, that I could not be instrumental in eliciting his powerful aid in behalf of those for whom I mourned so deeply.

This may provoke a smile from some who profess to be the friends of the slave, but who have a lower estimate of experimental Christianity than I believe is due to it; but I am not the less confident that sincere prayer to God, proceeding from a few hearts deeply imbued with experimental Christianity about *that time*, has had much to do with subsequent happy results. At that time the 800,000 bondmen in the British Isles had not seen the beginning of the end of their sufferings—at that time, 20,000 who are now free in Canada, were in bonds—at that time, there was no Vigilance Committee to aid the flying slave—at that time, the two powerful Anti-Slavery Societies of America had no being.

I distinctly remember that I felt the need of en-

listing the sympathy of God, in behalf of my enslaved
brethren ; but when I attempted it day after day,
and night after night, I was made to feel, that whatever else I might do, I was not qualified to do that,
as I was myself alienated from him by wicked works.
In short, I felt that I needed the powerful aid of
some in my behalf with God, just as much as I did
that of my dear friend in Pennsylvania, when flying
from man. "If one man sin against another, the
judge shall judge him, but if a man sin against God,
who shall entreat for him ?"

Day after day, for about two weeks, I found myself
more deeply convicted of personal guilt before God.
My heart, soul and body were in the greatest distress ;
I thought of neither food, drink or rest, for days and
nights together.   Burning with a recollection of the
wrongs man had done me—mourning for the injuries
my brethren were still enduring, and deeply convicted
of the guilt of my own sins against God.   One evening, in the third week of the struggle, while alone in
my chamber, and after solemn reflection for several
hours, I concluded that I could never be happy or useful in that state of mind, and resolved that I would
try to become reconciled to God.   I was then living in
the family of an Elder of the Presbyterian Church.
I had not made known my feelings to any one, either
in the family or out of it ; and I did not suppose
that any one had discovered my feelings.   To my
surprise, however, I found that the family had not
only been aware of my state for several days, but
were deeply anxious on my behalf.   The following
Sabbath, Dr. Cox was on a visit in Brooklyn to preach,
and was a guest in the family ; hearing of my case,
he expressed a wish to converse with me, and with-

out knowing the plan, I was invited into a room and left alone with him. He entered skilfully and kindly into my feelings, and after considerable conversation he invited me to attend his service that afternoon. I did so, and was deeply interested.

Without detaining the reader with too many particulars, I will only state that I heard the doctor once or twice after this, at his own place of worship in New York City, and had several personal interviews with him, as the result of which, I hope, I was brought to a saving acquaintance with Him, of whom Moses in the Law and the Prophets did write; and soon connected myself with the church under his pastoral care.

I now returned with all my renewed powers to the great theme—slavery. It seemed now as I looked at it, to be more hideous than ever. I saw it now as an evil under the moral government of God—as a sin not only against man, but also against God. The great and engrossing thought with me was, how shall I now employ my time and my talents so as to tell most effectually upon this system of wrong! As I have stated, there was no Anti-Slavery Society then—there was no Vigilance Committee. I had, therefore, to select a course of action, without counsel or advice from any one who professed to sympathize with the slave. Many, many lonely hours of deep meditation have I passed during the years 1828 and 1829, before the great anti-slavery movement. On the questions, What shall I do for the slave? How shall I act so that he will reap the benefit of my time and talents? At one time I had resolved to go to Africa, and to react from there; but without bias or advice from any mortal, I soon gave up that, as looking too much like feeding a hungry man with a long spoon.

At length, finding that the misery, ignorance, and wretchedness of the free coloured people was by the whites tortured into an argument for slavery ; finding myself now among the free people of colour in New York, where slavery was so recently abolished; and finding much to do for their elevation, I resolved to give my strength in that direction. And well do I remember the great movement which commenced among us about this time, for the holding of General Conventions, to devise ways and means for their elevation, which continued with happy influence up to 1834, when we gave way to anti-slavery friends, who had then taken up the labouring oar. And well do I remember that the first time I ever saw those tried friends, Garrison, Jocelyn, and Tappan, was in one of those Conventions, where they came to make our acquaintance, and to secure our confidence in some of their preliminary labours.

My particular mode of labour was still a subject of deep reflection ; and from time to time I carried it to the Throne of Grace. Eventually my mind fixed upon the ministry as the desire of my whole heart. I had mastered the preliminary branches of English education, and was engaged in studying logic, rhetoric, and the Greek Testament, without a master. While thus struggling in my laudable work, an opening presented itself which was not less surprising than gratifying. Walking on the street one day, I met a friend, who said to me, " I have just had an application to supply a teacher for a school, and I have recommended you." I said, "My dear friend, I am obliged to you for the kindness ; but I fear I cannot sustain an examination for that station." " Oh," said he, " try." I said, " I will," and we separated.

Two weeks afterwards, I met the trustees of the
school, was examined, accepted, and agreed with them
for a salary of two hundred dollars per annum ; commenced my school, and succeeded.   This was five
years, three months, and thirteen days after I came
from the South.

As the events of my life since that have been of a
public professional nature, I will say no more about
it.   My object in writing this tract is now completed.
It has been to shew the reader the hand of God with
a slave ; and to elicit your sympathy in behalf of the
fugitive slave, by shewing some of the untold dangers
and hardships through which he has to pass to gain
liberty, and how much he needs friends on free soil ;
and that men who have felt the yoke of slavery, even
in its mildest form, cannot be expected to speak of
the system otherwise than in terms of the most unqualified condemnation.

There is one sin that slavery committed against me,
which I never can forgive.   It robbed me of my education ; the injury is irreparable ; I feel the embarrassment more seriously now than I ever did before.
It cost me two years' hard labour, after I fled, to un-
shackle my mind ; it was three years before I had
purged my language of slavery's idioms ; it was four
years before I had thrown off the crouching aspect of
slavery ; and now the evil that besets me is a great
lack of that general information, the foundation of
which is most effectually laid in that part of life
which I served as a slave.   When I consider how
much now, more than ever, depends upon sound and
thorough education among coloured men, I am
grievously overwhelmed with a sense of my deficiency,
and more especially as I can never hope now to make

it up. If I know my own heart, I have no ambition but to serve the cause of suffering humanity ; all that I have desired or sought, has been to make me more efficient for good. So far I have some consciousness that I have done my utmost ; and should my future days be few or many, I am reconciled to meet the last account, hoping to be acquitted of any wilful neglect of duty ; but I shall have to go to my last account with this charge against the system of slavery, " *Vile monster! thou hast hindered my usefulness, by robbing me of my early education.*"

Oh ! what might I have been now, but for this robbery perpetrated upon me as soon as I saw the light. When the monster heard that a man child was born, he laughed, and said, "It is mine." When I was laid in the cradle, he came and looked on my face, and wrote down my name upon his barbarous list of chattels personal, on the same list where he registered his horses, hogs, cows, sheep, and even his *dogs !* Gracious Heaven, is there no repentance for the misguided men who do these things !

The only harm I wish to slaveholders is, that they may be speedily delivered from the guilt of a sin, which, if not repented of, must bring down the judgment of Almighty God upon their devoted heads. The least I desire for the slave is, that he may be speedily released from the pain of drinking a cup whose bitterness I have sufficiently tasted, to know that it is insufferable.

CHAPTER VI.

SOME ACCOUNT OF THE FAMILY I LEFT IN SLAVERY— PROPOSAL TO PURCHASE MYSELF AND PARENTS—HOW MET BY MY OLD MASTER.

IT is but natural that the reader should wish to hear a word about the family I left behind.

There are frequently large slave families with whom God seems to deal in a remarkable manner. I believe my family is an instance.

I have already stated that when I fled, I left a father, mother, and eleven brothers and sisters. These were all, except my oldest brother, owned by the man from whom I fled. It will be seen at once then how the fear of implicating them embarrassed me in the outset. They suffered nothing, however, but a strong suspicion, until about six months after I had left; when the following circumstance took place :—

When I left my friend W. W. in Pennsylvania to go on north, I ventured to write a letter back to one of my brothers, informing him how I was ; and this letter was directed to the care of a white man who was hired on the plantation, who worked in the garden with my father, and who professed a warm friendship to our family ; but instead of acting in good faith, he handed the letter to my master. I am sorry that truth compels me to say that that man was an Englishman.

From that day the family were handled most strangely. The history begins thus : they were all sold into Virginia, the adjoining state. This was done lest I should have some plan to get them off; but God so ordered that they fell into kinder hands. After a few years, however, their master became much embarrassed, so that he was obliged to pass them into other hands, at least for a term of years. By this change the family was divided, and my parents, with the greater part of their children, were taken to New Orleans. After remaining there several years at hard labour,—my father being in a situation of considerable trust, they were again taken back to Virginia ; and by this means became entitled by the laws of that state to their freedom. Before justice, however, could take its course, their old master in Maryland, as if intent to doom them for ever to bondage, repurchased them ; and in order to defeat a similar law in Maryland, by which they would have been entitled to liberty, he obtained from the General Assembly of that state the following special act. This will show not only something of his character as a slaveholder, but also his political influence in the state. It is often urged in the behalf of slaveholders, that the law interposes an obstacle in the way of emancipating their slaves when they wish to do so, but here is an instance which lays open the real philosophy of the whole case. They make the law themselves, and when they find the laws operate more in favour of the slaves than themselves, they can easily evade or change it. Maryland being a slave-exporting state, you will see why they need a law to prohibit the importation of slaves ; it is a protection to that sort of trade. This law he wished to evade.

" *An act for the Relief of* ——— *of* ——— *County.*
Passed January 17th, 1842.

" Whereas it is represented to this General Assembly that ——— of ——— county, brought into this state from the state of Virginia, sometime in the month of March last, two negro slaves, to wit, ———

and ——— his wife, who are slaves for life, and who were acquired by the said ——— by purchase, and whereas, the said ——— is desirous of retaining said slaves in this state. THEREFORE, BE IT ENACTED, *by the General Assembly* of Maryland, that the said ——— be, and he is hereby authorized to retain said negroes as slaves for life within this state, provided that the said ——— shall within thirty days after the passage of this act, file with the clerk of the ——— county court, a list of said slaves so brought into this state, stating their ages, with an affidavit thereto attached, that the same is a true and faithful list of the slaves so removed, and that they were not brought into this state for the purpose of sale, and that they are slaves for life. And *provided also,* that the sum of fifteen dollars for each slave, between the ages of twelve and forty-five years, and the sum of five dollars for each slave above the age of forty-five years and under twelve years of age, so brought into this state, shall be paid to the said clerk of ——— county court : to be paid over by him to the treasurer of the western shore, for the use and benefit of the Colonization Society of this state.

State of Connecticut.
Office of Secretary of State.

" I hereby certify, that the foregoing is a true copy of an act passed by the General Assembly of Maryland, January 17th, 1842, as it appears in the printed acts of the said Maryland, in the Library of the state.

In testimony whereof, I have hereunto set my hand and seal of said state, at Hartford, this 17th day of August, 1846.

CHARLES W. BRADLEY,
Secretary of State.

(SEAL.)

Thus, the whole family after being twice fairly entitled to their liberty, even by the laws of two slave states, had the mortification of finding themselves again, not only recorded as slaves for life, but also a premium paid upon them, professedly to aid in establishing others of their fellow-beings in a free republic on the coast of Africa; but the hand of God seems to have been heavy upon the man who could plan such a stratagem to wrong his fellows.

The immense fortune he possessed when I left him, (bating one thousand dollars I brought with me in my own body,) and which he seems to have retained till that time, began to fly, and in a few years he was insolvent, so that he was unable to hold the family, and was compelled to think of selling them again. About this time I heard of their state by an underground railroad passenger, who came from that neighbourhood, and resolved to make an effort to obtain the freedom of my parents, and to relieve myself from liability. For this purpose, after arranging for the means to purchase, I employed counsel to make a definite offer for my parents and myself. To his proposal, the following evasive and offensive answer was returned.

January 12*th*, 1846.

J. H——, Esq.

" Sir,—Your letter is before me. The ungrateful servant in whose behalf you write, merits no clemency from me. He was guilty of theft when he departed, for which I hope he has made due amends. I have heard he was a respectable man, and calculated to do some good to his fellow-beings. Servants are selling from five hundred and fifty to seven hundred dollars. I will take five hundred and fifty dollars, and liberate

him.   If my proposition is acceded to, and the
money lodged in Baltimore, I will execute the necessary instrument, and deliver it in Baltimore, to be
given up on payment being made.

"Yours, &c.,
"   ."

" Jim was a first-rate mechanic, (blacksmith) and
was worth to me one thousand dollars."

Here he not only refuses to account for my parents,
by including them in his return and proposition, but
he at the same time attempts to intimidate me by
mooting the charge of theft.

I confess I was not only surprised, but mortified,
at this result.   The hope of being once more united
to parents whom I had not seen for sixteen years, and
whom I still loved dearly, had so excited my mind,
that I disarranged my business relations, disposed of
a valuable library of four hundred volumes, and by
additional aid obtained among the liberal people of
Jamaica, I was prepared to give the extravagant sum
of five hundred dollars each for myself, and my father
and mother.   This I was willing to do, not because I
approve of the principle involved as a general rule.
But supposing that, as my former master was now an
old man not far from his grave, (about which I was
not mistaken) and as he knew, by his own shewing,
that I was able to do some good, he would be inclined,
whatever might have been our former relations and
misunderstandings, to meet my reasonable desire to
see my parents, and to part this world in reconcilia-
tion with each other, as well as with God.   I should
have rejoiced had his temper permitted him to accede
to my offer.   But I thought it too bad, a free man of

Jesus Christ, living on " free soil," to give a man five hundred dollars for the privilege of being let alone, and to be branded as a thief into the bargain, and that too after I had served him twenty prime years, without the benefit of being taught so much as the alphabet.

I wrote him with my own hand, sometime after this, stating that no proposition would be acceded to by me, which did not include my parents ; and likewise fix the sum for myself more reasonable, and also retract the offensive charge ; to this he maintained a dignified silence. The means I had acquired by the contributions of kind friends to redeem myself, I laid by, in case the worst should come ; and that designed for the purchase of my parents, I used in another kind of operation, as the result of which, my father and two brothers are now in Canada. My mother was sold a second time, south, but she was eventually found. Several of my sisters married free men, who purchased their liberty; and three brothers are owned, by what may be called conscience slaveholders, who hold slaves only for a term of years. My old master has since died ; my mother and he are now in the other world together, she is at rest from him. Sometime after his death, I received information from a gentleman, intimate with his heirs, (who are principally females) that the reduced state of the family, afforded not only a good opportunity to obtain a release upon reasonable terms, but also to render the children of my oppressor some pecuniary aid ; and much as I had suffered, I must confess this latter was the stronger motive with me, for acceding to their offer made by him.

I have many other deeply interesting particulars

touching our family history, but I have detailed as
many as prudence will permit, on account of those
members who are yet south of Mason and Dixon's
line.

I have faith in the hand that has dealt with us so
strangely, that all our remaining members will in
time be brought together ; and then the case may
merit a reviewed and enlarged edition of this tract,
when other important matter will be inserted.

CHAPTER VII.

THE slaves are generally fed upon salt pork, herrings and Indian corn.

The manner of dealing it out to them is as follows: —Each working man, on Monday morning, goes to the cellar of the master where the provisions are kept, and where the overseer takes his stand with some one to assist him, when he, with a pair of steel-yards, weighs out to every man the amount of three-and-a-half pounds, to last him till the ensuing Monday— allowing him just half-a-pound per day. Once in a few weeks there is a change made, by which, instead of the three-and-a-half pounds of pork, each man receives twelve herrings, allowing two a-day. The only bread kind the slaves have is that made of Indian meal. In some of the lower counties, the masters usually give their slaves the corn in the ear ; and they have to grind it for themselves by night at hand-mills. But my master had a quantity sent to the grist mill at a time, to be ground into coarse meal, and kept it in a large chest in his cellar, where the woman who cooked for the boys could get it daily. This was baked in large loaves, called "steel poun bread." Sometimes as a change it was made into "Johnny Cake," and then at others into mush.

The slaves had no butter, coffee, tea, or sugar; occa-

F

sionally they were allowed milk, but not statedly; the only exception to this statement was the "harvest provisions." In harvest, when cutting the grain, which lasted from two to three weeks in the heat of summer, they were allowed some fresh meat, rice, sugar, and coffee; and also their allowance of whiskey.

At the beginning of winter, each slave had one pair of coarse shoes and stockings, one pair of pantaloons, and a jacket.

At the beginning of summer, he had two pair of coarse linen pantaloons and two shirts.

Once in a number of years, each slave, or each man and his wife, had one coarse blanket and enough coarse linen for a "bed-tick." He never had any bedstead or other furniture kind. The men had no hats, waistcoats or handkerchiefs given them, or the women any bonnets. These they had to contrive for themselves. Each labouring man had a small "patch" of ground allowed him; from this he was expected to furnish himself and his boys hats, &c. These patches they had to work by night; from these, also, they had to raise their own provisions, as no potatoes, cabbage, &c., were allowed them from the plantation. Years ago the slaves were in the habit of raising broom-corn, and making brooms to supply the market in the towns; but now of later years great quantities of these and other articles, such as scrubbing-brushes, wooden trays, mats, baskets, and straw hats which the slaves made, are furnished by the shakers and other small manufacturers, from the free states of the north.

Neither my master or any other master, within my acquaintance, made any provisions for the religious instruction of his slaves. They were not worked on the Sabbath. One of the "boys" was required to stay at home and "feed," that is, take care of the stock, every Sabbath ; the rest went to see their friends. Those men whose families were on other plantations usually spent the Sabbath with them ; some would lie about at home and rest themselves.

When it was pleasant weather my master would ride "into town" to church, but I never knew him to say a word to one of us about going to church, or about our obligations to God, or a future state. But there were a number of pious slaves in our neighbourhood, and several of these my master owned ; one of these was an exhorter. He was not connected with a religious body, but used to speak every Sabbath in some part of the neighbourhood. When slaves died, their remains were usually consigned to the grave without any ceremony ; but this old gentleman, wherever he heard of a slave having been buried in that way, would send notice from plantation to plantation, calling the slaves together at the grave on the Sabbath, where he'd sing, pray, and exhort. I have known him to go ten or fifteen miles voluntarily to attend these services. He could not read, and I never heard him refer to any Scripture, and state and discourse upon any fundamental doctrine of the gospel ; but he knew a number of " spiritual songs by heart," of these he would give two lines at a time very exact, set and lead the tune himself ; he would pray with great fervour, and his exhortations were amongst the most impressive I have heard.

The Methodists at one time attempted to evangelize the slaves in our neighbourhod, but the effort was sternly resisted by the masters. They held a Camp Meeting in the neighbourhood, where many of the slaves attended. But one of their preachers for ad-

dressing words of comfort to the slaves, was arrested
and tried for his life.

My master was very active in this disgraceful affair,
but the excellent man, Rev. Mr. G., was acquitted and
escaped out of their hands.   Still, it was deemed by
his brethren to be imprudent for him to preach any
more in the place, as some of the more reckless masters
swore violence against him.   This good man's name
is remembered dearly, till this day, by slaves in that
county.   I met with a fugitive about a year ago, who
remembered distinctly the words spoken by Mr. G.,
and by which his own mind was awakened to a sense
of the value of his soul.   He said, in the course of his
preaching, addressing himself to the slaves, " You
have precious immortal souls, that are worth far more
to you than your bodies are to your masters ;" or
words to that effect.   But while these words interested
many slaves, they also made many masters exceedingly angry, and they tortured his words into an
attempt to excite the slaves to rebellion.

Some of my master's slaves who had families, were
regularly married, and others were not ; the law makes
no provision for such marriages, and the only provision
made by the master was, that they should obtain his
leave.   In some cases, after obtaining leave to take his
wife, the slave would ask further leave to go to a minister and be married.   I never knew him to deny such
a request, and yet, in those cases where the slave did
not ask it, he never required him to be married by a
minister.   Of course, no Bibles, Tracts, or religious
books of any kind, were ever given to the slaves ; and
no ministers or religious instructors were ever known
to visit our plantation at any time, either in sickness or
in health.   When a slave was sick, my master being

himself a physician, sometimes attended, and sometimes he called other physicians. Slaves frequently sickened and died, but I never knew any provision made to administer to them the comforts, or to offer to them the hopes of the gospel, or to their friends after their death.

———————

There is no one feature of slavery to which the mind recurs with more gloomy impressions, than to its disastrous influence upon the families of the masters, physically, pecuniarily, and mentally.

It seems to destroy families as by a powerful blight, large and opulent slave-holding families, often vanish like a group of shadows at the third or fourth generation. This fact arrested my attention some years before I escaped from slavery, and of course before I had any enlightened views of the moral character of the system. As far back as I can recollect, indeed, it was a remark among slaves, that every generation of slaveholders are more and more inferior. There were several large and powerful families in our county, including that of my master, which affords to my mind a melancholy illustration of this remark. One of the wealthiest slaveholders in the county, was General R., a brother-in-law to my master. This man owned a large and highly valuable tract of land, called R.'s Manor. I do not know how many slaves he owned, but the number was large. He lived in a splendid mansion, and drove his coach and four. He was for some years a member of Congress. He had a numerous family of children.

The family showed no particular signs of decay until he had married a second time, and had considerably increased his number of children. It then became evident that his older children were not educated for active business, and were only destined to be a charge. Of sons, (seven or eight,) not one of them reached the eminence once occupied by the father. The only one that approached to it, was the eldest, who became an officer in the navy, and obtained the doubtful glory of being killed in the Mexican war.

General R. himself ran through his vast estate, died intemperate, and left a widow and large number of daughters, some minors, destitute, and none of his sons fitted for any employment but in the army and navy.

Slaves have a superstitious dread of passing the dilapidated dwelling of a man who has been guilty of great cruelties to his slaves, and who is dead, or moved away. I never felt this dread deeply but once, and that was one Sabbath about sunset, as I crossed the yard of General R.'s residence, which was about two miles from us, after he had been compelled to leave it.

To see the once fine smooth gravel walks, overgrown with grass—the redundances of the shrubbery neg-lected—the once finely painted pricket fences, rusted and fallen down—a fine garden in splendid ruins—the lofty ceiling of the mansion thickly curtained with cobwebs—the spacious apartments abandoned, while the only music heard within as a substitute for the voices of family glee that once filled it, was the crying cricket and cockroaches! Ignorant slave as I was at that time, I could but pause for a moment, and recur in silent horror to the fact that, a strange reverse of fortune, had lately driven from that proud mansion, a large and once opulent family. What advantage was it now to the members of that family, that the father and head had for near half a century stood high in the counsels of the state, and had the benefit of the unrequited toil of hundreds of his fellowmen, when they were already grappling with the annoyances of that poverty, which he had entailed upon others.

My master's family, in wealth and influence, was not inferior to General R.'s originally. His father was a member of the convention that framed the present constitution of the state ; he was, also, for some years chief justice of the state.

My master was never equal to his father, although he stood high at one time. He once lacked but a few votes of being elected Governor of the state : he once sat in the Assembly, and was generally a leading man in his own county. His influence was found to be greatest when exerted in favour of any measure in regard to the control of slaves. He was the first mover in several cruel and rigid municipal regulations in the county, which prohibited slaves from going over a certain number of miles from their master's places on the Sabbath, and from being seen about the town. He once instigated the authorities of the town where he attended service, to break up a Sabbath-school some humane members of the Methodist and Lutheran denominations had set up to teach the free negroes, lest the slaves should get some benefit of it.

But there was a still wider contrast between my master and his own children, eight in number, when I left him. His eldest daughter, the flower of the family, married a miserable and reckless gambler. His eldest son was kind-hearted, and rather a favourite with the slaves on that account; but he had no strength of mind or weight of character. His education was limited, and he had no disposition or tact for business of any kind. He died at thirty-six, intestate; leaving his second wife (a sister to his father's second wife) with several orphan children, a widow with a small estate deeply embarrassed. The second son was once sent to West Point to fit for an officer. After being there a short time, however, he became unsteady, and commenced the study of medicine, but he soon gave that up and preferred to live at home and flog the slaves; and by them was cordially dreaded and disliked, and among themselves he was vulgarly nicknamed on account of his cruel and filthy habits.

These two families will afford a fair illustration of the gloomy history of many others that I could name. This decline of slaveholding families is a subject of observation and daily remark among slaves; they are led to observe every change in the pecuniary, moral, and social state of the families they belong to, from the fact, that as the old master declines, or as his children are married off, they are expecting to fall into their hands, or in case of insolvency on the part of the old master, they expect to be sold; in either case, it involves a change of master—a subject to which they cannot be indifferent. And it is very rarely the case that a slave's condition is benefited by passing from the old master into the hands of one of his children. Owing to the causes I have mentioned, the decline is so rapid and marked, in almost every point of view, that the children of slaveholders are universally inferior to themselves, mentally, morally, physically, as well as pecuniarily, especially so in the latter point of view ; and this is a matter of most vital concern to the slaves. The young master not being able to own as many slaves as his father, usually works what he has more severely, and being more liable to embarrassment, the slaves' liability to be sold at an early day is much greater. For the same reason, slaves have a deep interest, generally, in the marriage of a young mistress. Very generally the daughters of slaveholders marry inferior men ; men who seek to better their own condition by a wealthy connection. The slaves who pass into the hands of the young master has had some chance to become acquainted with his character, bad as it may be ; but the young mistress brings her slaves a new, and sometimes an unknown master. Sometimes these are the sons of already broken down slaveholders. In other cases they are adventurers from the north who remove to the south, and who readily become the most cruel masters.

APPENDIX.

These two letters are simply introduced to show what the state of my feelings was with reference to slavery at the time they were written. I had just heard several facts with regard to my parents, which had awakened my mind to great excitement.

TO MY FATHER, MOTHER, BROTHERS, AND SISTERS.

The following was written in 1844 :

DEARLY BELOVED IN BONDS,

About seventeen long years have now rolled away, since in the Providence of Almighty God, I left your embraces, and set out upon a daring adventure in search of freedom. Since that time, I have felt most severely the loss of the sun and moon and eleven stars from my social sky. Many, many a thick cloud of anguish has pressed my brow and sent deep down into my soul the bitter waters of sorrow in consequence. And you have doubtless had your troubles and anxious seasons also about your fugitive star.

I have learned that some of you have been sold, and again taken back by Colonel ———. How many of you are living and together, I cannot tell. My great grief is, lest you should have suffered this or some additional punishment on account of my *Exodus.*

I indulge the hope that it will afford you some consolation to know that your son and brother is yet alive. That God has dealt wonderfully and kindly with me in all my way. He has made me a Christian, and a Christian Minister, and thus I have drawn my support and comfort from that blessed Saviour, who came *to preach good tidings unto the meek, to bind up the broken hearted, to proclaim liberty to the captives, and the opening of the prison to them that are bound. To proclaim the acceptable year of the Lord and the day of vengeance of our God ; to comfort all that mourn. To appoint unto them that mourn in Zion, to give unto them beauty for ashes, the oil of joy for mourning, the garment of praise for the spirit of heaviness, that they might be called trees of righteousness, the planting of the Lord that he might be glorified.*

If the course I took in leaving a condition which had become intolerable to me, has been made the occasion of making that condition worse to you in any way, I do most heartily regret such a change for the worse on your part. As I have no means, however, of knowing if such be the fact, so I have no means of making atonement, but by sincere prayer to Almighty God in your behalf, and also by taking this method of offering to you these consolations of the gospel to which I have just referred, and which I have found to be pre-eminently my own stay and support. My dear father and mother ; I have very often wished, while administering the Holy Ordinance of Baptism to some scores of children brought forward by doting parents, that I could see you with yours among the number. And you, my brothers and sisters, while teaching hundreds of children and youths in schools over which I have been placed, what unspeakable delight I should have had in having you among the number ; you may all judge of my feeling for these past years, when while preaching from Sabbath to Sabbath to congregations, I have not been so fortunate as even to see father, mother, brother, sister, uncle, aunt, nephew, niece, or cousin in my congregations. While visiting the sick, going to the house of mourning, and burying the dead, I have been a constant mourner for you. My sorrow has been that I know you are not in possession of those hallowed means of grace. I am thankful to you for those mild and gentle traits of character which you took such care to enforce upon me in my youthful days. As an evidence that I prize both you and them, I may say that at the age of thirty-seven, I find them as valuable as any lessons I have learned, nor am I ashamed to let it be known to the world, that I am the son of a bond man and a bond woman.

Let me urge upon you the fundamental truths of the Gospel of the Son of God. Let repentance towards God and faith in our Lord Jesus Christ have their perfect work in you, I beseech you. Do not be prejudiced against the gospel because it may be seemingly twisted into a support of slavery. The gospel rightly understood, taught, received, felt and practised, is anti-slavery as it is anti-sin. Just so far and so fast as the true spirit of the gospel obtains in the land, and especially in the lives of the oppressed, will the spirit of slavery sicken and become powerless like the serpent with his head pressed beneath the fresh leaves of the prickly ash of the forest.

There is not a solitary decree of the immaculate God that has been concerned in the ordination of slavery, nor does any possible development of his holy will sanctify it.

He has permitted us to be enslaved according to the invention of wicked men, instigated by the devil, with intention to bring good out of the evil, but He does not, He cannot approve of it. He has no need to approve of it, even on account of the good which He will bring out of it, for He could have brought about that very good in some other way.

God is never straitened ; He is never at a loss for means to work. Could He not have made this a great and wealthy nation without making its riches to consist in our blood, bones, and souls ? And could He not also have given the gospel to us without making us slaves ?

My friends, let us then, in our afflictions, embrace and hold fast the gospel. The gospel is the fulness of God. We have the glorious and total weight of God's moral character in our side of the scale.

The wonderful purple stream which flowed for the healing of the nations, has a branch for us. Nay, is Christ divided ? " The grace of God that bringeth salvation hath appeared to (for) all men, teaching us that denying ungodliness and worldly lust, we should live soberly, righteously, and godly in this present world, looking for that blessed hope and glorious appearing of the great God and our Saviour Jesus Christ, who gave himself for us that he might redeem us from all iniquity, and purify unto himself a peculiar people, zealous of good works."—Titus ii. 11–14.

But you say you have not the privilege of hearing of this gospel of which I speak. I know it; and this is my great grief. But you shall have it ; I will send it to you by my humble prayer ; I can do it ; I will beg our heavenly Father, and he will preach this gospel to you in his holy providence.

You, dear father and mother cannot have much longer to live in this troublesome and oppressive world ; you cannot bear the yoke much longer. And as you approach another world, how desirable it is that you should have the prospect of a different destiny from what you have been called to endure in this world during a long life.

But it is the gospel that sets before you the hope of such a blessed rest as is spoken of in the word of God, Job iii. 17, 19. "There the wicked cease from troubling, and there the weary be at rest; there the prisoners rest together; they hear not the voice of the oppressors. The small and great are there; and the servant is free from his master."

Father, I know thy eyes are dim with age and weary with weeping, but look, dear father, yet a little while toward that haven. Look unto Jesus, "the author and finisher of thy faith," for the moment of thy happy deliverance is at hand.

Mother, dear mother, I know, I feel, mother, the pangs of thy bleeding heart, that thou hast endured, during so many years of vexation. Thy agonies are by a genuine son-like sympathy mine; I will, I must, I do share daily in those agonies of thine. But I sincerely hope that with me you bear your agonies to Christ who carries our sorrows.

O come then with me, my beloved family, of weary heart-broken and care-worn ones, to Jesus Christ, "casting all your care upon him, for he careth for you." —2 Peter v. 7.

With these words of earnest exhortation, joined with fervent prayer to God that He may smooth your rugged way, lighten your burden, and give a happy issue out of all your troubles, I must bid you adieu.

Your son and brother,

JAS. P.

Alias J. W. C. PENNINGTON.

To Colonel F—— T——, of H——, Washington
County, Md. 1844.

Dear Sir,

It is now, as you are aware, about seventeen years
since I left your house and service, at the age of
twenty. Up to that time, I was, according to your
rule and claim, your slave. Till the age of seven
years, I was, of course, of little or no service to you.
At that age, however, you hired me out, and for
three years I earned my support; at the age of ten
years, you took me to your place again, and in a short
time after you put me to work at the blacksmith's
trade, at which, together with the carpentering trade,
&c., I served you peaceably until the day I left you,
with exception of the short time you had sold me to
S—— H——, Esq., for seven hundred dollars. It is
important for me to say to you, that I have no consciousness of having done you any wrong. I called
you master when I was with you from the mere force
of circumstances; but I never regarded you as my
master. The nature which God gave me did not
allow me to believe that you had any more right to
me than I had to you, and that was just none at all.
And from an early age, I had intentions to free myself from your claim. I never consulted any one
about it; I had no advisers or instigators; I kept
my own counsel entirely concealed in my own bosom.
I never meditated any evil to your person or property,
but I regarded you as my oppressor, and I deemed it
my duty to get out of your hands by peaceable means.

I was always obedient to your commands. I laboured for you diligently at all times. I acted with
fidelity in any matter which you entrusted me. As

you sometimes saw fit to entrust me with considerable money, to buy tools or materials, not a cent was ever coveted or kept.

During the time I served you in the capacity of blacksmith, your materials were used economically, your work was done expeditiously, and in the very best style, a style second to no smith in your neighbourhood. In short, sir, you well know that my habits from early life were advantageous to you. Drinking, gambling, fighting, &c., were not my habits. On Sabbaths, holidays, &c., I was frequently at your service, when not even your body-servant was at home.

Times and times again, I have gone on Sunday afternoon to H——, six miles, after your letters and papers, when it was as much my privilege to be "*out of the way*," as it was C——.

But what treatment did you see fit to return me for all this? You, in the most unfeeling manner, abused my father for no cause but speaking a word to you, as a man would speak to his fellow-man, for the sake simply of a better understanding.

You vexed my mother, and because she, as a tender mother would do, showed solicitude for the virtue of her daughters, you threatened her in an insulting brutal manner.

You abused my brother and sister without cause, and in like manner you did to myself ; you surmised evil against me. You struck me with your walking-cane, called me insulting names, threatened me, swore at me, and became more and more wrathy in your conduct, and at the time I quitted your place, I had good reason to believe that you were meditating serious evil against me.

Since I have been out of your hands, I have been signally favoured of God, whence I infer that in leaving you, I acted strictly in accordance with his holy will. I have a conscience void of offence towards God and towards all men, yourself not excepted. And I verily believe that I have performed a sacred duty to God and myself, and a kindness to you, in taking the blood of my soul peaceably off your soul. And now, dear sir, having spoken somewhat pointedly, I would, to convince you of my perfect good will towards you, in the most kind and respectful terms, remind you of your coming destiny. You are now over seventy years of age, pressing on to eternity with the weight of these seventy years upon you. Is not this enough without the blood of some half-score of souls?

You are aware that your right to property in man is now disputed by the civilized world. You are fully aware, also, that the question, whether the Bible sanctions slavery, has distinctly divided this nation in sentiment. On the side of Biblical Anti-slavery, we have many of the most learned, wise and holy men in the land. If the Bible affords no sanction to slavery, (and I claim that it cannot,) then it must be a sin of the deepest dye; and can you, sir, think to go to God in hope with a sin of such magnitude upon your soul?

But admitting that the question is yet doubtful, (which I do only for the sake of argument,) still, sir, you will have the critical hazard of this doubt pressing, in no very doubtful way, upon your declining years, as you descend the long and tedious hill of life.

Would it not seem to be exceedingly undesirable to close an eventful probation of seventy or eighty years, and leave your reputation among posterity suspended

G

upon so doubtful an issue? But what, my dear sir, is a reputation among posterity, who are but worms, compared with a destiny in the world of spirits? And it is in light of that destiny that I would now have you look at this subject. You and I, and all that you claim as your slaves, are in a state of probation; our great business is to serve God under His righteous moral government. Master and slave are the subjects of that government, bound by its immutable requirements, and liable to its sanctions in the next world, though enjoying its forbearance in this. You will pardon me then for pressing this point in earnest good faith. You should, at this stage, review your life without political bias, or adherence to long cherished prejudices, and remember that you are soon to meet those whom you have held, and do hold in slavery, at the awful bar of the impartial Judge of all who doeth right. Then what will become of your own doubtful claims? What will be done with those doubts that agitated your mind years ago; will you answer for threatening, swearing, and using the cowhide among your slaves?

What will become of those long groans and unsatisfied complaints of your slaves, for vexing them with insulting words, placing them in the power of dogish and abusive overseers, or under your stripling, misguided, hot-headed son, to drive and whip at pleasure, and for selling parts or whole families to Georgia? They will all meet you at that bar. Uncle James True, Charles Cooper, Aunt Jenny, and the native Africans; Jeremiah, London, and Donmore, have already gone a-head, and only wait your arrival—Sir, I shall meet you there. The account between us for the first twenty years of my life, will have a definite character upon which one or the other will be able to make out a case.

Upon such a review as this, sir, you will, I am quite sure, see the need of seriousness. I assure you that the thought of meeting you in eternity, and before the dread tribunal of God, with a complaint in my mouth against you, is to me of most weighty and solemn character. And you will see that the circumstances from which this thought arises are of equal moment to yourself. Can the pride of leaving your children possessed of long slave states, or the policy of sustaining in the state the institution of slavery, justify you in overlooking a point of moment to your future happiness?

What excuse could you offer at the bar of God, favoured as you have been with the benefits of a refined education, and through a long life with the gospel of love, should you, when arraigned there, find that you have, all your life long, laboured under a great mistake in regard to slavery, and that in this mistake you had died, and only lifted up your eyes in the light of eternity to be corrected, when it was too late to be corrected in any other way.

I could wish to address you (being bred, born, and raised in your family) *as a father in Israel, or as an elder brother in Christ, but I cannot; mockery is a sin.* I can only say then, dear sir, farewell, till I meet you at the bar of God, where Jesus, who died for us, will judge between us. Now his blood can wash out our stain, break down the middle wall of partition, and reconcile us not only to God but to each other, then the word of his mouth, the sentence will set us at one. As for myself, I am quite ready to meet you face to face at the bar of God. I have done you no wrong ; I have nothing to fear when we both fall into the hands of the just God.

I beseech you, dear sir, to look well and consider this matter soundly. In yonder world you can have no slaves—you can be no man's master—you can neither sell, buy, or whip, or drive. Are you then, by sustaining the relation of a slaveholder, forming a character to dwell with God in peace?

With kind regards,

I am, sir, yours respectfully,

J. W. C. PENNINGTON.

LIBERTY'S CHAMPION.

BY A FRIEND OF THE AUTHOR'S.

On the wings of the wind he comes, he comes!
    With the rolling billow's speed;
On his breast are the signs of peace and love,
And his soul is nerved with strength from above:
        While his eyes flash fire,
        He burns with desire
    To achieve the noble deed.

To the shores of the free he goes, he goes!
    And smiles as he passes on;
He hears the glad notes of Liberty's song,
And bids the brave sons of freedom be strong.
        While his heart bounds high
        To his crown in the sky,
    He triumphs o'er conquests won.

To the homes of the slave he flies, he flies!
    Where manacled mourners cry;
The bursting groan of the mind's o'erflow,
Transfixed on the dark and speaking brow:
        With a murmuring sound,
        Ascends from the ground,
    To the God that reigns on high.

To his loved Father's throne he hastes, he hastes !
   And pours forth his soul in grief :
Uprising he finds his strength renewed,
And his heart with fervent love is imbued ;
     While the heaving sigh,
     And the deep-toned cry,
   Appeal for instant relief.

To the hard oppressor he cries, he cries,
   And points to the bleeding slave ;
He tells of the rights of the human soul,
And his eyes with full indignation roll :
     While his heart is moved,
     And the truth is proved,
   He seeks the captive to save.

Again to the foeman he speaks, he speaks,
   But utters his cry in vain ;
He breathes no curse, no vengeance seeks,—
For the broken hearts or the anguished shrieks,
     For the mother's pains,
     Or the father's gains,—
   Upon the oppressor's name.

To nations of freemen once more he comes,
   To raise Liberty's banner high ;
He tells of the wrongs of the bonded slave,
And cries aloud, 'mid throngs of the brave,
     " O freemen, arise !
     Be faithful and wise,
   And answer the mourner's cry.

In melting strains of love he calls, he calls,
   To the great and good from afar ;
Till sympathy wakes to the truthful tale,
And the prayer of the faith, which cannot fail,
      Ascends to heaven,
      And grace is given,
   To nerve for the bloodless war.

The truth with a magic power prevails :
   All hearts are moved to the strife ;
In a holy phalanx, and with deathless aim,
   They seek a peaceful triumph to gain
      O'er the tyrant's sway,
      In his onward way,
   To raise the fallen to life.

At the mighty voice of the glorious free
   The chain of the oppressor breaks ;
The slave from his bondage springs forth to love,
And, standing erect, his eye fixed above,
      He honours his race,
      And in the world's face,
   The language of liberty speaks.

The oppressor no longer owns a right,
   Or property claims in the slave,
But the world, in the glory of freedom's light,
Beams out from the darkness of wide-spread night ;
      Throughout its length,
      In greatness and strength,
   The honour of the free and brave.

Printed for CHARLES GILPIN, 5, Bishopgate Street Without.

NARRATIVE

OF

WILLIAM W. BROWN,

Wm. W. Brown.

TO WELLS BROWN, OF OHIO.

———◆———

THIRTEEN years ago, I came to your door, a weary fugitive from chains and stripes. I was a stranger, and you took me in. I was hungry, and you fed me. Naked was I, and you clothed me. Even a name by which to be known among men, slavery had denied me. You bestowed upon me your own. Base indeed should I be, if I ever forget what I owe to you, or do anything to disgrace that honored name!

As a slight testimony of my gratitude to my earliest benefactor, I take the liberty to inscribe to you this little Narrative of the sufferings from which I was fleeing when you had compassion upon me. In the multitude that you have succored, it is very possible that you may not remember me ; but until I forget God and myself, I can never forget you.

Your grateful friend,

WILLIAM WELLS BROWN.

LETTER

FROM

EDMUND QUINCY, ESQ.

———

DEDHAM, JULY 1, 1847.

TO WILLIAM W. BROWN.

MY DEAR FRIEND : — I heartily thank you for the privilege of reading the manuscript of your Narrative. I have read it with deep interest and strong emotion. I am much mistaken if it be not greatly successful and eminently useful. It presents a different phase of the infernal slave-system from that portrayed in the admirable story of Mr. Douglass, and gives us a glimpse of its hideous cruelties in other portions of its domain.

Your opportunities of observing the workings of this accursed system have been singularly great. Your experiences in the Field, in the House, and especially on the River in the service of the slave-trader, Walker, have been such as few individuals have had ; — no one, certainly, who has been competent to describe them. What I have admired, and marvelled at, in your Narrative, is the simplicity and calmness with which you describe scenes and actions which might well "move the very stones to rise and mutiny" against the National Institution which makes them possible.

You will perceive that I have made very sparing use of your flattering permission to alter what you had written. To correct a few errors, which appeared to be merely clerical ones, committed in the hurry of composition, under unfavorable circumstances, and to suggest a few curtailments, is all that I have ventured to do. I should be a bold man, as well as a vain one, if I should attempt to improve your descriptions of what you have seen and suffered. Some of the scenes are not unworthy of De Foe himself.

I trust and believe that your Narrative will have a wide circulation. I am sure it deserves it. At least, a man must be differently constituted from me, who can rise from the perusal of your Narrative without feeling that he understands slavery better, and hates it worse, than he ever did before.

I am, very faithfully and respectfully,

Your friend,

EDMUND QUINCY.

PREFACE.

THE friends of freedom may well congratulate each other on the appearance of the following Narrative. It adds another volume to the rapidly increasing anti-slavery literature of the age. It has been remarked by a close observer of human nature, "Let me make the songs of a nation, and I care not who makes its laws;" and it may with equal truth be said, that, among a reading people like our own, their books will at least give character to their laws. It is an influence which goes forth noiselessly upon its mission, but fails not to find its way to many a warm heart, to kindle on the altar thereof the fires of freedom, which will one day break forth in a living flame to consume oppression.

This little book is a voice from the prison-house, unfolding the deeds of darkness which are there perpetrated. Our cause has received efficient aid from this source. The names of those who have come from thence, and battled manfully for the right, need not to be recorded here. The works of some of them are an enduring monument of praise, and their perpetual record shall be found in the grateful hearts of the redeemed bondman.

Few persons have had greater facilities for becoming
acquainted with slavery, in all its horrible aspects, than
WILLIAM W. BROWN. He has been behind the curtain·
He has visited its secret chambers. Its iron has entered his
own soul. The dearest ties of nature have been riven in his
own person. A mother has been cruelly scourged before
his own eyes. A father, — alas! slaves have no father. A
brother has been made the subject of its tender mercies. A
sister has been given up to the irresponsible control of the
pale-faced oppressor. This nation looks on approvingly.
The American Union sanctions the deed. The Constitution
shields the criminals. American religion sanctifies the
crime. But the tide is turning. Already, a mighty under-
current is sweeping onward. The voice of warning, of
remonstrance, of rebuke, of entreaty, has gone forth. Hand
is linked in hand, and heart mingles with heart, in this great
work of the slave's deliverance.

The convulsive throes of the monster, even now, give
evidence of deep wounds.

The writer of this Narrative was hired by his master to a
"*soul-driver,*" and has witnessed all the horrors of the traffic,
from the buying up of human cattle in the slave-breeding
States, which produced a constant scene of separating the
victims from all those whom they loved, to their final sale
in the southern market, to be worked up in seven years, or
given over to minister to the lust of southern *Christians*.

Many harrowing scenes are graphically portrayed; and
yet with that simplicity and ingenuousness which carries
with it a conviction of the truthfulness of the picture.

This book will do much to unmask those who have "clothed themselves in the livery of the court of heaven" to cover up the enormity of their deeds.

During the past three years, the author has devoted his entire energies to the anti-slavery cause. Laboring under all the disabilities and disadvantages growing out of his education in slavery — subjected, as he had been from his birth, to all the wrongs and deprivations incident to his condition — he yet went forth, impelled to the work by a love of liberty — stimulated by the remembrance of his own sufferings — urged on by the consideration that a mother, brothers, and sister, were still grinding in the prison-house of bondage, in common with three millions of our Father's children — sustained by an unfaltering faith in the omnipotence of truth and the final triumph of justice — to plead the cause of the slave, and by the eloquence of earnestness carried conviction to many minds, and enlisted the sympathy and secured the co-operation of many to the cause.

His labors have been chiefly confined to Western New York, where he has secured many warm friends, by his untiring zeal, persevering energy, continued fidelity, and universal kindness.

Reader, are you an Abolitionist? What have you done for the slave? What are you doing in his behalf? What do you purpose to do? There is a great work before us Who will be an idler now? This is the great humanitary movement of the age, swallowing up, for the time being, all other questions, comparatively speaking. The course of human events, in obedience to the unchangeable laws of our being, is fast hastening the final crisis, and

> " Have ye chosen, O my people, on whose party ye shall stand,
> Ere the Doom from its worn sandal shakes the dust against our land? "

Are you a Christian? This is the carrying out of practical Christianity; and there is no other. Christianity is *practical* in its very nature and essence. It is a life, springing out of a soul imbued with its spirit. Are you a friend of the missionary cause? This is the greatest missionary enterprize of the day. Three millions of *Christian*, law-manufactured heathen are longing for the glad tidings of the Gospel of freedom. Are you a friend of the Bible? Come, then, and help us to restore to these millions, whose eyes have been bored out by slavery, their sight, that they may see to read the Bible. Do you love God whom you have not seen? Then manifest that love, by restoring to your brother whom you have seen, his rightful inheritance, of which he has been so long and so cruelly deprived.

It is not for a single generation alone, numbering three millions — sublime as would be that effort — that we are working. It is for HUMANITY, the wide world over, not only now, but for all coming time, and all future generations: —

> " For he who settles Freedom's principles,
> Writes the death-warrant of all tyranny."

It is a vast work — a glorious enterprize — worthy the unswerving devotion of the entire life-time of the great and the good.

Slaveholding and slaveholders must be rendered disreputable and odious. They must be stripped of their respectability and Christian reputation. They must be treated as "MEN-STEALERS — guilty of the highest kind of theft, and sinners of the first rank." Their more guilty accomplices in the persons of *northern apologists*, both in Church and State, must be placed in the same category. Honest men must be made to look upon their crimes with the same abhorrence and loathing, with which they regard the less guilty robber and assassin, until

> "The common damned shun their society,
> And look upon themselves as fiends less foul."

When a just estimate is placed upon the crime of slaveholding, the work will have been accomplished, and the glorious day ushered in —

> "When man nor woman in all our wide domain,
> Shall buy, or sell, or hold, or be a slave."

J. C. HATHAWAY.

Farmington, N. Y., 1847.

NARRATIVE.

CHAPTER I.

I was born in Lexington, Ky. The man who stole me as soon as I was born, recorded the births of all the infants which he claimed to be born his property, in a book which he kept for that purpose. My mother's name was Elizabeth. She had seven children, viz: Solomon, Leander, Benjamin, Joseph, Millford, Elizabeth, and myself. No two of us were children of the same father. My father's name, as I learned from my mother, was George Higgins. He was a white man, a relative of my master, and connected with some of the first families in Kentucky.

My master owned about forty slaves, twenty-five of whom were field hands. He removed from

Kentucky to Missouri, when I was quite young, and
settled thirty or forty miles above St. Charles, on
the Missouri, where, in addition to his practice as a
physician, he carried on milling, merchandizing and
farming.   He had a large farm, the principal pro-
ductions of which were tobacco and hemp.   The
slave cabins were situated on the back part of the
farm, with the house of the overseer, whose name
was Grove Cook, in their midst.   He had the entire
charge of the farm, and having no family, was
allowed a woman to keep house for him, whose
business it was to deal out the provisions for the
hands.

A woman was also kept at the quarters to do the
cooking for the field hands, who were summoned
to their unrequited toil every morning at four o'clock,
by the ringing of a bell, hung on a post near the
house of the overseer.   They were allowed half an
hour to eat their breakfast, and get to the field.   At
half past four, a horn was blown by the overseer,
which was the signal to commence work; and every
one that was not on the spot at the time, had to
receive ten lashes from the negro-whip, with which
the overseer always went armed.   The handle was

about three feet long, with the butt-end filled with
lead, and the lash six or seven feet in length, made
of cowhide, with platted wire on the end of it.
This whip was put in requisition very frequently and
freely, and a small offence on the part of a slave furnished an occasion for its use.   During the time that
Mr. Cook was overseer, I was a house servant — a
situation preferable to that of a field hand, as I was
better fed, better clothed, and not obliged to rise at
the ringing of the bell, but about half an hour after.
I have often laid and heard the crack of the whip,
and the screams of the slave.   My mother was a
field hand, and one morning was ten or fifteen minutes behind the others in getting into the field.   As
soon as she reached the spot where they were at
work, the overseer commenced whipping her.   She
cried, "Oh! pray — Oh! pray — Oh! pray" —
these are generally the words of slaves, when imploring mercy at the hands of their oppressors.   I
heard her voice, and knew it, and jumped out of my
bunk, and went to the door.   Though the field was
some distance from the house, I could hear every
crack of the whip, and every groan and cry of my
poor mother.   I remained at the door, not daring

to venture any farther. The cold chills ran over me, and I wept aloud. After giving her ten lashes, the sound of the whip ceased, and I returned to my bed, and found no consolation but in my tears. It was not yet daylight.

CHAPTER II.

My master being a political demagogue, soon found those who were ready to put him into office, for the favors he could render them ; and a few years after his arrival in Missouri, he was elected to a seat in the Legislature. In his absence from home, everything was left in charge of Mr. Cook, the overseer, and he soon became more tyrannical and cruel. Among the slaves on the plantation, was one by the name of Randall. He was a man about six feet high, and well-proportioned, and known as a man of great strength and power. He was considered the most valuable and able-bodied slave on the plantation ; but no matter how good or useful a slave may be, he seldom escapes the lash. But it was not so with Randall. He had been on the plantation since my earliest recollection, and I had never known of his being flogged. No thanks were due to the master or overseer for this. I have

2

often heard him declare, that no white man should
ever whip him — that he would die first.

Cook, from the time that he came upon the plantation, had frequently declared, that he could and
would flog any nigger that was put into the field to
work under him. My master had repeatedly told
him not to attempt to whip Randall, but he was
determined to try it. As soon as he was left sole
dictator, he thought the time had come to put his
threats into execution. He soon began to find fault
with Randall, and threatened to whip him, if he did
not do better. One day he gave him a very hard
task, — more than he could possibly do; and at
night, the task not being performed, he told Randall
that he should remember him the next morning.
On the following morning, after the hands had taken
breakfast, Cook called out to Randall, and told him
that he intended to whip him, and ordered him to
cross his hands and be tied. Randall asked why
he wished to whip him. He answered, because he
had not finished his task the day before. Randall
said that the task was too great, or he should have
done it. Cook said it made no difference, — he
should whip him. Randall stood silent for a

moment, and then said, "Mr. Cook, I have always tried to please you since you have been on the plantation, and I find you are determined not to be satisfied with my work, let me do as well as I may. No man has laid hands on me, to whip me, for the last ten years, and I have long since come to the conclusion not to be whipped by any man living." Cook, finding by Randall's determined look and gestures, that he would resist, called three of the hands from their work, and commanded them to seize Randall, and tie him. The hands stood still; — they knew Randall — and they also knew him to be a powerful man, and were afraid to grapple with him. As soon as Cook had ordered the men to seize him, Randall turned to them, and said — "Boys, you all know me; you know that I can handle any three of you, and the man that lays hands on me shall die. This white man can't whip me himself, and therefore he has called you to help him." The overseer was unable to prevail upon them to seize and secure Randall, and finally ordered them all to go to their work together.

Nothing was said to Randall by the overseer, for more than a week. One morning, however, while the hands were at work in the field, he came into it, accompanied by three friends of his, Thompson, Woodbridge and Jones. They came up to where Randall was at work, and Cook ordered him to leave his work, and go with them to the barn. He refused to go; whereupon he was attacked by the overseer and his companions, when he turned upon them, and laid them, one after another, prostrate on the ground. Woodbridge drew out his pistol, and fired at him, and brought him to the ground by a pistol ball. The others rushed upon him with their clubs, and beat him over the head and face, until they succeeded in tying him. He was then taken to the barn, and tied to a beam. Cook gave him over one hundred lashes with a heavy cowhide, had him washed with salt and water, and left him tied during the day. The next day he was untied, and taken to a blacksmith's shop, and had a ball and chain attached to his leg. He was compelled to labor in the field, and perform the same amount of work that the other hands did. When his master returned home, he was much pleased to find that Randall had been subdued in his absence.

CHAPTER III.

Soon afterwards, my master removed to the city of St. Louis, and purchased a farm four miles from there, which he placed under the charge of an overseer by the name of Friend Haskell. He was a regular Yankee from New England. The Yankees are noted for making the most cruel overseers.

My mother was hired out in the city, and I was also hired out there to Major Freeland, who kept a public house. He was formerly from Virginia, and was a horse-racer, cock-fighter, gambler, and withal an inveterate drunkard. There were ten or twelve servants in the house, and when he was present, it was cut and slash — knock down and drag out. In his fits of anger, he would take up a chair, and throw it at a servant; and in his more rational moments, when he wished to chastise one, he would tie them up in the smoke-house, and whip them; after which, he would cause a fire to be made of

tobacco stems, and smoke them.   This he called
" *Virginia play.*"

I complained to my master of the treatment which
I received from Major Freeland; but it made no
difference.   He cared nothing about it, so long as
he received the money for my labor.   After living
with Major Freeland five or six months, I ran away,
and went into the woods back of the city; and when
night came on, I made my way to my master's
farm, but was afraid to be seen, knowing that if Mr.
Haskell, the overseer, should discover me, I should
be again carried back to Major Freeland; so I kept
in the woods.   One day, while in the woods, I
heard the barking and howling of dogs, and in a
short time they came so near, that I knew them to
be the bloodhounds of Major Benjamin O'Fallon.
He kept five or six, to hunt runaway slaves with.

As soon as I was convinced that it was them, I
knew there was no chance of escape.   I took refuge
in the top of a tree, and the hounds were soon at its
base, and there remained until the hunters came up
in a half or three quarters of an hour afterwards.
There were two men with the dogs, who, as soon
as they came up, ordered me to descend.   I came

down, was tied, and taken to St. Louis jail. Major
Freeland soon made his appearance, and took me
out, and ordered me to follow him, which I did.
After we returned home, I was tied up in the smoke-
house, and was very severely whipped. After the
Major had flogged me to his satisfaction, he sent out
his son Robert, a young man eighteen or twenty
years of age, to see that I was well smoked. He
made a fire of tobacco stems, which soon set me to
coughing and sneezing. This, Robert told me, was
the way his father used to do to his slaves in Virginia. After giving me what they conceived to be a
decent smoking, I was untied and again set to work.

Robert Freeland was a "chip of the old block."
Though quite young, it was not unfrequently that
he came home in a state of intoxication. He is
now, I believe, a popular commander of a steamboat
on the Mississippi river. Major Freeland soon after
failed in business, and I was put on board the
steamboat Missouri, which plied between St. Louis
and Galena. The commander of the boat was
William B. Culver. I remained on her during the
sailing season, which was the most pleasant time for
me that I had ever experienced. At the close of

navigation, I was hired to Mr. John Colburn, keeper of the Missouri Hotel. He was from one of the Free States; but a more inveterate hater of the negro, I do not believe ever walked on God's green earth. This hotel was at that time one of the largest in the city, and there were employed in it twenty or thirty servants, mostly slaves.

Mr. Colburn was very abusive, not only to the servants, but to his wife also, who was an excellent woman, and one from whom I never knew a servant to receive a harsh word; but never did I know a kind one to a servant from her husband. Among the slaves employed in the hotel, was one by the name of Aaron, who belonged to Mr. John F. Darby, a lawyer. Aaron was the knife-cleaner. One day, one of the knives was put on the table, not as clean as it might have been. Mr. Colburn, for this offence, tied Aaron up in the wood-house, and gave him over fifty lashes on the bare back with a cowhide, after which, he made me wash him down with rum. This seemed to put him into more agony than the whipping. After being untied, he went home to his master, and complained of the treatment which he had received. Mr. Darby would give no heed to anything he had to say, but sent him directly back. Colburn, learning that he had been to his master with complaints, tied him up again, and gave him a more severe whipping than before. The poor fellow's back was literally cut to pieces; so much so, that he was not able to work for ten or twelve days.

There was also, among the servants, a girl whose master resided in the country. Her name was Patsey. Mr. Colburn tied her up one evening, and whipped her until several of the boarders came out and begged him to desist. The reason for whipping her was this. She was engaged to be married to a man belonging to Major William Christy, who resided four or five miles north of the city. Mr. Colburn had forbid her to see John Christy. The reason of this was said to be the regard which he himself had for Patsey. She went to meeting that evening, and John returned home with her. Mr. Colburn had intended to flog John, if he came within the inclosure; but John knew too well the temper of his rival, and kept at a safe distance; — so he took vengeance on the poor girl. If all the slave-drivers had been called together, I do not think a more cruel man than John Colburn, — and he too a northern man, — could have been found among them.

While living at the Missouri Hotel, a circumstance occurred which caused me great unhappiness. My master sold my mother, and all her children, except myself. They were sold to different persons in the city of St. Louis.

CHAPTER IV.

I WAS soon after taken from Mr. Colburn's, and hired to Elijah P. Lovejoy, who was at that time publisher and editor of the " St. Louis Times." My work, while with him, was mainly in the printing office, waiting on the hands, working the press, &c. Mr. Lovejoy was a very good man, and decidedly the best master that I had ever had. I am chiefly indebted to him, and to my employment in the printing office, for what little learning I obtained while in slavery.

Though slavery is thought, by some, to be mild in Missouri, when compared with the cotton, sugar and rice growing States, yet no part of our slave-holding country, is more noted for the barbarity of its inhabitants, than St. Louis. It was here that Col. Harney, a United States officer, whipped a slave woman to death. It was here that Francis McIntosh, a free colored man from Pittsburgh, was taken from the steamboat Flora, and burned at the stake. During a residence of eight years in this city, numerous cases of extreme cruelty came under my own observation ; — to record them all, would occupy more space than could possibly be allowed in this little volume. I shall, therefore, give but a few more, in addition to what I have already related.

Capt. J. B. Brunt, who resided near my master, had a slave named John. He was his body servant, carriage driver, &c. On one occasion, while driving his master through the city, — the streets being very muddy, and the horses going at a rapid rate, — some mud spattered upon a gentleman by the name of Robert More. More was determined to be re- venged. Some three or four months after this occurrence, he purchased John, for the express pur- pose, as he said, "to tame the d—d nigger." After the purchase, he took him to a blacksmith's shop, and had a ball and chain fastened to his leg, and then put him to driving a yoke of oxen, and kept him at hard labor, until the iron around his leg was so worn into the flesh, that it was thought mortifica- tion would ensue. In addition to this, John told me that his master whipped him regularly three times a

week for the first two months : — and all this to
"*tame him.*" A more noble looking man than he,
was not to be found in all St. Louis, before he fell
into the hands of More ; and a more degraded and
spirit-crushed looking being was never seen on a
southern plantation, after he had been subjected to
this "*taming*" process for three months. The
last time that I saw him, he had nearly lost the entire use of his limbs.

While living with Mr. Lovejoy, I was often sent
on errands to the office of the "Missouri Republican," published by Mr. Edward Charles. Once,
while returning to the office with type, I was
attacked by several large boys, sons of slave-holders,
who pelted me with snow-balls. Having the heavy
form of type in my hands, I could not make my escape by running ; so I laid down the type and gave
them battle. They gathered around me, pelting me
with stones and sticks, until they overpowered me,
and would have captured me, if I had not resorted
to my heels. Upon my retreat, they took possession
of the type ; and what to do to regain it I could not
devise. Knowing Mr. Lovejoy to be a very humane
man, I went to the office, and laid the case before

him.   He told me to remain in the office.   He took
one of the apprentices with him, and went after the
type, and soon returned with it ; but on his return
informed me that Samuel McKinney had told him
that he would whip me, because I had hurt his boy.
Soon after, McKinney was seen making his way to
the office by one of the printers, who informed me
of the fact, and I made my escape through the back
door.

McKinney not being able to find me on his
arrival, left the office in a great rage, swearing that
he would whip me to death.   A few days after, as
I was walking along Main Street, he seized me by
the collar, and struck me over the head five or six
times with a large cane, which caused the blood to
gush from my nose and ears in such a manner that
my clothes were completely saturated with blood.
After beating me to his satisfaction, he let me go,
and I returned to the office so weak from the loss
of blood, that Mr. Lovejoy sent me home to my
master.   It was five weeks before I was able to
walk again.   During this time, it was necessary to
have some one to supply my place at the office,
and I lost the situation.

After my recovery, I was hired to Capt. Otis Reynolds, as a waiter on board the steamboat Enterprize, owned by Messrs. John and Edward Walsh, commission merchants at St. Louis. This boat was then running on the upper Mississippi. My employment on board was to wait on gentlemen, and the captain being a good man, the situation was a pleasant one to me; — but in passing from place to place, and seeing new faces every day, and knowing that they could go where they pleased, I soon became unhappy, and several times thought of leaving the boat at some landing place, and trying to make my escape to Canada, which I had heard much about as a place where the slave might live, be free, and be protected.

But whenever such thoughts would come into my mind, my resolution would soon be shaken by the remembrance that my dear mother was a slave in St. Louis, and I could not bear the idea of leaving her in that condition. She had often taken me upon her knee, and told me how she had carried me upon her back to the field when I was an infant — how often she had been whipped for leaving her work to nurse me — and how happy I would appear when she would take me into her arms. When these thoughts came over me, I would resolve never to leave the land of slavery without my mother. I thought that to leave her in slavery, after she had undergone and suffered so much for me, would be proving recreant to the duty which I owed to her. Besides this, I had three brothers and a sister there, — two of my brothers having died.

My mother, my brothers Joseph and Millford, and my sister Elizabeth, belonged to Mr. Isaac Mansfield, formerly from one of the Free States, (Massachusetts, I believe.) He was a tinner by trade, and carried on a large manufacturing establishment. Of all my relatives, mother was first, and sister next. One evening, while visiting them, I made some allusion to a proposed journey to Canada, and sister took her seat by my side, and taking my hand in hers, said, with tears in her eyes, —

"Brother, you are not going to leave mother and your dear sister here without a friend, are you?"

I looked into her face, as the tears coursed swiftly down her cheeks, and bursting into tears myself, said —

" No, I will never desert you and mother."

She clasped my hand in hers, and said —

" Brother, you have often declared that you would not end your days in slavery. I see no possible way in which you can escape with us; and now, brother, you are on a steamboat where there is some chance for you to escape to a land of liberty. I beseech you not to let us hinder you. If we cannot get our liberty, we do not wish to be the means of keeping you from a land of freedom."

I could restrain my feelings no longer, and an outburst of my own feelings, caused her to cease speaking upon that subject. In opposition to their wishes, I pledged myself not to leave them in the hand of the oppressor. I took leave of them, and returned to the boat, and laid down in my bunk; but " sleep departed from my eyes, and slumber from my eyelids."

A few weeks after, on our downward passage, the boat took on board, at Hannibal, a drove of slaves, bound for the New Orleans market. They numbered from fifty to sixty, consisting of men and women from eighteen to forty years of age. A drove of slaves on a southern steamboat, bound for

3

the cotton or sugar regions, is an occurrence so common, that no one, not even the passengers, appear to notice it, though they clank their chains at every step. There was, however, one in this gang that attracted the attention of the passengers and crew. It was a beautiful girl, apparently about twenty years of age, perfectly white, with straight light hair and blue eyes. But it was not the whiteness of her skin that created such a sensation among those who gazed upon her — it was her almost unparalleled beauty. She had been on the boat but a short time, before the attention of all the passengers, including the ladies, had been called to her, and the common topic of conversation was about the beautiful slave-girl. She was not in chains. The man who claimed this article of human merchandize was a Mr. Walker, — a well known slave-trader, residing in St. Louis. There was a general anxiety among the passengers and crew to learn the history of the girl. Her master kept close by her side, and it would have been considered impudent for any of the passengers to have spoken to her, and the crew were not allowed to have any conversation with them. When we reached St. Louis, the slaves were removed to a boat bound for New Orleans, and the history of the beautiful slave-girl remained a mystery.

I remained on the boat during the season, and it was not an unfrequent occurrence to have on board gangs of slaves on their way to the cotton, sugar and rice plantations of the South.

Toward the latter part of the summer, Captain Reynolds left the boat, and I was sent home. I was then placed on the farm under Mr. Haskell, the overseer. As I had been some time out of the field, and not accustomed to work in the burning sun, it was very hard; but I was compelled to keep up with the best of the hands.

I found a great difference between the work in a steamboat cabin and that in a corn-field.

My master, who was then living in the city, soon after removed to the farm, when I was taken out of the field to work in the house as a waiter. Though his wife was very peevish, and hard to please, I much preferred to be under her control than the overseer's. They brought with them Mr. Sloane, a Presbyterian minister; Miss Martha Tulley, a neice of theirs from Kentucky; and their nephew William. The latter had been in the family a number of years, but the others were all new-comers.

Mr. Sloane was a young minister, who had been at the South but a short time, and it seemed as if his whole aim was to please the slaveholders, especially my master and mistress. He was intending to make a visit during the winter, and he not only tried to please them, but I think he succeeded admirably. When they wanted singing, he sung; when they wanted praying, he prayed; when they wanted a story told, he told a story. Instead of his teaching my master theology, my master taught theology to him. While I was with Captain Reynolds, my master "got religion," and new laws were made on the plantation. Formerly, we had the privilege of hunting, fishing, making splint brooms, baskets, &c. on Sunday; but this was all stopped. Every Sunday, we were all compelled to attend meeting. Master was so religious, that he induced some others to join him in hiring a preacher to preach to the slaves.

CHAPTER V.

My master had family worship, night and morning. At night, the slaves were called in to attend;
but in the mornings, they had to be at their work,
and master did all the praying. My master and
mistress were great lovers of mint julep, and every
morning, a pitcher-full was made, of which they all
partook freely, not excepting little master William.
After drinking freely all round, they would have
family worship, and then breakfast. I cannot say
but I loved the julep as well as any of them, and
during prayer was always careful to seat myself
close to the table where it stood, so as to help myself when they were all busily engaged in their
devotions. By the time prayer was over, I was
about as happy as any of them. A sad accident
happened one morning. In helping myself, and at
the same time keeping an eye on my old mistress, I
accidentally let the pitcher fall upon the floor,

breaking it in pieces, and spilling the contents. This was a bad affair for me; for as soon as prayer was over, I was taken and severely chastised.

My master's family consisted of himself, his wife, and their nephew, William Moore. He was taken into the family, when only a few weeks of age. His name being that of my own, mine was changed, for the purpose of giving precedence to his, though I was his senior by ten or twelve years. The plantation being four miles from the city, I had to drive the family to church. I always dreaded the approach of the Sabbath; for, during service, I was obliged to stand by the horses in the hot broiling sun, or in the rain, just as it happened.

One Sabbath, as we were driving past the house of D. D. Page, a gentleman who owned a large baking establishment, as I was sitting upon the box of the carriage, which was very much elevated, I saw Mr. Page pursuing a slave around the yard, with a long whip, cutting him at every jump. The man soon escaped from the yard, and was followed by Mr. Page. They came running past us, and the slave perceiving that he would be overtaken, stopped suddenly, and Page stumbled over him, and falling on the stone pavement, fractured one of his legs, which crippled him for life. The same gentleman, but a short time previous, tied up a woman of his, by the name of Delphia, and whipped her nearly to death; yet he was a deacon in the Baptist church, in good and regular standing. Poor Delphia! I was well acquainted with her, and called to see her while upon her sick bed; and I shall never forget her appearance. She was a member of the same church with her master.

Soon after this, I was hired out to Mr. Walker; the same man whom I have mentioned as having carried a gang of slaves down the river, on the steamboat Enterprize. Seeing me in the capacity of steward on the boat, and thinking that I would make a good hand to take care of slaves, he determined to have me for that purpose; and finding that my master would not sell me, he hired me for the term of one year.

When I learned the fact of my having been hired to a negro speculator, or a "soul-driver" as they are generally called among slaves, no one can tell my emotions. Mr. Walker had offered a high price for me, as I afterwards learned, but I suppose

my master was restrained from selling me by the
fact that I was a near relative of his.   On entering
the service of Mr. Walker, I found that my opportunity of getting to a land of liberty was gone, at
least for the time being.   He had a gang of slaves
in readiness to start for New Orleans, and in a few
days we were on our journey.   I am at a loss for
language to express my feelings on that occasion.
Although my master had told me that he had not
sold me, and Mr. Walker had told me that he had
not purchased me, I did not believe them ; and not
until I had been to New Orleans, and was on my
return, did I believe that I was not sold.

There was on the boat a large room on the lower
deck, in which the slaves were kept, men and
women, promiscuously — all chained two and two,
and a strict watch kept that they did not get loose ;
for cases have occurred in which slaves have got
off their chains, and made their escape at landing-
places, while the boats were taking in wood ; — and
with all our care, we lost one woman who had been
taken from her husband and children, and having
no desire to live without them, in the agony of her
soul jumped overboard, and drowned herself.   She
was not chained.

It was almost impossible to keep that part of the boat clean.

On landing at Natchez, the slaves were all carried to the slave-pen, and there kept one week, during which time, several of them were sold. Mr. Walker fed his slaves well. We took on board, at St. Louis, several hundred pounds of bacon (smoked meat) and corn-meal, and his slaves were better fed than slaves generally were in Natchez, so far as my observation extended.

At the end of a week, we left for New Orleans, the place of our final destination, which we reached in two days. Here the slaves were placed in a negro-pen, where those who wished to purchase could call and examine them. The negro-pen is a small yard, surrounded by buildings, from fifteen to twenty feet wide, with the exception of a large gate with iron bars. The slaves are kept in the buildings during the night, and turned out into the yard during the day. After the best of the stock was sold at private sale at the pen, the balance were taken to the Exchange Coffee House Auction Rooms, kept by Isaac L. McCoy, and sold at public auction. After the sale of this lot of slaves, we left New Orleans for St. Louis.

CHAPTER VI.

On our arrival at St. Louis, I went to Dr.
Young, and told him that I did not wish to live
with Mr. Walker any longer.   I was heart-sick at
seeing my fellow-creatures bought and sold.   But
the Dr. had hired me for the year, and stay I must.
Mr Walker again commenced purchasing another
gang of slaves.   He bought a man of Colonel John
O'Fallon, who resided in the suburbs of the city.
This man had a wife and three children.   As soon
as the purchase was made, he was put in jail for
safe keeping, until we should be ready to start for
New Orleans.   His wife visited him while there,
several times, and several times when she went for
that purpose was refused admittance.

In the course of eight or nine weeks Mr. Walker
had his cargo of human flesh made up.   There
was in this lot a number of old men and women,
some of them with gray locks.   We left St. Louis

in the steamboat Carlton, Captain Swan, bound for New Orleans. On our way down, and before we reached Rodney, the place where we made our first stop, I had to prepare the old slaves for market. I was ordered to have the old men's whiskers shaved off, and the grey hairs plucked out, where they were not too numerous, in which case he had a preparation of blacking to color it, and with a blacking-brush we would put it on. This was new business to me, and was performed in a room where the passengers could not see us. These slaves were also taught how old they were by Mr. Walker, and after going through the blacking process, they looked ten or fifteen years younger; and I am sure that some of those who purchased slaves of Mr. Walker, were dreadfully cheated, especially in the ages of the slaves which they bought.

We landed at Rodney, and the slaves were driven to the pen in the back part of the village. Several were sold at this place, during our stay of four or five days, when we proceeded to Natchez. There we landed at night, and the gang were put in the warehouse until morning, when they were

driven to the pen. As soon as the slaves are put
in these pens, swarms of planters may be seen in
and about them. They knew when Walker was
expected, as he always had the time advertised
beforehand when he would be in Rodney, Natchez,
and New Orleans. These were the principal
places where he offered his slaves for sale.

When at Natchez the second time, I saw a slave
very cruelly whipped. He belonged to a Mr.
Broadwell, a merchant who kept a store on the
wharf. The slave's name was Lewis. I had
known him several years, as he was formerly from
St. Louis. We were expecting a steamboat down
the river, in which we were to take passage for
New Orleans. Mr. Walker sent me to the landing
to watch for the boat, ordering me to inform him
on its arrival. While there, I went into the store
to see Lewis. I saw a slave in the store, and asked
him where Lewis was. Said he, "They have got
Lewis hanging between the heavens and the earth."
I asked him what he meant by that. He told me
to go into the warehouse and see. I went in, and
found Lewis there. He was tied up to a beam,
with his toes just touching the floor. As there was

no one in the warehouse but himself, I inquired the reason of his being in that situation. He said Mr. Broadwell had sold his wife to a planter six miles from the city, and that he had been to visit her, — that he went in the night, expecting to return before daylight, and went without his master's permission. The patrol had taken him up before he reached his wife. He was put in jail, and his master had to pay for his catching and keeping, and that was what he was tied up for.

Just as he finished his story, Mr. Broadwell came in, and inquired what I was doing there. I knew not what to say, and while I was thinking what reply to make, he struck me over the head with the cowhide, the end of which struck me over my right eye, sinking deep into the flesh, leaving a scar which I carry to this day. Before I visited Lewis, he had received fifty lashes. Mr. Broadwell gave him fifty lashes more after I came out, as I was afterwards informed by Lewis himself.

The next day we proceeded to New Orleans, and put the gang in the same negro-pen which we occupied before. In a short time, the planters came flocking to the pen to purchase slaves. Be-

fore the slaves were exhibited for sale, they were
dressed and driven out into the yard. Some were
set to dancing, some to jumping, some to singing,
and some to playing cards. This was done to
make them appear cheerful and happy. My
business was to see that they were placed in those
situations before the arrival of the purchasers, and I
have often set them to dancing when their cheeks
were wet with tears. As slaves were in good
demand at that time, they were all soon disposed
of, and we again set out for St. Louis.

On our arrival, Mr. Walker purchased a farm
five or six miles from the city. He had no family,
but made a housekeeper of one of his female
slaves. Poor Cynthia! I knew her well. She was
a quadroon, and one of the most beautiful women
I ever saw. She was a native of St. Louis, and
bore an irreproachable character for virtue and
propriety of conduct. Mr. Walker bought her for
the New Orleans market, and took her down with
him on one of the trips that I made with him.
Never shall I forget the circumstances of that voyage! On the first night that we were on board the
steamboat, he directed me to put her into a state-

room he had provided for her, apart from the other slaves. I had seen too much of the workings of slavery, not to know what this meant. I accordingly watched him into the state-room, and listened to hear what passed between them. I heard him make his base offers, and her reject them. He told her that if she would accept his vile proposals, he would take her back with him to St. Louis, and establish her as his housekeeper at his farm. But if she persisted in rejecting them, he would sell her as a field hand on the worst plantation on the river. Neither threats nor bribes prevailed, however, and he retired, disappointed of his prey.

The next morning, poor Cynthia told me what had past, and bewailed her sad fate with floods of tears. I comforted and encouraged her all I could; but I foresaw but too well what the result must be. Without entering into any farther particulars, suffice it to say that Walker performed his part of the contract, at that time. He took her back to St. Louis, established her as his mistress and house-keeper at his farm, and before I left, he had two children by her. But, mark the end! Since I have been at the North, I have been credibly informed that Walker has been married, and, as a previous measure, sold poor Cynthia and her four children (she having had two more since I came away) into hopeless bondage!

He soon commenced purchasing to make up the third gang. We took steamboat, and went to Jefferson City, a town on the Missouri river. Here we landed, and took stage for the interior of the State. He bought a number of slaves as he passed the different farms and villages. After getting twenty-two or twenty-three men and women, we arrived at St. Charles, a village on the banks of the Missouri. Here he purchased a woman who had a child in her arms, appearing to be four or five weeks old.

We had been travelling by land for some days, and were in hopes to have found a boat at this place for St. Louis, but were disappointed. As no boat was expected for some days, we started for St. Louis by land. Mr. Walker had purchased two horses. He rode one, and I the other. The slaves were chained together, and we took up our line of march, Mr. Walker taking the lead, and I bringing up the rear. Though the distance was not more thah twenty miles, we did not reach it the first day. The road was worse than any that I have ever travelled.

Soon after we left St. Charles, the young child grew very cross, and kept up a noise during the greater part of the day. Mr. Walker complained of its crying several times, and told the mother to stop the child's d——d noise, or he would. The woman tried to keep the child from crying, but could not. We put up at night with an acquaintance of Mr. Walker, and in the morning, just as we were about to start, the child again commenced crying. Walker stepped up to her, and told her to give the child to him. The mother tremblingly obeyed. He took the child by one arm, as you would a cat by the leg, walked into the house, and said to the lady,

"Madam, I will make you a present of this little nigger; it keeps such a noise that I can't bear it."

"Thank you, sir," said the lady.

The mother, as soon as she saw that her child was to be left, ran up to Mr. Walker, and falling upon her knees begged him to let her have her child; she clung around his legs, and cried, "Oh,

4

my child! my child! master, do let me have my
child! oh, do, do, do.   I will stop its crying, if you
will only let me have it again."   When I saw this
woman crying for her child so piteously, a shudder, — a feeling akin to horror, shot through my
frame.   I have often since in imagination heard
her crying for her child: —

> "O, master, let me stay to catch
>   My baby's sobbing breath,
> His little glassy eye to watch,
>   And smooth his limbs in death,
>
> And cover him with grass and leaf,
>   Beneath the large oak tree :
> It is not sullenness, but grief, —
>   O, master, pity me !
>
> The morn was chill — I spoke no word,
>   But feared my babe might die,
> And heard all day, or thought I heard,
>   My little baby cry.
>
> At noon, oh, how I ran and took
>   My baby to my breast !
> I lingered — and the long lash broke
>   My sleeping infant's rest.
>
> I worked till night — till darkest night,
>   In torture and disgrace ;
> Went home and watched till morning light,
>   To see my baby's face.

Then give me but one little hour —
    O! do not lash me so!
One little hour — one little hour —
    And gratefully I'll go."

Mr. Walker commanded her to return into the ranks with the other slaves. Women who had children were not chained, but those that had none were. As soon as her child was disposed of, she was chained in the gang.

The following song I have often heard the slaves sing, when about to be carried to the far south. It is said to have been composed by a slave.

" See these poor souls from Africa
Transported to America;
We are stolen, and sold to Georgia,
Will you go along with me?
We are stolen, and sold to Georgia,
Come sound the jubilee!

See wives and husbands sold apart,
Their children's screams will break my heart; —
There 's a better day a coming,
Will you go along with me?
There 's a better day a coming,
Go sound the jubilee!

O, gracious Lord! when shall it be,
That we poor souls shall all be free;

Lord, break them slavery powers —
Will you go along with me?
Lord break them slavery powers,
Go sound the jubilee!

Dear Lord, dear Lord, when slavery 'll cease,
Then we poor souls will have our peace; —
There 's a better day a coming,
Will you go along with me?
There 's a better day a coming,
Go sound the jubilee! "

We finally arrived at Mr. Walker's farm. He had a house built during our absence to put slaves in. It was a kind of domestic jail. The slaves were put in the jail at night, and worked on the farm during the day. They were kept here until the gang was completed, when we again started for New Orleans, on board the steamboat North America, Capt. Alexander Scott. We had a large number of slaves in this gang. One, by the name of Joe, Mr. Walker was training up to take my place, as my time was nearly out, and glad was I. We made our first stop at Vicksburg, where we remained one week and sold several slaves.

Mr. Walker, though not a good master, had not flogged a slave since I had been with him, though he had threatened me. The slaves were kept in the pen, and he always put up at the best hotel, and kept his wines in his room, for the accommodation of those who called to negotiate with him for the purchase of slaves. One day while we were at Vicksburg, several gentlemen came to see him for this purpose, and as usual the wine was called for. I took the tray and started around with it, and having accidentally filled some of the glasses too full, the gentlemen spilled the wine on their clothes as they went to drink. Mr. Walker apologized to them for my carelessness, but looked at me as though he would see me again on this subject.

After the gentlemen had left the room, he asked me what I meant by my carelessness, and said that he would attend to me. The next morning, he gave me a note to carry to the jailer, and a dollar in money to give to him. I suspected that all was not right, so I went down near the landing where I met with a sailor, and walking up to him, asked him if he would be so kind as to read the note for me. He read it over, and then looked at me. I asked him to tell me what was in it. Said he,

" They are going to give you hell."

" Why ? " said I.

He said, " This is a note to have you whipped, and says that you have a dollar to pay for it."

He handed me back the note, and off I started. I knew not what to do, but was determined not to be whipped. I went up to the jail — took a look at it, and walked off again. As Mr. Walker was acquainted with the jailer, I feared that I should be found out if I did not go, and be treated in consequence of it still worse.

While I was meditating on the subject, I saw a colored man about my size walk up, and the thought struck me in a moment to send him with my note. I walked up to him, and asked him who he belonged to. He said he was a free man, and had been in the city but a short time. I told him I had a note to go into the jail, and get a trunk to carry to one of the steamboats; but was so busily engaged that I could not do it, although I had a dollar to pay for it. He asked me if I would not give him the job. I handed him the note and the dollar, and off he started for the jail.

I watched to see that he went in, and as soon as I saw the door close behind him, I walked around the corner, and took my station, intending to see how my friend looked when he came out. I had been there but a short time, when a colored man came around the corner, and said to another colored man with whom he was acquainted —

"They are giving a nigger scissors in the jail."

"What for?" said the other. The man continued,

"A nigger came into the jail, and asked for the jailer. The jailer came out, and he handed him a note, and said he wanted to get a trunk. The jailer told him to go with him, and he would give him the trunk. So he took him into the room, and told the nigger to give up the dollar. He said a man had given him the dollar to pay for getting the trunk. But that lie would not answer. So they made him strip himself, and then they tied him down, and are now whipping him."

I stood by all the while listening to their talk, and soon found out that the person alluded to was my customer. I went into the street opposite the jail, and concealed myself in such a manner that I could not be seen by any one coming out. I had been there but a short time, when the young man made his appearance, and looked around for me.

I, unobserved, came forth from my hiding-place, behind a pile of brick, and he pretty soon saw me and came up to me complaining bitterly, saying that I had played a trick upon him. I denied any knowledge of what the note contained, and asked him what they had done to him. He told me in substance what I heard the man tell who had come out of the jail.

"Yes," said he, "they whipped me and took my dollar, and gave me this note."

He showed me the note which the jailer had given him, telling him to give it to his master. I told him I would give him fifty cents for it, — that being all the money I had. He gave it to me, and took his money. He had received twenty lashes on his bare back, with the negro-whip.

I took the note and started for the hotel where I had left Mr. Walker. Upon reaching the hotel, I handed it to a stranger whom I had not seen before, and requested him to read it to me. As near as I can recollect, it was as follows: —

"DEAR SIR: — By your direction, I have given your boy twenty lashes. He is a very saucy boy, and tried to make me believe that he did not belong to you, and I put it on to him well for lying to me.

>   I remain,
>   Your obedient servant."

It is true that in most of the slave-holding cities, when a gentleman wishes his servants whipped, he can send him to the jail and have it done.   Before I went in where Mr. Walker was, I wet my cheeks a little, as though I had been crying.   He looked at me, and inquired what was the matter.   I told him that I had never had such a whipping in my life, and handed him the note.   He looked at it and laughed; — "and so you told him that you did not belong to me." "Yes, sir," said I. "I did not know that there was any harm in that."   He told me I must behave myself, if I did not want to be whipped again.

This incident shows how it is that slavery makes its victims lying and mean; for which vices it afterwards reproaches them, and uses them as arguments to prove that they deserve no better fate.   I have often, since my escape, deeply regretted the deception I practised upon this poor fellow ; and I heartily desire that it may be, at some time or other, in my power to make him amends for his vicarious sufferings in my behalf.

CHAPTER VII

In a few days we reached New Orleans, and arriving there in the night, remained on board until morning. While at New Orleans this time, I saw a slave killed; an account of which has been published by Theodore D. Weld, in his book entitled, "Slavery as it is." The circumstances were as follows. In the evening, between seven and eight o'clock, a slave came running down the levee, followed by several men and boys. The whites were crying out, "Stop that nigger; stop that nigger;" while the poor panting slave, in almost breathless accents, was repeating, "I did not steal the meat — I did not steal the meat." The poor man at last took refuge in the river. The whites who were in pursuit of him, run on board of one of the boats to see if they could discover him. They finally espied him under the bow of the steamboat Trenton. They got a pike-pole, and tried to drive him from his hiding place. When they would strike at him, he would dive under the water. The water was so cold, that it soon became evident that he must come out or be drowned.

While they were trying to drive him from under the bow of the boat or drown him, he would in broken and imploring accents say, "I did not steal the meat; I did not steal the meat. My master lives up the river. I want to see my master. I did not steal the meat. Do let me go home to master." After punching him, and striking him over the head for some time, he at last sunk in the water, to rise no more alive.

On the end of the pike-pole with which they were striking him was a hook which caught in his clothing, and they hauled him up on the bow of the boat. Some said he was dead, others said he was *"playing possum,"* while others kicked him to make him get up, but it was of no use — he was dead.

As soon as they became satisfied of this, they commenced leaving, one after another. One of the hands on the boat informed the captain that they had killed the man, and that the dead body was

lying on the deck. The captain came on deck, and
said to those who were remaining, " You have
killed this nigger; now take him off of my boat."
The captain's name was Hart. The dead body was
dragged on shore and left there. I went on board
of the boat where our gang of slaves were, and
during the whole night my mind was occupied with
what I had seen. Early in the morning, I went on
shore to see if the dead body remained there. I
found it in the same position that it was left the
night before. I watched to see what they would
do with it. It was left there until between eight
and nine o'clock, when a cart, which takes up the
trash out of the streets, came along, and the body
was thrown in, and in a few minutes more was
covered over with dirt which they were removing
from the streets. During the whole time, I did not
see more than six or seven persons around it, who,
from their manner, evidently regarded it as no
uncommon occurrence.

During our stay in the city, I met with a young
white man with whom I was well acquainted in St.
Louis. He had been sold into slavery, under the
following circumstances. His father was a drunk-

ard, and very poor, with a family of five or six children. The father died, and left the mother to take care of and provide for the children as best she might. The eldest was a boy, named Burrill, about thirteen years of age, who did chores in a store kept by Mr. Riley, to assist his mother in procuring a living for the family. After working with him two years, Mr. Riley took him to New Orleans to wait on him while in that city on a visit, and when he returned to St. Louis, he told the mother of the boy that he had died with the yellow fever. Nothing more was heard from him, no one supposing him to be alive. I was much astonished when Burrill told me his story. Though I sympathized with him, I could not assist him. We were both slaves. He was poor, uneducated, and without friends; and if living, is, I presume, still held as a slave.

After selling out this cargo of human flesh, we returned to St. Louis, and my time was up with Mr. Walker. I had served him one year, and it was the longest year I ever lived.

CHAPTER VIII.

I was sent home, and was glad enough to leave the service of one who was tearing the husband from the wife, the child from the mother, and the sister from the brother, — but a trial more severe and heart-rending than any which I had yet met with awaited me. My dear sister had been sold to a man who was going to Natchez, and was lying in jail awaiting the hour of his departure. She had expressed her determination to die, rather than go to the far south, and she was put in jail for safe keeping. I went to the jail the same day that I arrived, but as the jailor was not in, I could not see her.

I went home to my master, in the country, and the first day after my return, he came where I was at work, and spoke to me very politely. I knew from his appearance that something was the matter. After talking about my several journeys to New

Orleans with Mr. Walker, he told me that he was hard pressed for money, and as he had sold my mother and all her children except me, he thought it would be better to sell me than any other one, and that as I had been used to living in the city, he thought it probable that I would prefer it to a country life. I raised up my head, and looked him full in the face. When my eyes caught his, he immediately looked to the ground. After a short pause, I said,

"Master, mother has often told me that you are a near relative of mine, and I have often heard you admit the fact; and after you have hired me out, and received, as I once heard you say, nine hundred dollars for my services, — after receiving this large sum, will you sell me to be carried to New Orleans or some other place?"

"No," said he, "I do not intend to sell you to a negro trader. If I had wished to have done that, I might have sold you to Mr. Walker for a large sum, but I would not sell you to a negro trader. You may go to the city, and find you a good master."

"But," said I, "I cannot find a good master in the whole city of St. Louis."

"Why?" said he.

"Because there are no good masters in the State."

"Do you not call me a good master?"

"If you were, you would not sell me."

"Now I will give you one week to find a master in, and surely you can do it in that time."

The price set by my evangelical master upon my soul and body was the trifling sum of five hundred dollars. I tried to enter into some arrangement by which I might purchase my freedom; but he would enter into no such arrangement.

I set out for the city with the understanding that I was to return in a week with some one to become my new master. Soon after reaching the city, I went to the jail, to learn if I could once more see my sister; but could not gain admission. I then went to mother, and learned from her that the owner of my sister intended to start for Natchez in a few days.

I went to the jail again the next day, and Mr. Simonds, the keeper, allowed me to see my sister for the last time. I cannot give a just description of the scene at that parting interview. Never, never can be erased from my heart the occurrences of

5

that day! When I entered the room where she was, she was seated in one corner, alone. There were four other women in the same room, belonging to the same man. He had purchased them, he said, for his own use. She was seated with her face towards the door where I entered, yet she did not look up until I walked up to her. As soon as she observed me, she sprung up, threw her arms around my neck, leaned her head upon my breast, and, without uttering a word, burst into tears. As soon as she recovered herself sufficiently to speak, she advised me to take mother, and try to get out of slavery. She said there was no hope for herself, — that she must live and die a slave. After giving her some advice, and taking from my finger a ring and placing it upon hers, I bade her farewell forever, and returned to my mother, and then and there made up my mind to leave for Canada as soon as possible.

I had been in the city nearly two days, and as I was to be absent only a week, I thought best to get on my journey as soon as possible. In conversing with mother, I found her unwilling to make the attempt to reach a land of liberty, but she counselled me to get my liberty if I could. She said, as all her children were in slavery, she did not wish to leave them. I could not bear the idea of leaving her among those pirates, when there was a prospect of being able to get away from them. After much persuasion, I succeeded in inducing her to make the attempt to get away.

The time fixed for our departure was the next night. I had with me a little money that I had received, from time to time, from gentlemen for whom I had done errands. I took my scanty means and purchased some dried beef, crackers and cheese, which I carried to mother, who had provided herself with a bag to carry it in. I occasionally thought of my old master, and of my mission to the city to find a new one. I waited with the most intense anxiety for the appointed time to leave the land of slavery, in search of a land of liberty.

The time at length arrived, and we left the city just as the clock struck nine. We proceeded to the upper part of the city, where I had been two or three times during the day, and selected a skiff to carry us across the river. The boat was not mine, nor did I know to whom it did belong; neither

did I ca⁻e. The boat was fastened with a small
pole, which, with the aid of a rail, I soon loosened
from its moorings.   After hunting round and finding a board to use as an oar, I turned to the city,
and bidding it a long farewell, pushed off my boat.
The current running very swift, we had not reached
the middle of the stream before we were directly
opposite the city.

We were soon upon the Illinois shore, and, leap-
ing from the boat, turned it adrift, and the last
I saw of it, it was going down the river at good
speed. We took the ma·n road to Alton, and passed
through just at daylight, when we made for the
woôds, where we remained during the day.   Our
reason for going into the woods was, that we expected that Mr. Mansfield (the man who owned
my mother) would start in pursuit of her as soon as
he discovered that she was missing.   He also knew
that I had been in the city looking for a new master, and we thought probably he would go out to
my master's to see if he could find my mother, and
in so doing, Dr. Young might be led to suspect that
I had gone to Canada to find a purchaser.

We remained in the woods during the day, and as soon as darkness overshadowed the earth, we started again on our gloomy way, having no guide but the NORTH STAR. We continued to travel by night, and secrete ourselves in woods by day ; and every night, before emerging from our hiding-place, we would anxiously look for our friend and leader, — the NORTH STAR.

CHAPTER IX.

As we travelled towards a land of liberty, my heart would at times leap for joy.   At other times, being, as I was, almost constantly on my feet, I felt as though I could travel no further.   But when I thought of slavery with its Democratic whips — its Republican chains — its evangelical blood-hounds, and its religious slave-holders — when I thought of all this paraphernalia of American Democracy and Religion behind me, and the prospect of liberty before me, I was encouraged to press forward, my heart was strengthened, and I forgot that I was tired or hungry.

On the eighth day of our journey, we had a very heavy rain, and in a few hours after it commenced, we had not a dry thread upon our bodies.   This made our journey still more unpleasant.   On the tenth day, we found ourselves entirely destitute of provisions, and how to obtain any we could not tell. We finally resolved to stop at some farm-house, and try to get something to eat. We had no sooner determined to do this, than we went to a house, and asked them for some food. We were treated with great kindness, and they not only gave us something to eat, but gave us provisions to carry with us. They advised us to travel by day, and lye by at night. Finding ourselves about one hundred and fifty miles from St. Louis, we concluded that it would be safe to travel by daylight, and did not leave the house until the next morning. We travelled on that day through a thickly settled country, and through one small village. Though we were fleeing from a land of oppression, our hearts were still there. My dear sister and two beloved brothers were behind us, and the idea of giving them up, and leaving them forever, made us feel sad. But with all this depression of heart, the thought that I should one day be free, and call my body my own, buoyed me up, and made my heart leap for joy. I had just been telling mother how I should try to get employment as soon as we reached Canada, and how I intended to purchase us a little farm, and how I would earn money enough to buy

sister and brothers, and how happy we would be in
our own FREE HOME, — when three men came up
on horseback, and ordered us to stop.

I turned to the one who appeared to be the
principal man, and asked him what he wanted.
He said he had a warrant to take us up.   The
three immediately dismounted, and one took from
his pocket a handbill, advertising us as runaways,
and offering a reward of two hundred dollars for
our apprehension, and delivery in the city of St.
Louis.   The advertisement had been put out by
Isaac Mansfield and John Young.

While they were reading the advertisement,
mother looked me in the face, and burst into tears.
A cold chill ran over me, and such a sensation I
never experienced before, and I hope never to
again.   They took out a rope and tied me, and we
were taken back about six miles, to the house of
the individual who appeared to be the leader.   We
reached there about seven o'clock in the evening,
had supper, and were separated for the night.   Two
men remained in the room during the night.   Before the family retired to rest, they were all called
together to attend prayers.   The man who but a

few hours before had bound my hands together with a strong cord, read a chapter from the Bible, and then offered up prayer, just as though God sanctioned the act he had just committed upon a poor panting, fugitive slave.

The next morning, a blacksmith came in, and put a pair of handcuffs on me, and we started on our journey back to the land of whips, chains and Bibles. Mother was not tied, but was closely watched at night. We were carried back in a wagon, and after four days travel, we came in sight of St. Louis. I cannot describe my feelings upon approaching the city.

As we were crossing the ferry, Mr. Wiggins, the owner of the ferry, came up to me, and inquired what I had been doing that I was in chains. He had not heard that I had run away. In a few minutes, we were on the Missouri side, and were taken directly to the jail. On the way thither, I saw several of my friends, who gave me a nod of recognition as I passed them. After reaching the jail, we were locked up in different apartments.

CHAPTER X.

I HAD been in jail but a short time when I heard
that my master was sick, and nothing brought more
joy to my heart than that intelligence. I prayed
fervently for him — not for his recovery, but for
his death. I knew he would be exasperated at
having to pay for my apprehension, and knowing
his cruelty, I feared him. While in jail, I learned
that my sister Elizabeth, who was in prison when
we left the city, had been carried off four days
before our arrival.

I had been in jail but a few hours when three
negro-traders, learning that I was secured thus for
running away, came to my prison-house and looked
at me, expecting that I would be offered for sale.
Mr. Mansfield, the man who owned mother, came
into the jail as soon as Mr. Jones, the man who
arrested us, informed him that he had brought her
back. He told her that he would not whip her,

but would sell her to a negro-trader, or take her to
New Orleans himself.   After being in jail about
one week, master sent a man to take me out of jail,
and send me home.   I was taken out and carried
home, and the old man was well enough to sit up.
He had me brought into the room where he was,
and as I entered, he asked me where I had been?
I told I had acted according to his orders.   He
had told me to look for a master, and I had been
to look for one.   He answered that he did not tell
me to go to Canada to look for a master.   I told
him that as I had served him faithfully, and had
been the means of putting a number of hundreds of
dollars into his pocket, I thought I had a right to
my liberty.   He said he had promised my father
that I should not be sold to supply the New Orleans market, or he would sell me to a negro-
trader.

I was ordered to go into the field to work, and
was closely watched by the overseer during the day,
and locked up at night.   The overseer gave me a
severe whipping on the second day that I was in
the field.   I had been at home but a short time,
when master was able to ride to the city; and on

his return, he informed me that he had sold me to Samuel Willi, a merchant tailor. I knew Mr. Willi. I had lived with him three or four months some years before, when he hired me of my master.

Mr. Willi was not considered by his servants as a very bad man, nor was he the best of masters. I went to my new home, and found my new mistress very glad to see me. Mr. Willi owned two servants before he purchased me, — Robert and Charlotte. Robert was an excellent white-washer, and hired his time from his master, paying him one dollar per day, besides taking care of himself. He was known in the city by the name of Bob Music. Charlotte was an old woman, who attended to the cooking, washing, &c. Mr. Willi was not a wealthy man, and did not feel able to keep many servants around his house; so he soon decided to hire me out, and as I had been accustomed to service in steamboats, he gave me the privilege of finding such employment.

I soon secured a situation on board the steamer Otto, Capt. J. B. Hill, which sailed from St. Louis to Independence, Missouri. My former master, Dr. Young, did not let Mr. Willi know that I had run away, or he would not have permitted me to go on board a steamboat. The boat was not quite ready to commence running, and therefore I had to remain with Mr. Willi. But during this time, I had to undergo a trial, for which I was entirely unprepared. My mother, who had been in jail since her return until the present time, was now about being carried to New Orleans, to die on a cotton, sugar, or rice plantation!

I had been several times to the jail, but could obtain no interview with her. I ascertained, however, the time the boat in which she was to embark would sail, and as I had not seen mother since her being thrown into prison, I felt anxious for the hour of sailing to come. At last, the day arrived when I was to see her for the first time after our painful separation, and, for aught that I knew, for the last time in this world!

At about ten o'clock in the morning I went on board of the boat, and found her there in company with fifty or sixty other slaves. She was chained to another woman. On seeing me, she immediately dropped her head upon her heaving bosom. She moved not, neither did she weep. Her emotions

were too deep for tears. I approached, threw my
arms around her neck, kissed her, and fell upon
my knees, begging her forgiveness, for I thought
myself to blame for her sad condition; for if I had
not persuaded her to accompany me, she would not
then have been in chains.

She finally raised her head, looked me in the
face, (and such a look none but an angel can give!)
and said, "*My dear son, you are not to blame for
my being here. You have done nothing more
nor less than your duty. Do not, I pray you,
weep for me. I cannot last long upon a cotton
plantation. I feel that my heavenly master will
soon call me home, and then I shall be out of the
hands of the slave-holders!*"

I could bear no more — my heart struggled to
free itself from the human form. In a moment she
saw Mr. Mansfield coming toward that part of the
boat, and she whispered into my ear, "*My child,
we must soon part to meet no more this side of the
grave. You have ever said that you would not
die a slave; that you would be a freeman. Now
try to get your liberty! You will soon have no
one to look after but yourself!*" and just as she

whispered the last sentence into my ear, Mansfield came up to me, and with an oath, said, "Leave here this instant; you have been the means of my losing one hundred dollars to get this wench back," — at the same time kicking me with a heavy pair of boots. As I left her, she gave one shriek, saying, "God be with you!" It was the last time that I saw her, and the last word I heard her utter.

I walked on shore. The bell was tolling. The boat was about to start. I stood with a heavy heart, waiting to see her leave the wharf. As I thought of my mother, I could but feel that I had lost

> "———— the glory of my life,
> My blessing and my pride !
> I half forgot the name of slave,
> When she was by my side."

CHAPTER XI.

THE love of liberty that had been burning in my bosom, had well nigh gone out. I felt as though I was ready to die. The boat moved gently from the wharf, and while she glided down the river, I realized that my mother was indeed

> " Gone, — gone, — sold and gone,
> To the rice swamp dank and lone ! "

After the boat was out of sight, I returned home; but my thoughts were so absorbed in what I had witnessed, that I knew not what I was about half of the time. Night came, but it brought no sleep to my eyes.

In a few days, the boat upon which I was to work being ready, I went on board to commence. This employment suited me better than living in the city, and I remained until the close of navigation ; though it proved anything but pleasant. The captain was a drunken, profligate, hard-hearted creature, not knowing how to treat himself, or any other person.

The boat, on its second trip, brought down Mr. Walker, the man of whom I have spoken in a previous chapter, as hiring my time. He had between one and two hundred slaves, chained and manacled. Among them was a man that formerly belonged to my old master's brother, Aaron Young. His name was Solomon. He was a preacher, and belonged to the same church with his master. I was glad to see the old man. He wept like a child when he told me how he had been sold from his wife and children.

The boat carried down, while I remained on board, four or five gangs of slaves. Missouri, though a comparatively new State, is very much engaged in raising slaves to supply the southern market. In a former chapter, I have mentioned that I was once in the employ of a slave-trader, or driver, as he is called at the south. For fear that some may think that I have misrepresented a slave-driver, I will here give an extract from a

6

paper published in a slaveholding State, Tennes-
see, called the "Millennial Trumpeter."

"Droves of negroes, chained together in dozens
and scores, and hand-cuffed, have been driven
through our country in numbers far surpassing any
previous year, and these vile slave-drivers and deal-
ers are swarming like buzzards around a carrion.
Through this county, you cannot pass a few miles
in the great roads without having every feeling of
humanity insulted and lacerated by this spectacle,
nor can you go into any county or any neighborhood, scarcely, without seeing or hearing of some
of these despicable creatures, called negro-drivers.

"Who is a negro-driver?   One whose eyes
dwell with delight on lacerated bodies of helpless
men, women and children ; whose soul feels dia-
bolical raptures at the chains, and hand-cuffs, and
cart-whips, for inflicting tortures on weeping mothers torn from helpless babes, and on husbands and
wives torn asunder forever!"

Dark and revolting as is the picture here drawn,
it is from the pen of one living in the midst of
slavery.   But though these men may cant about
negro-drivers, and tell what despicable creatures

they are, who is it, I ask, that supplies them with the human beings that they are tearing asunder? I answer, as far as I have any knowledge of the State where I came from, that those who raise slaves for the market are to be found among all classes, from Thomas H. Benton down to the lowest political demagogue, who may be able to purchase a woman for the purpose of raising stock, and from the Doctor of Divinity down to the most humble lay member in the church.

It was not uncommon in St. Louis to pass by an auction-stand, and behold a woman upon the auction-block, and hear the seller crying out, "*How much is offered for this woman? She is a good cook, good washer, a good obedient servant. She has got religion!*" Why should this man tell the purchasers that she has religion? I answer, because in Missouri, and as far as I have any knowledge of slavery in the other States, the religious teaching consists in teaching the slave that he must never strike a white man; that God made him for a slave; and that, when whipped, he must not find fault, — for the Bible says, "He that knoweth his master's will, and doeth it not, shall be beaten with many stripes!" And slaveholders find such religion very profitable to them.

After leaving the steamer Otto, I resided at home, in Mr. Willi's family, and again began to lay my plans for making my escape from slavery. The anxiety to be a freeman would not let me rest day or night. I would think of the northern cities that I had heard so much about; — of Canada, where so many of my acquaintances had found refuge. I would dream at night that I was in Canada, a freeman, and on waking in the morning, weep to find myself so sadly mistaken.

> "I would think of Victoria's domain,
>   And in a moment I seemed to be there!
> But the fear of being taken again,
>   Soon hurried me back to despair."

Mr. Willi treated me better than Dr. Young ever had; but instead of making me contented and happy, it only rendered me the more miserable, for it enabled me better to appreciate liberty. Mr. Willi was a man who loved money as most men do, and without looking for an opportunity to sell me, he found one in the offer of Captain Enoch Price, a steamboat owner and commission mer-

chant, living in the city of St. Louis. Captain
Price tendered seven hundred dollars, which was
two hundred more than Mr. Willi had paid. He
therefore thought best to accept the offer. I was
wanted for a carriage driver, and Mrs. Price was
very much pleased with the captain's bargain. His
family consisted besides of one child. He had
three servants besides myself — one man and two
women.

Mrs. Price was very proud of her servants,
always keeping them well dressed, and as soon as I
had been purchased, she resolved to have a new
carriage. And soon one was procured, and all
preparations were made for a turn-out in grand
style, I being the driver.

One of the female servants was a girl some
eighteen or twenty years of age, named Maria.
Mrs. Price was very soon determined to have us
united, if she could so arrange matters. She
would often urge upon me the necessity of having
a wife, saying that it would be so pleasant for me
to take one in the same family ! But getting married, while in slavery, was the last of my thoughts;
and had I been ever so inclined, I should not have

married Maria, as my love had already gone in another quarter. Mrs. Price soon found out that her efforts at this match-making between Maria and myself would not prove successful. She also discovered (or thought she had) that I was rather partial to a girl named Eliza, who was owned by Dr. Mills. This induced her at once to endeavor the purchase of Eliza, so great was her desire to get me a wife!

Before making the attempt, however, she deemed it best to talk to me a little upon the subject of love, courtship, and marriage. Accordingly one afternoon she called me into her room — telling me to take a chair and sit down. I did so, thinking it rather strange, for servants are not very often asked thus to sit down in the same room with the master or mistress. She said that she had found out that I did not care enough about Maria to marry her. I told her that was true. She then asked me if there was not a girl in the city that I loved. Well, now, this was coming into too close quarters with me! People, generally, don't like to tell their love stories to everybody that may think fit to ask about them, and it was so with me. But, after blushing awhile and recovering myself, I told her that I did not want a wife. She then asked me, if I did not think something of Eliza. I told her that I did. She then said that if I wished to marry Eliza, she would purchase her if she could.

I gave but little encouragement to this proposition, as I was determined to make another trial to get my liberty, and I knew that if I should have a wife, I should not be willing to leave her behind; and if I should attempt to bring her with me, the chances would be difficult for success. However, Eliza was purchased, and brought into the family.

CHAPTER XII.

But the more I thought of the trap laid by Mrs. Price to make me satisfied with my new home, by getting me a wife, the more I determined never to marry any woman on earth until I should get my liberty. But this secret I was compelled to keep to myself, which placed me in a very critical position. I must keep upon good terms with Mrs. Price and Eliza. I therefore promised Mrs. Price that I would marry Eliza; but said that I was not then ready. And I had to keep upon good terms with Eliza, for fear that Mrs. Price would find out that I did not intend to get married.

I have here spoken of marriage, and it is very common among slaves themselves to talk of it. And it is common for slaves to be married; or at least have the marriage ceremony performed. But there is no such thing as slaves being lawfully married. There has never yet a case occurred where a slave has been tried for bigamy. The man may have as many women as he wishes, and the women as many men ; and the law takes no cognizance of such acts among slaves. And in fact some masters, when they have sold the husband from the wife, compel her to take another.

There lived opposite Captain Price's, Doctor Farrar, well known in St. Louis. He sold a man named Ben, to one of the traders. He also owned Ben's wife, and in a few days he compelled Sally (that was her name) to marry Peter, another man belonging to him. I asked Sally " why she married Peter so soon after Ben was sold." She said, " because master made her do it."

Mr. John Calvert, who resided near our place, had a woman named Lavinia. She was quite young, and a man to whom she was about to be married was sold, and carried into the country near St. Charles, about twenty miles from St. Louis. Mr. Calvert wanted her to get a husband ; but she had resolved not to marry any other man, and she refused. Mr. Calvert whipped her in such a manner that it was thought she would die. Some of the citizens had him arrested, but it was soon

hushed up. And that was the last of it. The
woman did not die, but it would have been the
same if she had.

Captain Price purchased me in the month of
October, and I remained with him until December,
when the family made a voyage to New Orleans, in
a boat owned by himself, and named the "Chester."
I served on board, as one of the stewards. On
arriving at New Orleans, about the middle of the
month, the boat took in freight for Cincinnati;
and it was decided that the family should go up the
river in her, and what was of more interest to me,
I was to accompany them.

The long looked for opportunity to make my
escape from slavery was near at hand.

Captain Price had some fears as to the propriety
of taking me near a free State, or a place where it
was likely I could run away, with a prospect of
liberty. He asked me if I had ever been in a free
State. "Oh yes," said I, "I have been in Ohio;
my master carried me into that State once, but I
never liked a free State."

It was soon decided that it would be safe to
take me with them, and what made it more safe,

Eliza was on the boat with us, and Mrs. Price, to try me, asked if I thought as much as ever of Eliza. I told her that Eliza was very dear to me indeed, and that nothing but death should part us. It was the same as if we were married. This had the desired effect. The boat left New Orleans, and proceeded up the river.

I had at different times obtained little sums of money, which I had reserved for a "rainy day." I procured some cotton cloth, and made me a bag to carry provisions in. The trials of the past were all lost in hopes for the future. The love of liberty, that had been burning in my bosom for years, and had been well nigh extinguished, was now resuscitated. At night, when all around was peaceful, I would walk the decks, meditating upon my happy prospects.

I should have stated, that before leaving St. Louis, I went to an old man named Frank, a slave, owned by a Mr. Sarpee. This old man was very distinguished (not only among the slave population, but also the whites) as a fortune-teller. He was about seventy years of age, something over six feet high, and very slender. Indeed, he was so small around his body that it looked as though it was not strong enough to hold up his head.

Uncle Frank was a very great favorite with the young ladies, who would go to him in great numbers to get their fortunes told. And it was generally believed that he could really penetrate into the mysteries of futurity. Whether true or not, he had the *name,* and that is about half of what one needs in this gullible age. I found Uncle Frank seated in the chimney corner, about ten o'clock at night. As soon as I entered, the old man left his seat. I watched his movement as well as I could by the dim light of the fire. He soon lit a lamp, and coming up, looked me full in the face, saying, " Well, my son, you have come to get uncle to tell your fortune, have you ? " " Yes," said I. But how the old man should know what I had come for, I could not tell. However, I paid the fee of twenty-five cents, and he commenced by looking into a gourd, filled with water. Whether the old man was a prophet, or the son of a prophet, I cannot say ; but there is one thing certain, many of his predictions were verified.

I am no believer in soothsaying; yet I am sometimes at a loss to know how Uncle Frank could tell
so accurately what would occur in the future.
Among the many things he told was one which was
enough to pay me for all the trouble of hunting him
up. It was that *I should be free!* He further
said, that in trying to get my liberty, I would meet
with many severe trials. I thought to myself, any
fool could tell me that!

The first place in which we landed in a free
State was Cairo, a small village at the mouth of the
Ohio river. We remained here but a few hours,
when we proceeded to Louisville. After unloading
some of the cargo, the boat started on her upward
trip. The next day was the first of January. I
had looked forward to New Year's day as the com-
mencement of a new era in the history of my life.
I had decided upon leaving the peculiar institution
that day.

During the last night that I served in slavery, I
did not close my eyes a single moment. When
not thinking of the future, my mind dwelt on the
past. The love of a dear mother, a dear sister, and
three dear brothers, yet living, caused me to shed

many tears. If I could only have been assured of their being dead, I should have felt satisfied; but I imagined I saw my dear mother in the cotton-field, followed by a merciless task-master, and no one to speak a consoling word to her! I beheld my dear sister in the hands of a slave-driver, and compelled to submit to his cruelty!   None but one placed in such a situation can for a moment imagine the intense agony to which these reflections subjected me.

CHAPTER XIII.

At last the time for action arrived. The boat landed at a point which appeared to me the place of all others to start from. I found that it would be impossible to carry anything with me, but what was upon my person. I had some provisions, and a single suit of clothes, about half worn. When the boat was discharging her cargo, and the passengers engaged carrying their baggage on and off shore, I improved the opportunity to convey myself with my little effects on land. Taking up a trunk, I went up the wharf, and was soon out of the crowd. I made directly for the woods, where I remained until night, knowing well that I could not travel, even in the State of Ohio, during the day, without danger of being arrested.

I had long since made up my mind that I would not trust myself in the hands of any man, white or colored. The slave is brought up to look upon every white man as an enemy to him and his race; and twenty-one years in slavery had taught me that there were traitors, even among colored people. After dark, I emerged from the woods into a narrow path, which led me into the main travelled road. But I knew not which way to go. I did not know North from South, East from West. I looked in vain for the North Star; a heavy cloud hid it from my view. I walked up and down the road until near midnight, when the clouds disappeared, and I welcomed the sight of my friend, — truly the slave's friend, — the North Star!

As soon as I saw it, I knew my course, and before daylight I travelled twenty or twenty-five miles. It being in the winter, I suffered intensely from the cold; being without an overcoat, and my other clothes rather thin for the season. I was provided with a tinder-box, so that I could make up a fire when necessary. And but for this, I should certainly have frozen to death; for I was determined not to go to any house for shelter. I knew of a man belonging to Gen. Ashly, of St. Louis, who had run away near Cincinnati, on the way to Washington, but had been caught and carried back into slavery; and I felt that a similar fate awaited me, should I be seen by any one. I travelled at night, and lay by during the day.

On the fourth day, my provisions gave out, and then what to do I could not tell. Have something to eat, I must; but how to get it was the question! On the first night after my food was gone, I went to a barn on the road-side, and there found some ears of corn. I took ten or twelve of them, and kept on my journey. During the next day, while in the woods, I roasted my corn and feasted upon it, thanking God that I was so well provided for.

My escape to a land of freedom now appeared certain, and the prospects of the future occupied a great part of my thoughts. What should be my occupation, was a subject of much anxiety to me; and the next thing what should be my name? I have before stated that my old master, Dr. Young, had no children of his own, but had with him a nephew, the son of his brother, Benjamin Young. When this boy was brought to Doctor Young, his name being William, the same as mine, my mother was ordered to change mine to something else. This, at the time, I thought to be one of the most

7

cruel acts that could be committed upon my rights ; and I received several very severe whippings for telling people that my name was William, after orders were given to change it.   Though young, I was old enough to place a high appreciation upon my name.   It was decided, however, to call me " Sandford," and this name I was known by, not only upon my master's plantation, but up to the time that I made my escape.   I was sold under the name of Sandford.

But as soon as the subject came to my mind, I resolved on adopting my old name of William, and let Sandford go by the board, for I always hated it. Not because there was anything peculiar in the name ; but because it had been forced upon me. It is sometimes common at the south, for slaves to take the name of their masters.   Some have a legitimate right to do so.   But I always detested the idea of being called by the name of either of my masters.   And as for my father, I would rather have adopted the name of " Friday," and been known as the servant of some Robinson Crusoe, than to have taken his name.   So I was not only hunting for my liberty, but also hunting for a name ;

though I regarded the latter as of little consequence, if I could but gain the former. Travelling
along the road, I would sometimes speak to myself,
sounding my name over, by way of getting used to
it, before I should arrive among civilized human
beings. On the fifth or sixth day, it rained very
fast, and it froze about as fast as it fell, so that my
clothes were one glare of ice. I travelled on at
night until I became so chilled and benumbed —
the wind blowing into my face — that I found it
impossible to go any further, and accordingly took
shelter in a barn, where I was obliged to walk about
to keep from freezing.

I have ever looked upon that night as the most
eventful part of my escape from slavery. Nothing
but the providence of God, and that old barn, saved
me from freezing to death. I received a very
severe cold, which settled upon my lungs, and from
time to time my feet had been frost-bitten, so that
it was with difficulty I could walk. In this situation I travelled two days, when I found that I must
seek shelter somewhere, or die.

The thought of death was nothing frightful to
me, compared with that of being caught, and again

carried back into slavery.   Nothing but the prospect of enjoying liberty could have induced me to undergo such trials, for

> " Behind I left the whips and chains,
> Before me were sweet Freedom's plains ! "

This, and this alone, cheered me onward.   But I at last resolved to seek protection from the inclemency of the weather, and therefore I secured myself behind some logs and brush, intending to wait there until some one should pass by; for I thought it probable that I might see some colored person, or, if not, some one who was not a slaveholder; for I had an idea that I should know a slaveholder as far as I could see him.

CHAPTER XIV.

THE first person that passed was a man in a buggy-wagon. He looked too genteel for me to hail him. Very soon, another passed by on horse-back. I attempted speaking to him, but fear made my voice fail me. As he passed, I left my hiding-place, and was approaching the road, when I observed an old man walking towards me, leading a white horse. He had on a broad-brimmed hat and a very long coat, and was evidently walking for exercise. As soon as I saw him, and observed his dress, I thought to myself, " You are the man that I have been looking for! " Nor was I mistaken. He was the very man!

On approaching me, he asked me, " if I was not a slave." I looked at him some time, and then asked him " if he knew of any one who would help me, as I was sick." He answered that he would; but again asked, if I was not a slave. I told him I was. He then said that I was in a very pro-slavery neighborhood, and if I would wait until he went home, he would get a covered wagon for me. I promised to remain. He mounted his horse, and was soon out of sight.

After he was gone, I meditated whether to wait or not; being apprehensive that he had gone for some one to arrest me. But I finally concluded to remain until he should return ; removing some few rods to watch his movements. After a suspense of an hour and a half or more, he returned with a two horse covered-wagon, such as are usually seen under the shed of a Quaker meeting-house on Sundays and Thursdays ; for the old man proved to be a Quaker of the George Fox stamp.

He took me to his house, but it was some time before I could be induced to enter it; not until the old lady came out, did I venture into the house. I thought I saw something in the old lady's cap that told me I was not only safe, but welcome, in her house. I was not, however, prepared to receive their hospitalities. The only fault I found with them was their being too kind. I had never had a white man to treat me as an equal, and the idea of a white lady waiting on me at the table was still worse! Though the table was loaded with the good things of this life, I could not eat. I thought if I could only be allowed the privilege of eating in the kitchen, I should be more than satisfied!

Finding that I could not eat, the old lady, who was a "Thompsonian," made me a cup of "composition," or "number six;" but it was so strong and hot, that I called it *"number seven!"* However, I soon found myself at home in this family. On different occasions, when telling these facts, I have been asked how I felt upon finding myself regarded as a man by a white family; especially just having run away from one. I cannot say that I have ever answered the question yet.

The fact that I was in all probability a freeman, sounded in my ears like a charm. I am satisfied that none but a slave could place such an appreciation upon liberty as I did at that time. I wanted to see mother and sister, that I might tell them "I was free!" I wanted to see my fellow slaves in St. Louis, and let them know that the chains were no longer upon my limbs. I wanted to see Captain Price, and let him learn from my own lips that I was no more a chattel, but a man! I was anxious, too, thus to inform Mrs. Price that she must get another coachman. And I wanted to see Eliza more than I did either Mr. or Mrs. Price!

The fact that I was a freeman — could walk, talk, eat and sleep as a man, and no one to stand over me with the blood-clotted cowhide — all this made me feel that I was not myself.

The kind friend that had taken me in was named Wells Brown. He was a devoted friend of the slave; but was very old, and not in the enjoyment of good health. After being by the fire awhile, I found that my feet had been very much frozen. I was seized with a fever which threatened to confine me to my bed. But my Thompsonian friends soon raised me, treating me as kindly as if I had been one of their own children. I remained with them twelve or fifteen days, during which time they made me some clothing, and the old gentleman purchased me a pair of boots.

I found that I was about fifty or sixty miles from Dayton, in the State of Ohio, and between one and two hundred miles from Cleaveland, on lake Erie, a place I was desirous of reaching on my way to

Canada.   This I know will sound strangely to the
ears of people in foreign lands, but it is nevertheless true.   An American citizen was fleeing from a
Democratic, Republican, Christian government, to
receive protection under the monarchy of Great
Britain.   While the people of the United States
boast of their freedom, they at the same time keep
three millions of their own citizens in chains; and
while I am seated here in sight of Bunker Hill
Monument, writing this narrative, I am a slave, and
no law, not even in Massachusetts, can protect me
from the hands of the slaveholder!

Before leaving this good Quaker friend, he inquired what my name was besides William.   I told
him that I had no other name.   " Well," said he,
" thee must have another name.   Since thee has
got out of slavery, thee has become a man, and
men always have two names."

I told him that he was the first man to extend the
hand of friendship to me, and I would give him the
privilege of naming me.

" If I name thee," said he, " I shall call thee
Wells Brown, after myself."

" But," said I, " I am not willing to lose my

name of William. As it was taken from me once against my will, I am not willing to part with it again upon any terms."

" Then," said he, " I will call thee William Wells Brown."

" So be it," said I ; and I have been known by that name ever since I left the house of my first white friend, Wells Brown.

After giving me some little change, I again started for Canada. In four days I reached a public house, and went in to warm myself. I there learned that some fugitive slaves had just passed through the place. The men in the bar-room were talking about it, and I thought that it must have been myself they referred to, and I was therefore afraid to start, fearing they would seize me ; but I finally mustered courage enough, and took my leave. As soon as I was out of sight, I went into the woods, and remained there until night, when I again regained the road, and travelled on until the next day.

Not having had any food for nearly two days, I was faint with hunger, and was in a dilemma what to do, as the little cash supplied me by my adopted father, and which had contributed to my comfort, was now all gone. I however concluded to go to a farm-house, and ask for something to eat. On approaching the door of the first one presenting itself, I knocked, and was soon met by a man who asked me what I wanted. I told him that I would like something to eat. He asked where I was from, and where I was going. I replied that I had come some way, and was going to Cleaveland.

After hesitating a moment or two, he told me that he could give me nothing to eat, adding, " that if I would work, I could get something to eat."

I felt bad, being thus refused something to sustain nature, but did not dare tell him that I was a slave.

Just as I was leaving the door, with a heavy heart, a woman, who proved to be the wife of this gentleman, came to the door, and asked her husband what I wanted? He did not seem inclined to inform her. She therefore asked me herself. I told her that I had asked for something to eat. After a few other questions, she told me to come in, and that she would give me something to eat.

I walked up to the door, but the husband remained in the passage, as if unwilling to let me enter.

She asked him two or three times to get out of the way, and let me in. But as he did not move, she pushed him on one side, bidding me walk in! I was never before so glad to see a woman push a man aside! Ever since that act, I have been in favor of "woman's rights!"

After giving me as much food as I could eat, she presented me with ten cents, all the money then at her disposal, accompanied with a note to a friend, a few miles further on the road. Thanking this angel of mercy from an overflowing heart, I pushed on my way, and in three days arrived at Cleaveland, Ohio.

Being an entire stranger in this place, it was difficult for me to find where to stop. I had no money, and the lake being frozen, I saw that I must remain until the opening of navigation, or go to Canada by way of Buffalo. But believing myself to be somewhat out of danger, I secured an engagement at the Mansion House, as a table waiter, in payment for my board. The proprietor, however, whose name was E. M. Segur, in a short time, hired me for twelve dollars per month; on which terms I remained until spring, when I found good employment on board a lake steamboat.

I purchased some books, and at leisure moments perused them with considerable advantage to myself. While at Cleaveland, I saw, for the first time, an anti-slavery newspaper. It was the " *Genius of Universal Emancipation*," published by Benjamin Lundy, and though I had no home, I subscribed for the paper. It was my great desire, being out of slavery myself, to do what I could for the emancipation of my brethren yet in chains, and while on Lake Erie, I found many opportunities of " helping their cause along."

It is well known, that a great number of fugitives make their escape to Canada, by way of Cleaveland; and while on the lake, I always made arrangement to carry them on the boat to Buffalo or Detroit, and thus effect their escape to the " promised land." The friends of the slave, knowing that I would transport them without charge, never failed to have a delegation when the boat arrived at Cleaveland. I have sometimes had four or five on board, at one time.

In the year 1842, I conveyed, from the first of May to the first of December, sixty-nine fugitives over Lake Erie to Canada. In 1843, I visited

Malden, in Upper Canada, and counted seventeen, in that small village, who owed their escape to my humble efforts.

Soon after coming North, I subscribed for the Liberator, edited by that champion of freedom, William Lloyd Garrison. I labored a season to promote the temperance cause among the colored people, but for the last three years, have been pleading for the victims of American slavery.

WILLIAM WELLS BROWN.

Boston, Mass., June, 1847.

MY LIFE IN THE SOUTH.

JACOB STROYER.

Rev. Jacob Stroyer's book is intensely interesting, because it is a story of personal experience. It is also a book of great educational worth, because it deals plainly and justly with slavery, as that institution existed both in time of peace and in time of war, from the standpoint of one who was himself a slave.

C. H. PUFFER,

Pastor First Universalist Church.
Salem, Mass., Nov. 9, 1898.

The author of this book—Mr. Stroyer—has been for years a worthy resident of this city, doing an excellent work among the colored people. His story, graphically told, is one of many which must interest every lover of the Nation's history, in both its dark and bright pages.

DE WITT S. CLARK, Salem.

OCT. 25, 1898.

Mr. Stroyer's account of his experiences in the War of the Rebellion is history at first hand. And his point of view is one from which little has been written. There have been any number of accounts by observers in both the Federal and the Confederate ranks. But not many have come from·the slaves who were forced to work against a cause which they knew was their own. This fact gives Mr. Stroyer's narrative an uncommon interest. I take pleasure in commending Mr. Stoyer as an earnest and worthy Christian man, who has deeply at heart the welfare of his people.

JAS. F. BRODIE.

Salem, Mass., September 19, 1898.

Mr. Stroyer's account of his experience in slavery and during the war is of great interest and value as a trustworthy description of the condition and life of slaves *by one of themselves*. His memory is remarkably keen and his narrative vivid and at times both touching and thrilling. The book is a great credit to its author and deserves a generous reception and a wide circulation.

John Wright Buckham.

August 13, 1879.

In this book Mr. Stroyer has given us, with a most simple and effective realism, the inside view of the institution of slavery. It is worth reading, to know how men, intelligent enough to report their experience, felt under the yoke. The time has come when American slavery can be studied historically, without passion, save such as mixes itself with the wonder that so great an evil could exist so long as a social form or a political idol. The time has not come when such study is unnecessary; for to deal justly by white or black in the United States, their previous relations must be understood, and nothing which casts light on the most universal and practical of those relations is without value today. I take pleasure, therefore, in saying that I consider Mr. Stroyer a competent and trustworthy witness to these details of plantation life.

E. C. Bolles.

(4)

CITY OF SALEM, MAYOR'S OFFICE, }
Nov. 5, 1884. }

This is to certify that since the year 1876 I have known Rev. Jacob Stroyer as a preacher and minister to the colored people of this city. He is earnest, devoted and faithful.

He is endeavoring by the sale of this book to realize the means to enable him, by a course of study, to better fit himself as a minister to preach in the South.

I most cheerfully commend him in his praiseworthy efforts.

WM. M. HILL, *Mayor.*

Mr. Stroyer's book is a setting forth in a fresh and unique manner of the old and bitter wrongs of American slavery. It is an inside view of a phase of our national life which has happily passed away forever. Although it concerns itself largely with incidents and details, it is not without the historical value which attaches to reliable personal reminiscences. The author has made commendable progress in intellectual culture, and is worthy of generous assistance in his effort to fit himself still more perfectly for labor among his needy brethren in the South.

E. S. ATWOOD.

(5)

PREFACE.

FOURTH EDITION.

When the author first presented his book to the public he did not anticipate the very great favor with which it would be received. The first edition was soon disposed of, a second and a third were called for, and those were as generously received as had been their predecessors. The present edition, the fourth, besides all that was in those former publications, contains some new material relating to the author's personal experiences in the Civil War.

Thanking the people for the support given, and hoping that this latest effort will meet approval, the author presents the story of himself and his once oppressed brethren.

CHAPTER I.

My father was born in Sierra Leone, Africa. Of his parents and his brothers and sisters I know nothing. I only remember that it was said that his father's name was Moncoso, and his mother's Mongomo, which names are known only among the native Africans. He was brought from Africa when but a boy, and sold to old Colonel Dick Singleton, who owned a great many plantations in South Carolina, and when the old colonel divided his property among his children, father fell to the second son, Col. M. R. Singleton.

Mother never was sold, but her parents were; they were owned by one Mr. Crough, who sold them and the rest of the slaves, with the plantation, to Col. Dick Singleton, upon whose place mother was born. I was born on this extensive plantation, twenty-eight miles southeast of Columbia, South Carolina, in the year 1849. I belonged to Col. M. R. Singleton, and was held in slavery up to the time of the emancipation proclamation issued by President Lincoln.

THE CHILDREN.

My father had fifteen children : four boys and three girls by his first wife and eight by his second. Their names were as follows : of the boys—Toney, Aszerine, Duke and Dezine ; of the girls—Violet, Priscilla, and Lydia. Those of his second wife were as follows : Footy, Embrus, Caleb, Mitchell, Cuffey and Jacob, and of the girls, Catherine and Retta.

SAND HILL DAYS.

Col. M. R. Singleton was like many other rich slave owners in the South, who had summer seats four, six or eight miles from the plantation, where they carried the little negro boys and girls too small to work.

Our summer seat, or the sand hill, as the slaves used to call it, was four miles from the plantation· Among the four hundred and sixty-five slaves owned by the colonel there were a great many children. If my readers had visited Col. Singleton's plantation the last of May or the first of June in the days of slavery, they would have seen three or four large plantation wagons loaded with little negroes of both sexes, of various complexions and conditions, who were being carried to this summer residence, and among them they would have found the author, of this little work in his sand-hill days.

My readers would naturally ask how many seasons these children were taken to the summer seats ? I answer, until, in the judgment of the overseer, they were large enough to work ; then they were kept at the plantation. How were they fed ? There were three or four women who were too old to work on the plantation who were sent as nurses to the summer seats with the children; they did the cooking. The way in which these old women cooked for 80, and sometimes 150 children, in my sand-hill days, was this :—they had two or three large pots, which held about a bushel each, in which they used to cook corn flour, stirred with large wooden paddles. The food was dealt out with the paddles into each child's little wooden tray or tin pail, which was furnished by the parents according to their ability.

With this corn flour, which the slaves called mush, each child used to get a gill of sour milk brought daily from the plantation in a large wooden pail on the head of a boy or man. We children used to like the sour milk, or hard clabber as it was called by the slaves; but that seldom changed diet, namely the mush, was hated worse than medicine. Our hatred was increased against the mush from the fact that they used to give us molasses to eat with it, instead of clabber. The hateful mixture made us anxious for Sundays to come, when our mothers, fathers, sisters and brothers would bring something from the plantation, which, however poor, we considered very nice, compared with what we had during the week days. Among the many desirable things our parents brought us the most delightful was cow pease, rice, and a piece of bacon, cooked together; the mixture was called by the slaves "hopping John."

THE STORY OF GILBERT.

A few large boys were sent yearly to the sand-hill among the smaller ones, as guides. At the time to which I am referring there was one by the name of Gilbert, who used to go around with the smaller boys in the woods to gather bushes and sticks for the old women to cook our food with.

Gilbert was a cruel boy. He used to strip his little fellow negroes while in the woods, and whip them two or three times a week, so that their backs were all scarred, and·threatened them with severer punishment if they told; this state of things had been going on for quite a while. As I was a favorite with Gilbert, I always had managed to escape a whipping, with the promise of keeping the secret of the punishment of the rest, which I did, not so much that I was afraid of Gilbert, as because I always was inclined to mind my own business. But finally, one day, Gilbert said to me, "Jake," as he used to call me, "you am a good boy, but I'm gwine to wip you some to-day, as I wip dem toder boys." Of course I was required to strip off my only garment, which was an Osnaburg linen shirt, worn by both sexes of the negro children in the summer. As I stood trembling before my merciless superior, who had a switch in his hand, thousands of thoughts went through my little mind as to how to get rid of the whipping. I finally fell upon a plan which I hoped would save me from a punishment that was near at hand. There were some carpenters in the woods, some distance from us, hewing timber; they were far away, but it was a clear morning, so we could hear their voices and the sound of the axes. Having resolved in my mind what I would do. I commenced reluctantly to take off my shirt, at the same time pleading with Gilbert, who paid no attention to my prayer, but said, " Jake, I is gwine to wip you to-day as I did dem toder boys." Having satisfied myself that no mercy was to be found with Gilbert, I drew my shirt off and threw it over his head, and bounded forward on a run in the direction of the sound of the carpenters. By the time he got from the entanglement of my garment, I had quite a little start of him. Between my starting point and the place where the carpenters were at work I jumped over some bushes five or six feet high. Gilbert soon gained upon me, and sometimes touched me with his hands, but as I had on nothing for him to hold to, he

could not take hold of me. As I began to come in
sight of the carpenters, Gilbert begged me not to go
to them, for he knew that it would be bad for him,
but as that was not a time for me to listen to his en-
treaties, I moved on faster. As I got near to the carpenters, one of them ran and met me, into whose
arms I jumped. The man into whose arms I ran was
Uncle Benjamin, my mother's uncle. As he clasped
me in his arms, he said, " Bres de Lo, my son, wat is
de matter ?" But I was so exhausted that it was
quite a while before I could tell him my trouble;
when recovered from my breathless condition, I told
him that Gilbert had been in the habit of stripping
the boys and whipping them two or three times a
week, when we went into the woods, and threatened
them with greater punishment if they told. I said
he had never whipped me before, but I was cautioned
to keep the secret, which I had done up to this time;
but he said he was going to whip me this morning, so
I threw my shirt over his head and ran here for protection. Gilbert did not follow me after I got in
sight of the carpenters, but sneaked away. Of course
my body was all bruised and scratched by the bushes.
Acting as a guide for Uncle Benjamin, I took him to
where I had left my garment.

At this time the children were scattered around in
the woods, waiting for what the trouble would bring;
They all were gathered up and taken to the sand-hill
house, examined, and it was found, as I have stated,
that their backs were all scarred. Gilbert was brought
to trial, severely whipped, and they made him
beg all the children to pardon him for his treatment to them. But he never was allowed to go into

the woods with the rest of the children during that season. My sand-hill associates always thanked me for the course I took, which saved them and myself from further punishment by him.

When master and mistress were to visit their little negroes at the sand-hill, the news was either brought by the overseer who resided at the above named place, and went back and forth to the plantation, or by one of master's house servants, a day ahead. The preparation required to receive our white guests was that each little negro was to be washed, and clad in the best dress he or she had. But before this was done, the unsuccessful attempt was made to straighten out our unruly wools with some small cards, or Jim-Crows as we called them.

On one occasion an old lady, by the name of Janney Cuteron, attempted to straighten out my wool with one of those Jim-crows; as she hitched the teeth of the instrument in my unyielding wool with her great masculine hand, of course I was jerked flat on my back. This was the common fate of most of my associates, whose wools were of the same nature, but with a little water and the strong application of the Jim-crow, the old lady soon combed out my wool into some sort of shape.

As our preparations were generally completed three-quarters of an hour before our guests came, we were placed in line, the boys together and the girls by themselves. We were then drilled in the art of addressing our expected visitors. The boys were required to bend the body forward with head down, and rest the body on the left foot, and scrape the right foot backward on the ground, while uttering the words, "how dy Massie and Missie." The girls were required to use the same words, accompanied with a courtesy. But when Master and Mistress had left, the little African wools were neglected until the news of their next visit.

Our sand-hill days were very pleasant, outside of the seldom changed diet, namely the mush, which we had sometimes to eat with molasses, the treatment of Gilbert, and the attempt to straighten out our unruly wools.

I said that my father was brought from Africa when but a boy, and was sold to old Col. Dick Singleton ; and when the children were of age, the Colonel divided his plantations among them, and father fell to Col. M. R. Singleten, who was the second son.

On this large plantation there were 465 slaves ; there were not so many when it was given to Col. M. R., but increased to the above stated number, up to the time of emancipation.

My father was not a field hand ; my first recollection of him was that he used to take care of hogs and cows in the swamp, and when too old for that work he was sent to the plantation to take care of horses and mules, as master had a great many for the use of his farm.

I have stated that father said that his father's name in Africa was Moncoso, and his mother's Mongomo, but I never learned what name he went by before he was brought to this country. I only know that he stated that Col. Dick Singleton gave him the name of William, by which he was known up to the day of his death. Father had a surname, Stroyer, which he could not use in public, as the surname Stroyer would be against the law ; he was known only by the name of William Singleton, because that was his master's name. So the title Stroyer was forbidden him, and could be used only by his children after the emancipation of the slaves.

There were two reasons given by the slave holders why they did not allow a slave to use his own name, but rather that of the master. The first was that, if he ran away, he would not be so easily detected by using his own name as by that of his master. The second was that to allow him to use his own name would be sharing an honor which was due only to his master, and that would be too much for a negro, said they, who was nothing more than a servant. So it was held as a crime for a slave to be caught using his own name, a crime which would expose him to severe punishment. But thanks be to God that those days have passed, and we now live under the sun of liberty.

MOTHER.

Mother's name was Chloe. She belonged to Col. M. R. Singleton too ; she was a field hand, and never was sold, but her parents were once.

Mr. Crough who, as I have said had owned this plantation on which mother lived, had sold the plantation to Col. Dick Singleton, with mother's parents on it, before she was born.

Most of the family from which mother came, had trades of some kind ; some were carpenters, some were blacksmiths, some house servants, and others were made drivers over the other negroes. Of course the negro drivers would be under a white man, who was called the overseer. Sometimes the negro drivers were a great deal worse to their fellow negroes than were the white men.

Mother had an uncle by the name of Esau, whom master thought more of than he did of the overseer. Uncle Esau was more cruel than was any white man master ever had on his plantation. Many of the slaves used to run away from him into the woods. I have known some of the negroes to run away from the cruel treatment of Uncle Esau, and to stay off eight or ten months. They were so afraid of him that they used to say that they would rather see the devil than to see him; they were glad when he died. But while so much was said of Uncle Esau, which was also true of many other negro drivers, the overseers themselves were not guiltless of cruelty to the defenceless slaves.

I have said that most of the family from which mother came had trades of some kind; but she had to take her chance in the field with those who had to weather the storm. But my readers are not to think that those whom I have spoken of as having trades were free from punishment, for they were not; some of them had more trouble than had the field hands. At times the overseer, who was a white man, would go to the shop of the blacksmith, or carpenter, and would pick a quarrel with him, so as to get an opportunity to punish him. He would say to the negro, " Oh, ye think yourself as good as ye master, ye—" Of course he knew what the overseer was after, so he was afraid to speak; the overseer, hearing no answer, would turn to him and cry out, "ye so big ye can't speak to me, ye—," and then the conflict would begin, and he would give that man such a punishment as would disable him for two or three months. The merciless overseer would say to him, " Ye think because ye have a trade ye are as good as ye master, ye —; but I will show ye that ye are nothing but a nigger."

I said that my father had two wives and fifteen children : four boys and three girls by the first, and six boys and two girls by the second wife. Of course he did not marry his wives as they do now, as it was not allowed among the slaves, but he took them as his wives by mutual agreement. He had my mother after the death of his first wife. I am the third son of his second wife.

My readers would very naturally like to know whether some of the slaves did not have more than one woman. I answer, they had ; for as they had no law to bind them to one woman, they could have as many as they pleased by mutual agreement. But notwithstanding, they had a sense of the moral law, for many of them felt that it was right to have but one woman ; they had different opinions about plurality of wives, as have the most educated and refined among the whites.

I met one of my fellow negroes one day, who lived next neighbor to us, and I said to him, " Well, Uncle William, how are you, to-day ?" His answer was " Thank God, my son, I have two wives now, and must try and make out with them until I get some more." But while you will find many like him, others would rebuke the idea of having more than one wife. But, thanks be to God, the day has come when no one need to plead ignorance, for master and servant are both bound by the same law.

I did not go to the sand-hill, or summer seat, my alloted time, but stopped on the plantation with father, as I said that he used to take care of horses and mules. I was around with him in the barn yard when but a very small boy; of course that gave me an early relish for the occupation of hostler, and I soon made known my preference to Col. Singleton, who was a sportsman, and an owner of fine horses. And, although I was too small to work, the Colonel granted my request; hence I was allowed to be numbered among those who took care of the fine horses, and learned to ride. But I soon found that my new occupation demanded a little more than I cared for.

It was not long after I had entered my new work before they put me upon the back of a horse which threw me to the ground almost as soon as I had reached his back. It hurt me a little, but that was not the worst of it, for when I got up there was a man standing near with a switch in hand, and he immediately began to beat me. Although I was a very bad boy, this was the first time I had been whipped by any one except father and mother, so I cried out in a tone of voice as if I would say, this is the first and last whipping you will give me when father gets hold of you.

When I had got away from him I ran to father with all my might, but soon found my expectation blasted, as father very coolly said to me, "Go back to your work and be a good boy, for I cannot do anything for you." But that did not satisfy me, so on I went to mother with my complaint and she came out to the man who had whipped me; he was a groom, a white man master had hired to train the horses. Mother

and he began to talk, then he took a whip and
started for her, and she ran from him, talking all the
time.   I ran back and forth between mother and him
until he stopped beating her. After the fight between
the groom and mother, he took me back to the stable
yard and gave me a severe flogging. And, although
mother failed to help me at first, still I had faith that
when he had taken me back to the stable yard, and
commenced whipping me, she would come and stop
him, but I looked in vain, for she did not come.

Then the idea first came to me that I, with my dear
father and mother and the rest of my fellow negroes,
was doomed to cruel treatment through life, and was
defenceless.   But when I found that father and
mother could not save me from punishment, as they
themselves had to submit to the same treatment, I
concluded to appeal to the sympathy of the groom,
who seemed to have full control over me ; but my
pitiful cries never touched his sympathy, for things
seemed to grow worse rather than better ; so I made
up my mind to stem the storm the best I could.

I have said that Col. Singleton had fine horses,
which he kept for racing, and he owned two very
noted ones, named Capt. Miner and Inspector. Perhaps some of my readers have already heard of Capt.
Miner, for he was widely known, having won many
races in Charlestown and Columbia, S. C., also in
Augusta, Ga., and New York. He was a dark bay,
with short tail. Inspector was a chestnut sorrel, and
had the reputation of being a very great horse. These
two horses have won many thousand dollars for the
the colonel. I rode these two horses a great many
times in their practice gallops, but never had the op-

portunity to ride them in a race before Col. Singleton died, for he did not live long after I had learned so that I could ride for money. The custom was, that when a boy had learned the trade of a rider, he would have to ride what was known as a trial, in the presence of a judge, who would approve or disapprove his qualifications to be admitted as a race rider, according to the jockey laws of South Carolina at that time.

I have said that I loved the business and acquired the skill very early, and this enabled me to pass my examination creditably, and to be accepted as a capable rider, but I passed through some very severe treatment before reaching that point.

This white man who trained horses for Col. Singleton was named Boney Young; he had a brother named Charles, who trained for the colonel's brother, John Singleton. Charles was a good man, but Boney our trainer, was as mean as Charles was good; he could smile in the face of one who was suffering the most painful death at his hands.

One day, about two weeks after Boney Young and mother had the conflict, he called me to him, as though he were in the pleasantest mood; he was singing. I ran to him as if to say by action, I will do anything you bid me, willingly. When I got to him he said, "Go and bring me a switch, sir." I answered, "yes, sir," and off I went and brought him one; then he said, "come in here, sir;" I answered, "yes, sir;" and I went into a horse's stall, but while I was going in a thousand thoughts passed through my mind as to what he wanted me to go into the stall for, but when I had got in I soon learned, for he gave me a first-class flogging.

A day or to after that he called me in the same way, and I went again, and he sent me for a switch. I brought him a short stubble that was worn out, which he took and beat me on the head with. Then he said to me, " Go and bring me a switch, sir ; " I answered " Yes, sir ; " and off I went the second time, and brought him one very little better than the first ; he broke that over my head also, saying, " Go and bring me a switch, sir ; " I answered, " Yes, sir," and off I went the third time, and brought one which I supposed would suit him. Then he said to me, " Come in here, sir." I answered, " Yes, sir." When I went into the stall, he told me to lie down, and I stooped down ; he kicked me around for a while, then, making me lie on my face, he whipped me to his satisfaction.

That evening when I went home to father and mother, I said to them, " Mr. Young is whipping me too much now, I shall not stand it, I shall fight him." Father said to me, " You must not do that, because if you do he will say that your mother and I advised you to do it, and it will make it hard for your mother and me, as well as for yourself. You must do as I told you, my son : do your work the best you can, and do not say anything." I said to father, " But I don't know what I have done that he should whip me ; he does not tell me what wrong I have done, he simply calls me to him and whips me when he gets ready." Father said, " I can do nothing more than to pray to the Lord to hasten the time when these things shall be done away ; that is all I can do." When mother had stripped me and looked at the wounds that were upon me she burst into tears, and said, " If he were not so small I would not mind it so much; this will break his constitution; I am going to master about it, because I know he will not allow Mr. Young to treat this child so.

And I thought to myself that had mother gone to master about it, it would have helped me some, for he and she had grown up together and he thought a great deal of her. But father said to mother, " You better not go to master, for while he might stop the child from being treated badly, Mr. Young may revenge himself through the overseer, for you know that they are very friendly to each other." So said father to mother, " You would gain nothing in the end; the best thing for us to do is to pray much over it, for I believe that the time will come when this boy with the rest of the children will be free, though we may not live to see it."

When father spoke of liberty his words were of great comfort to me, and my heart swelled with the hope of a future, which made every moment seem an hour to me.

Father had a rule, which was strictly carried out as far as possible under the slave law, which was to put his children to bed early; but that night the whole family sat up late, while father and mother talked over the matter. It was a custom among the slaves not to allow their children under certain ages to enter into conversation with them; hence we could take no part with father and mother. As I was the object of their sympathy, I was allowed the privilege of answering the questions about the whipping the groom gave me.

When the time came for us to go to bed we all

knelt down in family prayer, as was our custom; father's prayer seemed more real to me that night than ever before, especially in the words, "Lord, hasten the time when these children shall be their own free men and women."

My faith in father's prayer made me think that the Lord would answer him at the farthest in two or three weeks, but it was fully six years before it came, and father had been dead two years before the war.

After prayer we all went to bed; next morning father went to his work in the barn-yard, mother to hers in the field, and I to mine among the horses; before I started, however, father charged me carefully to keep his advice, as he said that would be the easiest way for me to get along.

But in spite of father's advice, I had made up my mind not to submit to the treatment of Mr. Young as before, seeing that it did not help me any. Things went smoothly for a while, until he called me to him, and ordered me to bring him a switch. I told him that I would bring him no more switches for him to whip me with, but that he must get them himself. After repeating the command very impatiently, and I refusing, he called to another boy named Hardy, who brought the switch, and then taking me into the stall he whipped me unmercifully.

After that he made me run back and forth every morning from a half to three quarters of an hour about two hundred and fifty yards, and every now and then he would run after me, and whip me to make me run faster. Besides that, when I was put upon a horse, if it threw me he would whip me, if it were five times a day. So I did not gain anything by refusing to bring switches for him to whip me with.

One very cold morning in the month of March, I came from home without washing my face, and Mr. Young made two of the slave boys take me down to a pond where the horses and mules used to drink; they threw me into the water and rubbed my face with sand until it bled, then I was made to run all the way to the stable, which was about a quarter of a mile. This cruel treatment soon hardened me so that I did not care for him at all.

A short time afterwards I was sent with the other boys about four or five miles from home, up the public road, to practice the horse, and they gave me a very wild animal to ride, which threw me very often. Mr. Young did not go with us, but sent a colored groom every morning, who was very faithful to every task alloted him; he was instructed to whip me every time the horse threw me while away from home. I got many little floggings by the colored groom, as the horse threw me a great many times, but the floggings I got from him were very feeble compared with those of the white man; hence I was better content to go away with the colored groom than to be at home where I should have worse punishment.

But the time was coming when they ceased to whip me for being thrown by horses. One day, as I was riding along the road, the horse that I was upon darted at the sight of a bird, which flew across the way, throwing me upon a pile of brush. The horse stepped on my cheek, and the head of a nail in his shoe went through my left cheek and broke a tooth, but it was done so quickly that I hardly felt it. It happened that he did not step on me with his whole weight, if he had my jaw would have been broken.

When I got up the colored groom was standing by me, but he could not whip me when he saw the blood flowing from my mouth, so he took me down to the creek, which was but a short distance from the place, and washed me, and then taking me home, sent for a doctor, who dressed the wound.

When Mr. Young saw my condition, he asked how it was done, and upon being told he said it ought to have killed me. After the doctor had dressed my face, of course I went home, thinking they would allow me to stay until I got well, but I had no sooner arrived than the groom sent for me; I did not answer, as my jaw pained me very much. When he found that I did not come, he came after me himself, and said if I did not come to the stable right away, he would whip me, so I went with him. He did not whip me while I was in that condition, but he would not let me lie down, so I suffered very much from exposure.

When mother came that night from the farm and saw my condition, she was overcome with grief; she said to father, "this wound is enough to kill the child, and that merciless man will not let him lie down until he gets well; this is too hard." Father said to her, "I know it is very hard, but what can we do? for if we try to keep this boy in the house it will cause us trouble." Mother said, "I wish they would take him out of the world, then he would be out of pain, and we should not have to fret about him, for he would be in heaven." Then she took hold of me and said, "Does it hurt you, son?" meaning my face, and I said, "Yes, mamma," and she shed tears; but she had no little toys to give me to comfort me;

she could only promise me such as she had, which were eggs and chickens.

Father did not show his grief for me as mother did, but he tried to comfort mother all he could, and at times would say to me, "Never mind, my son, you will be a man bye and bye," but he did not know what was passing through my mind at that time. Though I was very small I thought that if, while a boy, my treatment was so severe, it would be much worse when I became a man, and having had a chance to see how men were being punished, it was a very poor consolation to me.

Finally the time came for us to go to bed, and we all knelt in family prayer. Father thanked God for having saved me from a worse injury, and then he prayed for mother's comfort, and also for the time which he predicted would come, that is, the time of freedom, when I and the rest of the children would be our own masters and mistresses; then he commended us to God, and we all went to bed. The next morning I went to my work with a great deal of pain. They did not send me up the road with the horses in that condition, but I had to ride the old horses to water, and work around the stable until I was well enough to go with the other boys. But I am happy to say that from the time I got hurt by that horse I was never thrown except through carelessness, neither was I afraid of a horse after that.

Notwithstanding father and mother fretted very much about me, they were proud of my success as a rider, but my hardships did not end here.

A short time after, I was taken to Columbia and Charleston, S. C., where they used to have the races.

That year Col. Singleton won a large sum of money by the well-known horse, Capt. Miner, and that was the same season that I rode my trial race. The next year, before the time of racing, Col. Singleton died at his summer seat. After master's death, mistress sold all the race horses, and that put an end to sporting horses in that family.

I said that Boney Young, Col. Singleton's groom, had a brother by the name of Charles, who trained horses for the colonel's brother, John Singleton, Boney was a better trainer, but Charles was a better man to the negroes. It was against the law for a slave to buy spirituous liquors without a ticket, but Charles used to give the boys tickets to buy rum and whiskey with. He also allowed them to steal the neighbor's cows and hogs.

I remember that on one occasion his boys killed a cow belonging to a man by the name of Le Brun; soon after the meat was brought to the stable, Le Brun rode up on horseback with a loaded shot gun and threatened to shoot the party with whom the beef was found. Of course the negroes' apartments were searched; but as that had been anticipated, Mr. Young had made them put the meat in his apartment, and, as it was against the law of South Carolina for a white man to search another's house, or any apartment, without very strong evidence, the meat was not found. Before searching among the negroes, Mr. Young said to Le Brun, "You may search, but you won't find your beef here, for my boys don't steal." Le Brun answered, "Mr. Young, your word might be true, sir, but I would trust a nigger with money a great deal sooner than I would with cows and hogs."

Mr. Young answered, "That might be true, but you won't find your beef here."

After their rooms and clothes had been searched, blood was found under some of their finger nails, which increased Le Brun's suspicion that they were of the party who stole his cow; but Mr. Young answered, "that blood is from rabbits my boys caught today." Mr. Le Brun tried to scare one of the boys, to make him say it was the blood of his cow. Mr. Young said, "Mr. Le Brun, you have searched and did not find your beef, as I told you that you would not; also I told you that the blood under their finger nails is from rabbits caught today. You will have to take my word, sir, without going to further trouble; furthermore, these boys belong to Mr. Singleton, and if you want to take further steps you will have to see him." Finding that he was not allowed to do as he wanted to, Mr. Le Brun made great oaths and threats as he mounted his horse to leave, that he would shoot the very first one of those boys he should catch near his cattle. He and Mr. Young never did agree after that.

But poor Mr. Young, as good as he was to the negroes, was an enemy to himself, for he was a very hard drinker. People who knew him before I did said they never had seen him drink tea, coffee, or water, but rather rum and whiskey; he drank so hard that he used to go into a crazy fit; he finally put an end to his life by cutting his throat with a razor, at a place called O'Handly's race course, about three miles from Columbia, S. C. This was done just a few days before one of the great races.

Boney Young drank, too, but not so hard as Charles.

He lived until just after the late war, and, while walking one day through one of the streets of the above named city, dropped dead, with what was supposed to have been heart disease.

Boney had a mulatto woman, named Moriah, who had been originally brought from Virginia by negro traders, but had been sold to several different masters later. The trouble was that she was very beautiful, and wherever she was sold her mistresses became jealous of her, so that she changed owners very often. She was finally sold to Boney Young, who had no wife; and she lived with him until freed by the emancipation proclamation. She had two daughters; the elder's name was Annie, but we used to call her sissie; the younger's name was Josephine. Annie looked just like her father, Boney Young, while Josephine looked enough like Charles to have been his daughter. It was easy enough to tell that the mother had sprung from the negro race, but the girls could pass for white. Their mother, Moriah, died in Columbia some time after the war. Annie went off and was married to a white man, but I don't know what became of Josephine.

A short time before master's death he stood security for a northern man, who was cashier of one of the largest banks in the city of Charleston. This man ran away with a large sum of money, leaving the colonel embarassed, which fact made him very fretful and peevish. He had been none too good before to his slaves, and that made him worse, as you knew that the slave holders would revenge themselves on the slaves whenever they became angry. I had seen master whip his slaves a great many times, but never so severely as he did that spring before he died.

One day, before he went to his summer seat, he called a man to him, stripped and whipped him so that the blood ran from his body like water thrown upon him in cupfuls, and when the man stepped from the place where he had been tied, the blood ran out of his shoes. He said to the man, "You will remember me now, sir, as long as you live." The man answered, " Yes, master, I will."

Master went away that spring for the last time ; he never returned alive ; he died at his summer seat. When they brought his remains home all of the slaves were allowed to stop at home that day to see the last of him, and to lament with mistress. After all the slaves who cared to do so had seen his face, they gathered in groups around mistress to comfort her ; they shed false tears, saying, " Never mind, missis, massa gone home to heaven." While some were saying this, others said, " Thank God, massa gone home to hell." Of course the most of them were glad that he was dead ; but they were gathered there for the express purpose of comforting mistress. But after master's death mistress was a great deal worse than he had been.

When the master died there was a great change of things on the plantation ; the creditors came in for settlement, so all of the fine horses, and some others, such as carriage horses, and a few mules also, were sold. The slaves whom master had bought himself had to be sold, but those who had been born on the plantation, given to him by his father, old Col. Dick Singleton, could not be sold until the grandchildren were of age.

As I have stated, my hardships and trials did not end with the race horses ; you will now see them in another form.

After all the fine horses had been sold, mistress ordered the men and boys who were taking care of the horses to be put into the field, and I was among them, though small ; but I had become so attached to the horses that they could get no work out of me, so they began to whip me, but every time they whipped me I would leave the field and run home to the barn-yard.

Finally mistress engaged a very bad man as over-seer, in place of old Ben Usome, whose name was William Turner. Two or three days after his arrival he took me into the field and whipped me until I was sick, so I went home.

I went to mistress and told her that the overseer had whipped me ; she asked if I had done the work that he had given me. I told her that master had promised me that, when I got too heavy to ride race horses, he would send me to learn the carpenter's trade ; she asked me if, in case she put me to a trade, I would work, and I told her I would. So she con-sented.

But the overseer did not like the idea of having me work at the trade which was my choice. He said to mistress, "That is the worst thing you can do, madam, to allow a negro to have his choice about what he shall do. I have had some experience as an overseer for many years, and I think I am able to give a correct statement about the nature of negroes in general. I know a gentleman who allowed his negroes to have their own way about things on his plantation, and the result was that they got as high as their master. Besides that, madam, their influence rapidly spreads among the neighbors, and if such should be allowed, South Carolina would have all masters and mistresses, and no servants; and, as I have said, I know somewhat about the nature of negroes; I notice, madam, that this boy will put you to a great deal of trouble unless you begin to subdue him now while he is young. A very few years' delay will enable him to have a great influence among his fellow negroes, for that boy can read very well now, and you know, madam, it is against the law for a negro to get an education, and if you allow him to work at the carpenter's trade it will thus afford him the opportunity of acquiring a better education, because he will not be directly under the eye of one who will see that he makes no further advancement."

Then mistress asked me, "Can you read, Jacob?" I did not want her to know that I had taken notice of what they were saying, so I answered, "I don't know, ma'am." The overseer said, "He does not know what is meant, madam, but I can make him understand me." Then he took a newspaper from his pocket and said to me, "Can you say these words?" I took the paper and began to read, then he took it from me.

Mistress asked when I had learned to read and who had taught me. The overseer did not know, but said he would find out from me. Turning to me he took the paper from his pocket again, and said, "Jacob, who told you to say words in the book?" I answered, "Nobody, sir; I said them myself." He repeated the question three or four times, and I gave the same answer every time. Then mistress said, "I think it would be better to put him to trade than to have him in the field, because he will be away from his fellow-negroes, and will be less liable to influence them if we can manage to keep him away." The overseer said, "That might be true, madam, but if we can manage to keep him from gaining any more education he will eventually lose what little he has ; and now, madam, if you will allow me to take him in hand, I will bring him out all right without injuring him." Just at this juncture a carriage drove up to the gate, and I ran as usual to open it, the overseer went about his business, and mistress went to speak to the persons in the carriage. I never had a chance to hear their conclusion.

A few days after the conversation between the overseer and mistress, I was informed by one of the slaves, who was a carpenter, that she had ordered that I should go to work at the trade with him. This gave me great joy, as I was very anxious to know what they had decided to do with me. I went to my new trade with great delight, and soon began to imagine what a famous carpenter I should make, and what I should say and do when I had learned the trade. Everything seemed to run smoothly with me for about two months, when suddenly I was told one morning that I must go into the field to drop cotton seed, but I did not heed the call, as mistress was not at home, and I knew she had just put me to the trade, also that the overseer was trying to get mistress' consent to have me work out in the field.

The next morning the overseer came into the carpenter's shop and said, "Did I not order ye into the

field, sir ?" I answered, " Yes, sir." " Well, why
did ye not go ?" I answered, "Mistress has put me
here to learn the trade." He said, " I will give ye
trade." So he stripped me and gave me a severe
whipping, and told me that that was the kind of
trade I needed, and said he would give me many of
them. The next day I went into the field, and he put
me to drop cotton seed, as I was too small to do anything else. I would have made further resistance, but
mistress was very far away from home, and I had
already learned the lesson that father and mother
could render me no help, so I thought submission to
him the easiest for me.

When I had got through with the cotton seed, in
about three weeks, I went back to the carpenter's
shop to work ; so he came there and gave me another
severe whipping, and said to me, " Ye want to learn
the carpenter's trade, but I will have ye to the trade
of the field." But that was the last whipping he
gave me, and the last of his whip.

A few days after my last whipping the slaves were
ordered down into the swamp across the river to clear
up new grounds, while the already cleared lands were
too wet from rain that had fallen that night. Of
course I was among them to do my part ; that is,
while the men quartered up dry trees, which had
been already felled in the winter, and rolled the logs
together, the women, boys and girls piled the brushes
on the logs and burned them.

We had to cross the river in a flat boat, which was
too small to carry over all the slaves at once, so they
had to make several trips.

Mr. Turner, the overseer, went across in the first

flat; he did not ride down to the work place, but went on foot, while his horse, which was trained to stand alone without being hitched, was left at the landing place. My cousin and I crossed in the last boat. When we had got across we lingered behind the crowd at the landing; when they all were gone we went near the horse and saw the whip with which I was whipped a few days before fastened to the saddle. I said to him, "Here is the whip old Turner whipped me with the other day." He said, "It ought to be put where he will never get it to whip anybody with again." I answered my cousin, "If you will keep the secret I will put it where old Bill, as we used to call Mr. Turner, will never use it any more." He agreed to keep the secret, and then asked me how I would put the whip away. I told him if he would find me a string and a piece of iron I would show him how. He ran down to the swamp barn, which was a short distance from the margin of the river, and soon returned with the string and iron exactly suited for the work. I tied the iron to the whip, went into the flat boat, and threw it as far as I could into the river. My cousin and I watched it until it went out of sight under water; then, as guilty boys generally do after mischievous deeds, we dashed off in a run, hard as we could, among the other negroes, and acted as harmless as possible. Mr. Turner made several inquiries, but never learned what had become of his whip.

A short time after this, in the time of the war, in the year 1863, when a man was going round to the different plantations gathering slaves from their masters to carry off to work on fortifications and to wait on officers, there were ten slaves sent from Mrs. Singleton's plantation, and I was among them. They carried us to Sullivan's Island at Charleston, S. C., and I was there all of that year. I thanked God that it afforded me a better chance for an education than I had had at home, and so I was glad to be on the island. Though I had no one to teach me, as I was thrown among those of my fellow negroes who were fully as lame as I was in letters, yet I felt greatly relieved from being under the eye of the overseer, whose intention was to keep me from further advancement. The year after I had gone home I was sent back to Fort Sumpter—in the year 1864. I carried my spelling book with me, and, although the northerners were firing upon us, I tried to keep up my study.

In July of the same year I was wounded by the Union soldiers, on a Wednesday evening. I was taken to the city of Charleston, to Dr. Regg's hospital, and there I stayed until I got well enough to travel, when I was sent to Columbia, where I was when the hour of liberty was proclaimed to me, in 1865. This was the year of jubilee, the year which my father had spoken of in the dark days of slavery, when he and mother sat up late talking of it. He said to mother, "The time will come when this boy and the rest of the children will be their own masters and mistresses." He died six years before that day came, but mother is still enjoying liberty with her children.

And no doubt my readers would like to know how I was wounded in the war. We were obliged to do our work in the night, as they were firing on us in the day, and on a Wednesday night, just as we went out, we heard the cry of the watchman. " Look out." There was a little lime house near the southwest corner of the fort, and some twelve or thirteen of us ran into it, and all were killed but two ; a shell came down on the lime house and burst, and a piece cut my face open. But as it was not my time to die, I lived to enjoy freedom.

I said that when I got so I could travel I was sent from Dr. Ragg's hospital in Charleston to Col. Single-ton's plantation near Columbia, in the last part of the year 1864. I did not do any work during the remain-der of that year, because I was unwell from my wound received in the fort.

About that time Gen. Sherman came through Georgia with his hundred thousand men, and camped at Columbia, S. C. The slave holders were very un-easy as to how they should save other valuables, as they saw that slavery was a hopeless case. Mistress had some of her horses, mules, cows and hogs carried down into the swamp, while the others which were left on the plantation were divided out to the negroes for safe keeping, as she had heard that the Yankees would not take anything belonging to the slaves. A little pig of about fifty or sixty pounds was given to me for safe keeping. A few of the old horses and mules were taken from the plantation by the Union soldiers, but they did not trouble anything else.

After Columbia had been burned, and things had somewhat quieted, along in the year 1865, the negroes were asked to give up the cows and hogs given them for safe keeping ; all the rest gave up theirs, but mine was not found. No doubt but my readers want to

know what had become of it. Well, I will tell you.
You all know that Christmas was a great day with
both masters and slaves in the South, but the Christmas of 1864 was the greatest which had ever come to
the slaves, for, although the proclamation did not
reach us until 1865, we felt that the chains which had
bound us so long were well nigh broken.

So I killed the pig that Christmas, gathered all of
my associates, and had a great feast, after which we
danced the whole week. Mother would not let me
have my feast in her cabin, because she was afraid
that the white people would charge her with advising
me to kill the pig, so I had it in one of the other
slave's cabins.

When the overseer asked me for the pig given me,
I told him that I killed it for my Christmas feast.
Mistress said to me, " Jacob, why did you not ask me
for the pig if you wanted it, rather than take it without permission ?" I answered, " I would have asked,
but thought, as I had it in hand, it wasn't any use
asking for it." The overseer wanted to whip me for
it, but as Uncle Sam had already broken the right
arm of slavery, through the voice of the proclamation of 1863, he was powerless.

When the yoke had been taken from my neck I
went to school in Columbia, S. C., awhile, then to
Charleston. Afterward I came to Worcester, Mass.,
in February, 1869. I studied quite a while in the
evening schools at Worcester, and also a while in the
academy of the same place. During that time I was
licensed a local preacher of the African Methodist
Episcopal church, and sometime later was ordained
deacon at Newport, R. I.

A short time after my ordination I was sent to Salem, Mass., where I have remained, carrying on religious work among my people, trying in my feeble way to preach that gospel which our blessed Saviour intended for the redemption of all mankind, when he proclaimed, "Go ye into all the world and preach the gospel." In the meantime I have been striking steady blows for the improvement of my education, in preparing myself for a field of work among my more unfortunate brethren in the South.

I must say that I have been surrounded by many good friends, including the clergy, since I have been in Salem, whose aid has enabled me to serve a short term in the Wesleyan school at Wilbraham, Mass., also to begin a course of theological studies at Talladega college in Alabama, which I am endeavoring to complete by the sale of this publication.

CHAPTER II.—SKETCHES.

THE SALE OF MY TWO SISTERS.

I have stated that my father had fifteen children—four boys and three girls by his first wife, and six boys and two girls by his second. Their names are as follows: Toney, Azerine, Duke and Dezine, of the girls, Violet, Priscilla and Lydia; those of the second wife as follows: Footy, Embrus, Caleb, Mitchell, Cuffee, and Jacob, who is the author, and the girls, Catherine and Retta.

As I have said, old Col. Dick Singleton had two sons and two daughters, and each had a plantation. Their names were John, Matt, Marianna and Angelico. They were very agreeable together, so that if one wanted negro help from another's plantation, he or she could have it, especially in cotton picking time.

John Singleton had a place about twenty miles from master's, and master used to send him slaves to pick cotton. At one time my master, Col. M. R. Singleton, sent my two sisters, Violet and Priscilla, to his brother John, and while they were there they married two of the men on his place. By mutual consent master allowed them to remain on his brother's place. But some time after this John Singleton had some of his property destroyed by water, as is often the case in the South at the time of May freshets, what is known in the North as high tides.

One of these freshets swept away John Singleton's slave houses, his barns, with horses, mules and cows.

These caused his death by a broken heart, and since he owed a great deal of money his slaves had to be sold. A Mr. Manning bought a portion of them, and Charles Login the rest. These two men were known as the greatest slave traders in the South. My sisters were among the number that Mr. Manning bought.

He was to take them into the state of Louisiana for sale, but some of the men did not want to go with him, and he put those in prison until he was ready to start. My sisters' husbands were among the prisoners in the Sumterville jail, which was about twenty-five or thirty miles across the river from master's place. Those who did not show any unwillingness to go were allowed to visit their relatives and friends for the last time. So my sisters, with the rest of their unfortunate companions, came to master's place to visit us. When the day came for them to leave, some, who seemed to have been willing to go at first, refused, and were handcuffed together and guarded on their way to the cars by white men. The women and children were driven to the depot in crowds, like so many cattle, and the sight of them caused great excitement among master's negroes. Imagine a mass of uneducated people shedding tears and yelling at the top of their voices in anguish.

The victims were to take the cars at a station called Clarkson turnout, which was about four miles from master's place. The excitement was so great that the overseer and driver could not control the relatives and friends of those that were going away, as a large crowd of both old and young went down to the depot to see them off. Louisiana was considered by the slaves a place of slaughter, so those who were going did not expect to see their friends again. While passing along many of the negroes left their masters' fields and joined us as we marched to the cars ; some were yelling and wringing their hands, while others were singing little hymns that they had been accustomed to for the consolation of those that were going away, such as

> "When we all meet in heaven,
> There is no parting there;
> When we all meet in heaven,
> There is parting no more."

We arrived at the depot and had to wait for the cars to bring the others from the Sumterville jail, but they soon came in sight, and when the noise of the cars had died away, we heard wailing and shrieks from those in the cars. While some were weeping, others were fiddling, picking banjo, and dancing as they used to do in their cabins on the plantations. Those who were so merry had very bad masters, and even though they stood a chance of being sold to one as bad or even worse, yet they were glad to be rid of the one they knew.

While the cars were at the depot a large crowd of white people gathered, laughing and talking about the prospect of negro traffic; but when the cars began to start, and the conductor cried out, " All who are going on this train must get on board without delay," the colored people cried out with one voice as though the heavens and earth were coming together, and it was so pitiful that those hard-hearted white men, who had been accustomed to driving slaves all their lives, shed tears like children. As the cars moved away we heard the weeping and wailing from the slaves as far as human voice could be heard; and from that time to the present I have neither seen nor heard from my two sisters, nor any of those who left Clarkson depot on that memorable day.

THE WAY THE SLAVES LIVED.

Most of the cabins in the time of slavery were built so as to contain two families; some had partitions, while others had none. When there were no partitions each family would fit up its own part as it could; sometimes they got old boards and nailed them up, stuffing the cracks with rags; when they could not get boards they hung up old clothes. When the family increased the children all slept together, both boys and girls, until one got married; then a part of another cabin was assigned to that one, but the rest would have to remain with their mother and father, as in childhood, unless they could get with some of their relatives or friends who had small families, or unless they were sold; but of course the rules of modesty were held in some degrees by the slaves, while it could not be expected that they could entertain the highest degree of it, on account of their condition. A portion of the time the young men slept in the apartment known as the kitchen, and the young women slept in the room with their mother and father. The two families had to use one fireplace. One who was accustomed to the way in which the slaves lived in their cabins could tell as soon as they entered whether they were friendly or not, for when they did not agree the fires of the two families did not meet on the hearth, but there was a vacancy between them, that was a sign of disagreement. In a case of this kind, when either of the families stole a hog, cow or sheep from the master, he had to carry it to some of his friends, for fear of being betrayed by the other family. On one occasion a man, who lived with one unfriendly, stole a hog, killed it, and carried some of the meat home. He was seen by some one of the other family, who reported him to the overseer, and he gave the man a severe whipping. Sometime afterward this man who had been betrayed thought he would get even with his enemy; so about two months later he killed another hog, and, after eating a part of it, stole into the apartment of the other family and hid a portion of the meat among the old clothes. Then he told the overseer that he had seen the man go out late that night and that he had not come home until the next morning; when he did come he had called his wife to the window and she had taken something in. He did not know what it was, but if the overseer would go there right away he would find it. The overseer went and searched and found the meat, so the man was whipped. He told the overseer that the other man put it in his apartment while the family were away, but the overseer told him that every man must be responsible for his own apartment.

No doubt you would like to know how the slaves could sleep in their cabins in summer, when it was so very warm. When it was too warm for them to sleep comfortably, they all slept under trees until it grew too cool, that is along in the month of October. Then they took up their beds and walked.

JOE AND THE TURKEY.

Joe was a boy who was waiter to his master, one

Mr. King, and he and his wife were very fond of company. Mrs. King always had chickens and turkey for dinner, but at one time the company was so large that they did not leave anything for the servants; so that day, finding that all had been eaten, while mistress and master were busy with the company, Joe killed a turkey, dressed it and put it into the pot, but, as he did not cut it up, the turkey's knees stuck out of the pot, and, as he could not cover them up, he put one of his shirts over them. When Mrs. King called Joe, he answered, but did not go right away as he generally did, and when he did go his mistress said, "Joe, what was the matter with you?" he answered, "Noffing, missis." Then he went and opened the gate for the company. Soon after, Joe was back in the kitchen again, and Mrs. King went down to see what he was doing; seeing the pot on she said, "Joe, what is in that pot?" he said, "noffing, missis, but my shirt; am gwine to wash it." She did not believe him, so she took a fork and stuck it in the pot, taking out the shirt, and she found the turkey. She asked him how the turkey had got into the pot; he said he did not know but reckoned the turkey got in himself, as the fowls were very fond of going into the kitchen. So Joe was whipped because he allowed the turkey to get into the pot.

THE CUSTOM OF CHRISTMAS.

Both masters and slaves regarded Christmas as a great day. When the slaveholders had made a large crop they were pleased, and gave the slaves from five to six days, which were much enjoyed by the negroes, especially by those who could dance. Christmas morning was held sacred both by master and slaves, but in the afternoon, or in a part of the next day, the slaves were required to devote themselves to the pleasure of their masters. Some of the masters would buy presents for the slaves, such as hats and tobacco for the men, handkerchiefs and little things for the women; these things were given after they had been pleased with them; after either dancing or something for their amusement.

When the slaves came up to their masters and mistresses, the latter would welcome them, the men would take off their hats and bow and the women would make a low courtesy. There would be two or three large pails filled with sweetened water, with a gallon or two of whiskey in each; this was dealt out to them until they were partly drunk; while this was going on, those who could talk very well would give tokens of well wishing to their master and mistress, and some who were born in Africa, would sing some of their songs, or tell different stories of the customs in Africa. After this they would spend half a day in dancing in some large cotton house or on a scaffold, the master providing fiddlers who came from other plantations if there were none on the place, and who received from fifteen to twenty dollars on these occasions.

A great many of the strict members of the church who did not dance would be forced to do it to please their masters; the favorite tunes were " The Fisher's Hornpipe," " The Devil's Dream," and " Black-eyed Susan." No one can describe the intense emotion in the negro's soul on those occasions when they were trying to please their masters and mistresses.

After the dancing was over we had our presents, master giving to the men, and mistress to the women; then the slaves would go to their quarters and continue to dance the rest of the five or six days, and would sometimes dance until eight o'clock Sunday morning. The cabins were mostly made of logs, and there were large cracks in them so that a person could see the light in them for miles in the night, and of course the sun's rays would shine through them in the daytime, so on Sunday morning when they were dancing and did not want to stop you would see them filling up the cracks with old rags. The idea was that it would not be Sunday inside if they kept the sun out, and thus they would not desecrate the Sabbath; and these things continued until the freedom of the slaves.

Perhaps my readers would like to know if most of the negroes were inclined to violate the Sabbath. They were; as the masters would make them do unnecessary work, they got into the habit of disregarding the day as one for rest, and did many things Sunday that would not be allowed in the North. At that time, if you should go through the South on those large cotton and rice plantations, while you would find some dancing on Sunday, others would be in the woods and fields hunting rabbits and other game, and some would be killing pigs belonging to their masters or neighbors. I remember when a small boy I went into the woods one Sunday morning with one of my fellow negroes whose name was Munson, but we called him Pash, and we killed one of master's pigs, hid it under the leaves until night, then took it home and dressed it. That was the only time I killed a pig, but I knew of thousands of cases like this in the time of slavery. But thank God, the year of Jubilee has come, and the negroes can return from dancing, from hunting, and from the master's pig pens on Sundays and become observers of the Sabbath, of good moral habits and men of equal rights before the law.

PUNISHMENTS INFLICTED ON DIFFERENT ONES.

One of my fellow negroes, who belonged to Col. M. R. Singleton, visited the plantation of the Col.'s sister ; the overseer of that plantation had forbidden strangers to go there, but this man, whose name was Harry, would go. The overseer heard of him but could not catch him, but the overseer of master's place sent him to Mr. Jackson (the overseer of master's sister's place). Mr. Jackson tied him and hit him three hundred lashes and then said to him, " Harry, if you were not such a good nigger I should have given you a first class whipping, but as you are a good fellow, and I like you so well, I thought I would give you a light flogging now ; you must be a good nigger and behave yourself, for if I ever have to take hold of you again, I shall give you a good whipping." When Mr. Jackson had loosed him from where he had tied him, Harry was so exhausted that he fell down, so Mr. Jackson sent him home in a cart, and he had to stay at home from work a month or two, and was never the same man again.

THE PUNISHMENT AND SALE OF MONDAY.

There was a man who belonged to master by the name of Monday, who was a good field hand ; in

summer the tasks generally performed by the slaves
were more than they could do, and in consequence
they were severely whipped, but Monday would not
wait to be whipped, but would run away before the
overseer or driver could get to him. Sometimes master would hire a white man who did nothing else but
hunt runaway slaves for a living; this man would
take from fifteen to twenty hounds with him to hunt
Monday, but often he would be out three or four
months; when he was caught and brought home, he
was put in prison and was whipped every day for a
week or two, but just as soon as he could he would
run away again

At one time when he had been brought home, one
of his arms was tied and he was put in care of a
keeper who made him work with the other slaves,
days, and put him in confinement nights, but
for all this he got away from his keeper and went
into the woods again. The last time he ran away
two white men were hired to hunt him ; they had
about twenty-five blood hounds, but this time Monday fell in with another slave who had ran away from
his master and had been in the woods seven years, and
they together were able to kill a greater portion of the
hounds. Finally the white men caught his companion, but did not catch Monday, though they chased
him two or three days longer, but he came home
himself; they did not whip him and he went to work
in the field. Things went on very nicely with him
for two or three weeks, until one day a white man
was seen riding through the fields with the overseer ;
of course the slaves did not mistrust his obj·ct, as
white men often visited master's plantation, but that

night, when all the slaves were sleeping, the man that was seen in the daytime went to the door of Monday's cabin and called him out of his bed, and when he had come to his door, the stranger, whom he had never seen before that day, handcuffed him and said, "You now belong to me." Most of the slaves found it out, as Monday was put in a cart and carried through the streets of the negro quarters, and there was quite an excitement, but Monday was never heard from again.

THE STORY OF JAMES HAY.

There was a slave named James Hay, who belonged to a neighbor of master's; he was punished a great many times because he could not get his task done. The other slaves pitied him because he seemed unable to perform his task. One evening he got a severe whipping; the next morning as the slaves were having their tasks assigned them, an old lady by the name of Aunt Patience went by, and said, "Never mind, Jim, my son, the Lord will help you with your task today;" he answered, "Yes, ma'am." He began his work very faithfully and continued until it was half done, then he lay down under a tree; the others, not understanding his motive, thought he was tired and was taking a rest, but he did not return to his task until the overseer called him and asked him why he did not have his work nearer done. He said, "Aunt Patience told me dis morning that the Lord would help me today, and I thought as I did half of the task, the Lord might have finished the other half if he intended to help me at all." The overseer said "You see that the Lord did not come to help you and we shall not wait for him, but we will help you;" so Jim got a severe punishment. Sometime after this, Jim Hay was called upon by some professors of religion; they asked him if he was not tired of serving the devil, and told him that the Lord was good and had helped many of his people, and would help all who asked him and then take them home to heaven. Jim said that if the Lord would not do half an acre of his task for him when he depended on him, he did not think he could trust him, and Jim never became a Christian to my knowledge.

THE STORY OF MR. USOM AND JACK.

One Sunday when the boys were at the overseer's, Mr. Usom's house, as we generally were, he said to one, "Jack, don't you think that hell is a very hot place, if it is as they describe it?" Jack said, "Yes, massa." Mr. Usom said, "Well, how do you think it will be with poor fellows that have to go there?" "Well, Massa Bob, I will tell you what I tinks about it, I tinks us niggers need not trouble usselves about hell, as the white folks." "How is that, Jack?" Jack answered, "Because us niggers have to work out in the hot sun, and if we go to hell it would not be so bad for us because us used to heat, but it will be bad for white folks because they is not used to hot weather."

THE STORY OF JAMES SWINE AND HIS DEATH.

There was a negro who belonged to one Mr. Clarkson; he was called Jim Swine; his right name was James, but he was called Jim Swine because he loved hog meat and would often steal hogs from his

master or from the neighbors; he was a very able-
bodied man, weighing about two hundred and twenty-
five pounds, and a very good field hand. Of course
it is generally known that a great many of the slaves
were poorly fed, so it was natural that they should
take anything they could to sustain life. As his
master had only a few hogs, he stole many from the
neighbors and was punished a great many times for
it.

Sometimes he was punished when a hog was missing, even though they did not find the meat with him.
Jim was not in the habit of running away much, but
if they whipped him when he had not stolen the hog
they accused him of taking, he would go away into
the woods and stay until he got ready to come home.
He was so strong that they were afraid of him; three
or four men would not attack him when in the woods.
The last time Jim stole hogs he was caught in the act
of taking one from my master, Col. Singleton.
They tied him, and Mr. Clarkson's overseer was sent
for, who was his own son, Thomas Clarkson. Jim
was taken home, whipped, and a cured middling of a
hog was tied around his neck; he was then made to
work along with the other slaves in the day and was
put in prison in the night for two weeks. One morning when the overseer went to his place of confinement to take him into the field, he found him dead,
with a large piece of meat hanging to his neck. The
news of his death soon went abroad, also the cause
of it, and when old Mr. Clarkson found it out he
was very angry at his son Thomas, and his punishment was, that he was driven from his plantation
with orders never to return, and that he should not

have any of his property. This seemed to grieve Thomas very much, and he made several attempts to regain his father's affections, but failed. Finally, one night, Thomas made an outcry that he had found a pearl of great price, that the Lord had pardoned his sins, and that he was at peace with all mankind. When his father heard of this, he sent for him to come home, and he gave him quite a sum of money and willed him the portion of property that he had said he should keep from him. But poor Jim was not there to forgive him.

A MAN MISTAKEN FOR A HOG.

Two negroes went to steal hogs from their masters. The swine were under a barn, as in the South barns were made high enough for hogs to stand under. The man who went under the barn said to the other, you must strike the hog that goes the slowest; then he went under the barn on his knees to drive them out while the other stood with his club ready to strike, but they ran out so fast he could not hit them, except the last as he thought, which came just slow enough, and he struck. While the supposed hog was kicking, he jumped upon it to stab it with his knife but found it was his companion.

CUSTOM OF WITCHES AMONG SLAVES.

The witches among slaves were supposed to have been persons who worked with them every day, and were called old hags or jack lanterns. Those, both men and women, who, when they had grown old looked old, were supposed to be witches. Sometimes, after eating supper, the negroes would gather in each

other's cabins which looked over the large openings
on the plantation, and when they would see a light
at a great distance and see it open and shut, they
would say, " there is an old hag," and if it came from
a direction in which those lived whom they called
witches, one would say, " Dat looks like old Aunt
Susan ; " another would say, " No, dat look like man
hag ; " still another, " I tink dat look like ole Uncle
Renty."

When the light had disappeared they said that the
witch had got into the plantation and changed itself
into a person and had gone about on the place talking
with the people like others until those whom it
wanted to bewitch went to bed, then it would change
itself to a witch again. They claimed that the
witches rode human beings like horses, and that the
spittle that ran on the side of the cheek when one
slept, was the bridle that the witch rode with. Sometimes a baby would be smothered by its mother, and
they would charge it to a witch. If they went out
hunting at night and were lost, it was believed that a
witch had led them off, especially if they fell into a
pond or creek. I was very much troubled with
witches when a little boy and am now sometimes,
but it is only when I eat a hearty supper and immediately go to bed. It was said by some of the slaves
that the witches would sometimes go into the rooms
of the cabins and hide themselves until the family
went to bed, and therefore when any one claimed that
he had gone into the apartment before bed time and
thought he had seen a witch, if he had an old
Bible in the cabin, that would be taken into the room,
and the person who carried the Bible would say as he

went in, " In de name of de Fader and of de Son and de Holy Gos wat you want ? " Then the Bible would be put in the corner where the person thought he had seen the witch, as it was generally believed that if this were done the witch could not stay. When they could not get the Bible they used red pepper and salt pounded together and scattered in the room, but in this case they generally felt the effects of it more than the witch, for when they went to bed it made them cough all night. When I was a little boy my mother sent me into the cabin room for something, and as I got in I saw something black and white, but did not stop to see what it was, and running out said there was a witch in the room. But father, having been born in Africa, did not believe in such things, so he called me a fool and whipped me and the witch got scared and ran out the door. It turned out to be our own black and white cat that we children played with every day. Although it proved to be the cat, and father did not believe in witches, still I held the idea that there were such things, for I thought the majority of the people believed it, and that they ought to know more than could one man. Sometime after I was free, in travelling from Columbia to Camden, a distance of about thirty-two miles, night overtook me when about half way there; it was very dark and rainy, and as I approached a creek I saw a great number of lights of those witches opening and shutting. I did not know what to do and thought of turning back, but when I looked behind I saw some witches in the distance, so I said, " If I turn back those will meet me and I shall be in as much danger as if I go on, and I thought of what some of my fel-

low negroes had said about their leading men into
ponds and creeks. There was a creek just ahead, so I
concluded that I should be drowned that night; however, I went on, as I saw no chance of turning back.
When I came near the creek one of the witches flew
into my face. I jumped back and grasped it, but it
proved to be one of those lightning bugs, and I thought
that if all the witches were like that one, I should not
be in any great danger from them.

THE DEATH OF CYRUS AND STEPNEY.

Old Col. Dick Singleton had several state places as
I have mentioned. In the South, the rich men who
had a great deal of money bought all the plantations
they could get and obtained them very cheap. The
Colonel had some ten or twenty places and had slaves
settled on each of them.

He had four children, and after each had received
a plantation, the rest were called state places, and
these could not be sold until all the grandchildren
should become of age; after they all had received
places, the rest could be sold.

One of the places was called Biglake. The slaves
on these places were treated more cruelly than on
those where the owner lived, for the overseers had
full sway.

One day the overseer at Biglake punished the
slaves so that some of them fell exhausted. When
he came to the two men, Cyrus and Stepney, they resisted, but were taken by force and severely punished. A few days afterwards the overseer died,
and those two men were taken up and hanged on the
plantation without judge or jury.

After that another overseer was hired, with orders to arm himself, and every slave who did not submit to his punishment was to be shot immediately. At times, when the overseer was angry with a man he would strike him on the head with a club and kill him instantly, and they would bury him in the field. Some would run away and come to M. R. Singleton, my master, but he would only tell them to go home and behave. Then they were handcuffed or chained and carried back to Biglake, and when we would hear from them again the greater part would have been murdered. When they were taken from master's place, they would bid us good bye and say they knew they should be killed when they got home.

Oh! who can paint the sad feeling in our minds when we saw these, our own race, chained and carried home to drink the bitter cup of death from their merciless oppressors, with no one near to say, "Spare him, God made him," or to say, "Have mercy on him, for Jesus died for him." His companions dared not groan above a whisper for fear of sharing the same fate; but thanks that the voice of the Lord was heard in the North, which said, "Go quickly to the South and let my prison-bound people go free, for I have heard their cries from cotton, corn and rice plantations, saying, how long before thou wilt come to deliver us from this chain?" and the Lord said to them, "Wait, I will send you John Brown who shall be the key to the door of your liberty, and I will harden the heart of Jefferson Davis, your *devil*, that I may show him and his followers my power; then shall I send you Abraham Lincoln, mine *angel*, who shall lead you from the land of bondage to the land of liberty." Our fathers all died in "the wilderness," but thank God, the children reached " the promised land."

THE WAY THE SLAVES DETECTED THIEVES AMONG THEMSELVES.

The slaves had three ways of detecting thieves, one with a Bible, one with a sieve, and another with graveyard dust. The first way was this :—four men were selected, one of whom had a Bible with a string attached, and each man had his own part to perform. Of course this was done in the night as it was the only time they could attend to such matters as concerned themselves. These four would commence at the first cabin with every man of the family, and one who held the string attached to the Bible would say, " John or Tom," whatever the person's name was, " you are accused of stealing a chicken or a dress from Sam at such a time," then one of the other two would say, " John stole the chicken," and another would say, " John did not steal the chicken." They would continue their assertions for at least five minutes, then the man would put a stick in the loop of the string that was attached to the Bible, and holding it as still as he could, one would say, " Bible, in the name of the Father and of the Son and of the Holy Ghost, if John stole that chicken, turn," that is, if the man had stolen what he was accused of, the Bible was to turn around on the string, and that would be a proof that he did steal it. This was repeated three times before they left that cabin, and it would take those men a month sometimes when the plantation was very large, that is if they did not find the right person before they got through the whole place.

The second way they had of detecting thieves **was** very much like the first, only they used a sieve instead of a Bible ; they stuck a pair of scissors in the sieve with a string hitched to it and a stick put through the loop of the string and the same words were used as for the Bible. Sometimes the Bible and the sieve would turn upon the names of persons whose characters were beyond suspicion. When this was the case they would either charge the mistake to the men who fixed the Bible and the sieve, or else the man who was accused by the turning of the Bible and the sieve, would say that he passed near the coop from which the fowl was stolen, then they would say, " Bro. John we see dis how dat ting work, you pass by de chicken coop de same night de hen went away."

But when the Bible or the sieve turned on the name of one whom they knew often stole, and he did not acknowledge that he had stolen the chicken of which he was accused, he would have to acknowledge his previously stolen goods or that he had thought of stealing at the time when the chicken or the dress was stolen. Then this examining committee would justify the turning of the Bible or sieve on the above statement of the accused person.

The third way of detecting thieves was taught by the fathers and mothers of the slaves. They said no matter how untrue a man might have been during his life, when he came to die he had to tell the truth and had to own everything he had ever done, and whatever dealing those alive had with anything pertaining to the dead, must be true, or they would immediately die and go to hell to burn in fire and brimstone. So in consequence of this, the graveyard dust was the truest of the three ways in detecting thieves. The dust would be taken from the grave of a person who had died last and put into a bottle with water. Then two of the men of the examining committee would use the same words as in the case of the Bible and the sieve, "John stole that chicken," "John did not steal that chicken," and after this had gone on for about five minutes, then one of the other two who attended to the Bible and the sieve would say, "John, you are accused of stealing that chicken that was taken from Sam's chicken coop at such a time." "In the name of the Father and the Son and the Holy Ghost, if you have taken Sam's chicken don't drink this water, for if you do you will die and go to hell and be burned in fire and brimstone, but if you have not you may take it and it will not hurt you." So if John had taken the chicken he would own it rather than take the water.

Sometimes those whose characters were beyond suspicion would be proven thieves when they tried the graveyard dust and water. When the right person was detected, if he had any chickens he had to give four for one, and if he had none he made it good by promising that he would do so no more. If all the men on the plantation passed through the examination and no one was found guilty, the stolen goods would be charged to strangers. Of course these customs were among the negroes for their own benefit, for they did not consider it stealing when they took anything from their master.

JOSH AND THE CORN.

A man engaged in stripping fodder put some green

ears of corn in the fire to roast as the slaves generally do in fodder stripping time, although they were whipped when caught. Before the ears were roasted enough, the overseer approached, and Josh took the ears out with some live coals stuck to them and put them in his shirt bosom. In running away his clothes took fire and Josh jumped into a creek to put it out. The overseer said to him, "Josh, what are you doing there ?" He answered, "It is so warm today I taught I would go in de creek to git cool off, sir." " Well, have you got cooled off, Josh?" " Oh ! yes, sir, very much cooler, sir."

Josh was a very hearty eater, so that the peck of corn flour allowed the slaves for a week's ration lasted him only a half. He used to lug large sticks of wood on his shoulders from the woods, which was from a mile to a mile and a half away, to first one and then another of his fellow negroes, who gave him something to eat; and in that way he made out his week's rations.

His habit was to bring the wood at night, throw it down at the cabin door, and, as he walked in, some one of the family would say, "Well, Josh, you fetched us a piece of wood." He would burst into one of his jolly laughs and answer, " Yes." Soon after they had given him something to eat, Josh would bid them good night, but when he went, the wood disappeared too. He would throw it down at another cabin door as before, go in and get something to eat ; but every time when he went away the wood would be missing until he had found enough to eat, when he would leave it at the last cabin. Those to whom Josh carried the wood accused others of stealing it, and when they asked him about it, he only laughed and said that the wood was at the door when he came out.

Josh continued the trick for quite a while. Finally one night he brought a stick of wood and threw it down at a cabin door, walked in and got something to eat as usual. But as he came in, the man of the family, to whom he carried the wood, bade him good night, and said that he had business out which would keep him so late, that Josh would be gone before he got back. While Josh was busy laughing and talking with the rest of the family the man went out, and secreted himself in the chimney corner of another cabin, and it was not long after he took his stand before Josh bade the family good night, came out whistling, and shouldered the wood, but as he started off the watchman cried out, " Is that you, Josh ?" Josh threw the wood down and answered, " O no, tisn't me." Of course Josh was so funny one couldn't get angry with him if he wanted to ; but the rest of the slaves found out after that how the wood Josh brought them, was missing.

But poor Josh died at last, away from home ; he was sent with some of the other negroes from Mrs. M. R. Singleton's plantation at Columbia, in the year 1864, to build fortifications as a defence, under Gen. Wade Hampton against Gen. Sherman, and while there he was taken sick and died, under the yoke of slavery, having heard of freedom but not living to enjoy it.

RUNAWAY SLAVES.

My readers, have, no doubt, already heard that there were men in the South who made it their business in the days of slavery to raise and train hounds especially to hunt slaves with. Most of the owners hired such men on condition that they were to capture and return their runaway slaves, without being bruised and torn by the dogs. The average sums paid hunters were ten, fifteen and twenty-five dollars for capturing a slave; very many times, these sums were taken from the overseer's salary, as they were more or less the cause of slaves running away.

My readers want to know whether the runaway slaves ever returned to the overseers and their masters without being caught by the hunters. Sometimes they did and sometimes they never returned. Some stayed their lifetime; others, who would have returned, fell sick and died in the woods.

My readers ask, how did the slaves at home know when their fellow negroes, the runaways, sickened or died in the woods. In general, some one on the plantation from which they ran away, or confidential friends on some other plantation, had communication with them, so that if anything happened to them the slaves at home would find out through such parties. And sometimes the masters and overseers would find out about their death, but indirectly, however, because if it was known that any one on the plantation had dealings with the runaway, he would be punished, even though the information should be gladly received by the master and overseer.

Sometimes groups of runaway slaves, of eight, ten and even twenty, belonging to different owners, got together in the woods, which made it very difficult and dangerous for slave hunters to capture those whom they were hired to hunt. In such cases sometimes these runaways killed both hunters and dogs. The thick forests in which they lived could not be searched on horseback, neither could man or dog run in them. The only chances the hunters had of catching runaway slaves were either to rout them from those' thick forests or attack them when they came out in the opening to seek food.

Of course the runaways were mostly armed, and when attacked in the forests they would fight. My readers ask, how had they obtained arms and what were those arms, since slaves were not allowed to have deadly weapons? Some had large knives made by their fellow negroes who were blacksmiths, others stole guns from white men who' were accustomed to lay them carelessly around when they were out hunting game. The runaways who stole the guns were kept in powder and shot by some of the other slaves at home, who bought such from poor white men who kept little country stores in the different parts of the South.

The runaway slaves generally had fathers, brothers, cousins, or confidential friends who met them at certain appointed places, and brought them such things as were needed. The most they wanted from their fellow negroes at home was salt and a little corn flour; for they lived principally on beef and swine meat, taken either from their own masters or some other's stock.

My readers ask, did not some of the slaves at home betray their fellow negroes, the runaways, to the white man? I answer, they did; but often such were well spotted, and if the runaway slaves got a chance at them while in the woods would mob or kill them. On the other hand when they met those whom they could trust, instead of injuring them, they exchanged beef and swine meat with them for bread, corn flour, and salt, such as they needed in the woods.

THE RUNAWAY SLAVES IN THE HOUSE.

Instead of going into the woods, sometimes runaway slaves lived right around the overseer's and master's houses for months. A slave, named Isom, ran away from Thomas Clarkson, his master's son, who was the overseer. Mr. Clarkson was satisfied, as he said, that the unaccustomed runaway, whom he thought was in the woods could not stay from home long, but finding that he stayed longer than expected, Mr. Clarkson hired a slave hunter with his dogs to hunt him.

The hunter came early to the plantation and took breakfast with Mr. Clarkson on the day they began to hunt for the runaway slave. While sitting at breakfast, Mr. Clarkson said to the hunter, " My father brought up that boy as a house servant, and petted him so that it takes all the salt in the country to cure him. Father had too much religion to keep his negroes straight; but I don't believe in that. I think a negro ought to be overhauled every little while to keep him in his place, and that is just the reason why I took the overseership on this plantation.

The Hunter. " Well, what caused your boy to run away, Mr. Clarkson ? "

Mr. Clarkson. " Well he ran away because I gave him an overhauling, to keep him in the place of a negro."

Mr. Clarkson's wife. "Well, Thomas, I told you the other day, before you did it, that I didn't see any need of your whipping Isom, because I thought he was a good boy."

Mr. Clarkson. "Yes, my dear, if South Carolina had many more such Presbyterians as you and Father Boston (he meant old Mr. Clarkson), in a short time there would be no slaves in the state; then who would you have to work for you?"

I wish to state a fact to my readers. While there were exceptions, as a general thing the Presbyterians made better masters than did any other denomination among the slave holders in the South.

Mrs. Clarkson. "Yes, Thomas, if you were such a Presbyterian as you charged Father Boston and me with being, you could have saved yourself the trouble and money which it will cost to hunt him."

Mr. Clarkson. "Well, we will not discuss the matter of religion any further." (To the hunter.) "That boy has been away now for several days since I whipped him. I thought that he would have returned home long before this time, as this is the first time he has ever run away; but I rather conclude that he got with some experienced runaways. Now do you think that you can capture him without his being hurt, or torn by your dogs?"

Mrs. Clarkson. "That is just what I am afraid will be done to that boy."

The Hunter. "O, no fear of that, madam, I shall use care in hunting him. I have but one dog which is dangerous for tearing runaway negroes; I will chain him here until I capture your boy."

The hunter blew his horn which gathered his dogs,

chained the one he spoke of, then he and Mr. Clarkson started on a chase for the runaway slave, who,
secreted in the house, had heard every word they had
said about him.

After the hunter and Mr. Clarkson had gone, Mrs.
Clarkson went to her room (as a general thing the
southern mistresses hardly ever knew what went on
in their dining rooms and kitchens after meal hours),
and Isom, the runaway slave, sat at the same table
and ate his breakfast.

After two or three days of vain search in the woods
for the runaway slave, Mr. Clarkson asked some of
the other negroes on the plantation, if they saw him,
to tell him if he came home he would not whip him.
Of course, as a general thing, when they stayed in
the woods until they were captured, they were
whipped but they were not when they came home
themselves. One morning after several days of
fruitless search in the woods for the runaway slave
by the overseer and the hunter, while at breakfast,
Isom came up to the door. As soon as Mr. Clarkson learned that the runaway slave was at the door
he got up from his breakfast and went out.

"Well, Isom," said Mr. Clarkson. "Well, Massa
Thomas," said Isom. "Where have you been?" said
Mr. Clarkson. "I been in the woods, sir," answered
Isom. Of course it would not have been well for
him to tell Mr. Clarksom that he was hidden and fed
right in the house, for it would have made it bad for
the other negroes who were house servants, among
whom he had a brother and sister.

Mr. Clarkson. "Isom, did you get with some other
runaways?" "Yes, sir," said Isom. Of course

Isom's answer was in keeping with the belief of **Mr.**
Clarkson that he had got in with some experienced
runaway in the woods. "How many were with you?"
asked Mr. Clarkson. "Two," answered Isom. "What
are their names, and to whom do they belong?" asked
Mr. Clarkson. "I don't know, sir," said Isom.
"Didn't you ask their names?" said Mr. Clarkson.
"No, sir," said Isom. "Can you describe them?"
asked Mr. Clarkson. "One is big, like you, and the
other was little like the man who was hunting me,"
said Isom. "Where did you see the hunter?" asked
Mr. Clarkson. "In the woods, sir," said Isom·
"Isom, do you want something to eat?" asked **Mr.**
Clarkson. "Yes, sir," said Isom. He sent him
around to the kitchen and told the cook to give him
something to eat.

Mrs. Clarkson thought a great deal of Isom, so
while he was in the kitchen eating, she went in and
had a long talk with him about how he got along
since he had been away, as they supposed.

As I have said, in general, when runaway slaves
came home themselves, they were not whipped, but
were either handcuffed or put in stocks, and locked
up for two or three days.

While Isom was eating and talking with **Mrs.**
Clarkson, Mr. Clarkson appeared at the kitchen door
with a pistol in one hand and handcuffs in the other.
Mrs. Clarkson said, "What are you going to do,
Thomas?" "I want Isom as soon as he is through
eating," said Mr. Clarkson. "You are not going to
lock him up, are you Thomas?" said Mrs. Clarkson.
Mrs. Clarkson's name was Henrietta, but her pet
name was Henie. Mr. Clarkson said. "Henie, I
shan't hurt Isom."

Isom, who had a smooth, black, round face, full eyes, white teeth, was a very beautiful negro. When he saw the pistol and handcuffs in Mr. Clarkson's hands, those large eyes of his were stretched so wide, one could see the white, like great sheets in them.

Mrs. Clarkson said, "Thomas, please don't lock up Isom; he won't run away again. You won't, will you Isom?" "No, mamma massie Henie, I won't," said Isom. "Yes, Henie," said Mr. Clarkson, "he says so, but will he not?" "Thomas," said Mrs. Clarkson, "I will take the responsibility if you do as I ask you to; I will keep Isom around the house and will assure you that he will not run away.

Mr. Clarkson wanted to lock Isom up very much, but he knew what a strong will his wife had, and how hard it would be to get her right when she had got wrong, hence he complied with her request. So Isom worked around the house for a long time. The hunter was to rest a few days, and then resume his work, but Mr. Clarkson wrote to him that his services would be no longer needed, as the runaway slave whom he was employed to hunt had returned himself. I never learned whether the hunter got paid for what he had done.

MR. BLACK, THE SLAVE HUNTER.

There was a white man in Richland County, South Carolina, named Mr. Black, who made his living by hunting runaway slaves. I knew him as well as I did one of my fellow negroes on Col. Singleton's plantation. He was of dark complexion, short stature, spare built, with long, jet black, coarse hair. He bore the description of what some would call a good man, but he was quite the reverse; he was one of the most heartless men I have ever seen.

Mr. Black was a very successful hunter, although sometimes all of his bloodhounds were killed by runaway slaves, and he barely escaped with his life. He used to ride a small bay mare in hunting, which was the only horse he owned. She was a thin, raw-boned creature and looked as though she could hardly walk, but knew the business about as well as her master; and in such troubles as above stated she used to carry him pretty fast out of danger. Mr. Black caught several runaway slaves belonging to Col. Singleton.

I have known him to chase runaway slaves out of the forest right through the colonel's plantation, through a crowd of other negroes, and his dogs would never mistake any among the crowd for the ones they were after. When these hound dogs chased the runaways through farms in that way, many of them were killed and buried in the cotton or corn field by some among the crowd of negroes through which they passed. In general the slaves hated bloodhounds, and would kill them any time they got a chance, but especially on such occasions as above stated, to keep them from capturing runaways.

Once eight slaves ran away from Col. Singleton's plantation, and Mr. Black, with twenty-five hound dogs, was hired to hunt them up. The dogs struck trail of the runaways late one afternoon, and chased them all that night, during which time they got scattered. Next morning three of the runaways were chased through a crowd of their fellow negroes, who were working in the cotton field. While chasing the runaways some among the crowd killed six of the dogs, including the two leading ones, and buried them in the cotton beds or rows, as we used to call them.

Mr. Black, the hunter, though a mile or more off, knew that something had happened from the irregular barking of the other dogs, and also because he did not hear the yelling of the two leading dogs. So he blew his horn, called the rest of his dogs, and gave up the chase until he had replaced his leading dogs by others, which he always had on hand at home.

Slave hunters generally had one or two among the pack of hound dogs, called trailers or leaders, which the others, fifty or more, were trained to follow. So if anything happened to the leaders while on chase, the rest would become confused, and could not follow the runaway. But if the leaders were hurt or killed after the runaways were captured, the rest would surround and guard them until the hunter reached them, as he was always a mile or more behind.

After the leading dogs had been replaced, Mr. Black resumed the chase, and caught some of the runaways, but the rest came home themselves.

The last runaway slave Mr. Black was hired to hunt belonged to Col. M. R. Singleton, and was named Dick, but instead of Dick he caught a slave belonging to a man in Sumterville county, who had been in the woods seven years. This runaway slave had another name at home, but while in the woods had assumed the name of Champion, for his success in keeping slave hunters from capturing him up to that time.

Mr. Black, the hunter, chased Dick and Champion

two days and nights; on the morning before the capture of the latter they swam across the Water-ree river. After they got across they were separated; the dogs followed Champion, and ran him down that morning about eleven o'clock. Champion had a gun and pistol; as the first dog ran up and opened his mouth to take hold of him he discharged the contents of the pistol in his mouth and killed him instantly. The rest of the dogs did not take hold of him, but surrounded him and held him at bay until the hunter reached the spot.

When Mr. Black rode up within gunshot, Champion aimed at him with a loaded double barrel gun, but the caps of both barrels snapped from being wet by running through the bushes. Mr. Black had a gun and pistol, too; he attempted to shoot the negro, but William Turner, Col. Singleton's overseer, who hired Mr. Black to hunt Dick, the runaway from the colonel's plantation, would not let him do it. Mr. Black then attempted to strike Champion with the breech of his gun, but Champion kicked him down, and as he drew his knife to stab Mr. Black, Mr. Turner, the overseer, struck him on the back of his head with the butt of a loaded whip. This stunned him for a few moments, and by the time he had regained his senses they had handcuffed him.

After the negro had been handcuffed, Mr. Black wanted to abuse him, because he had killed the dog, and attempted to shoot him, but Mr. Turner, the overseer, would not let him. Champion was taken to Col. Singleton's plantation, locked up in the dungeon under the overseer's house, and his master was notified of his capture; he was a mulatto negro, and his master, who was his father, sent for him at Col. Singleton's plantation; but I never learned whether Mr. Black, the hunter, was ever paid for capturing him. Dick, the runaway negro from Col. Singleton's place, came home himself sometime after Champion, his companion, had been captured.

Mr. Black, the slave hunter, was very poor, and had a large family; he had a wife, with eight or ten helpless children, whom I knew as well as I did my fellow negroes on the colonel's plantation. But as cruel as Mr. Black was to runaway slaves, his family was almost wholly supported by negroes; I have known in some cases that they stole from their masters to help this family. The negroes were so kind to Mr. Black's family that his wife turned against him for his cruelty to runaway slaves.

I have stated that some of the masters and overseers hired the hunters, on condition that they would capture and return the runaway slaves, unbruised and untorn by their dogs; while others, in a mad fit of passion, would say to them, " I want you to bring my runaway nigger home, dead or alive."

All of the slave hunters used to practice cruelty upon the runaway slaves; more especially upon those whose masters would say to hunters "bring them dead or alive." But among all the slave hunters in the part of South Carolina where the author of this work lived, Mr. Black was the most cruel.

It was rumored that many of the runaway slaves that were never heard of afterward, were captured and killed in the woods by Mr. Black, but no special clue to this could be found. Finally Mr. Black was hired to capture a runaway slave in Barnwell County,

S. C. This slave was with another, who was thought well of by his master, but hated by the overseer. In the chase, the two runaways separated, and the dogs followed the second instead of the one whom Mr. Black had been hired to hunt. Mr. Black had another hunter with him by the name of Motley. The negro killed several of the dogs, and gave Messrs. Black and Motley a hard fight. After the negro had been captured, they killed him, cut him up and gave his remains to the living dogs.

The companion of the murdered slave was not caught. A few days after the chase, while wandering around in the wood in a somewhat excited state, he came to a spot where the bushes and leaves seemed to have been in a stirred-up condition, as though there had been tussling by two parties. On looking around in this disordered spot, he found pieces of clothing here and there in rags, looking just like the suit worn by his companion, who was then a victim of a most cruel death from the hands of the hunters. On closer examination, he saw spots of blood here and there upon the leaves, which awakened his suspicion ; on looking a little way from this spot, he saw some leaves which looked as though they had been moved by hands and put there, and on removing the leaves, he found that the earth had been freshly dug and filled in again. Digging down in the spot, he soon discovered pieces of the person of a dead man, whom he could not identify, but was satisfied that it was the remains of his companion, from whom he had been compelled to separate a few days before. This sight frightened the runaway negro so, that he left the woods, went home to his master and told the story ;

but as a negro's word was not to be taken against a white man's in the days of slavery, no special notice was taken of what he had said. Still some of the white people were secretly watching Mr. Black, the slave hunter, as he had been before suspected of killing runaway slaves in the woods.

The master of the murdered negro was still ignorant of his death ; he was in hopes that his slave would return. But finding that his slave did not return as expected, the master became uneasy, and offered a reward to any one who could give a clue of his negro. In the meantime, he discharged the overseer who had been the cause of his slave running away ; and he also kept the overseer's salary of four hundred dollars, which was the annual pay for overseeing his plantation.

Mr. Black's house was in Richland county, and as he was the last who had hunted runaway slaves in Barnwell county before the murder, suspicion rested on him. Still no one said anything to him, but he was very closely watched by men of his own county, whose interest was not in the hatefulness of the crime committed, but rather in the reward offered by the master to any who could give information of his runaway slave.

Sometime after the case had occurred, another white man of Richland county became quite a friend to Mr. Black, the slave hunter ; this apparent friendship soon led Mr. Black to tell the secret, which speedily brought him to trial. While he and his pretended friend were on a drinking spree, in the midst of the merriment,—of course the conversation was how to control negroes, as that was the principal topic of the poor white men South, in the days of slavery.

In the conversation, this friend spoke of several plans which he said, if properly carried out, " would keep a nigger in his place." After the friend had said so much to Mr. Black, the slave hunter, the latter felt that he could tell his secret without endangering himself, so he answered : " The way to show a nigger that would resist a white man, his place, is to put him among the missing. Not long since, I went to Barnwell county to hunt a runaway nigger, and my dogs struck trail of another instead of the one I wanted to capture. After quite a long chase my dogs ran him down, and before I reached him he killed several of them, and gave me a hard fight when I got to him. Motley and I were together ; I shot him down, and Motley and I cut him up and gave the pieces to the remainder of my dogs ; that is the way I put a nigger in his place."

After the secret had been revealed, Mr. Black's friend excused himself, and the former saw him no more until he appeared as a witness against him. The companion of the murdered negro was summoned to carry the investigating party, including the murderer, to the spot where his companion had been buried.

Mr. Black was tried and found to be guilty. After sentence had been passed, he confessed the commission of that crime, and also told that he had killed several runaway negroes previously in his own county. So Mr. Black and Motley, his companion, were both hanged in Barnwell county, S. C. The system of slavery outlived Mr. Black, the slave hunter, just six years.

MANNING BROWN AND AUNT BETTY.

A man by the name of Manning Brown was nursed by an old colored woman he called mamma Betty. She was naturally good natured and a devout Christian, and Mr. Brown gained many of her good qualities when he was under her entire control, at which time he was said to be a boy of very fine sense of feeling and quite promising. But when approaching manhood Mr. Brown fell among a class of other white men who, in the days of slavery, were unbridled in their habits. With this class of men he began to drink, and step by step in this rapid stride he soon became a confirmed drunkard. This habit so overcoated the good influence he had gained from the colored woman, that it rendered him dangerous not only to his enemies, but also to his friends.

Manning Brown was feared by most of the other white men in Richland county, S. C., and, strange to say, although he was dangerous to white men, yet he never lost the respect he had for colored people in his boyhood days. He ate, drank and slept among colored people after he was a grown man, and in many cases when other white men, who were called patrols, caught colored people away from home without tickets, and were about to whip them, Mr. Brown would ride up and say, " The first man who raises a whip at one of those negroes I will blow his brains out." Knowing that he would shoot a man as quick as he would a bird, even if ten patrols were together, when Mr. Brown made such threats, they never would attempt to whip the negroes.

Mr. Brown owned a plantation with forty slaves on it; his good treatment of them enabled him to get more work out of them than most owners got out of their slaves. His slaves thought so much of their "Massa Manning," as they used to call him, that they did everything in their power to please him. But while he was so good to colored people, he was dangerous to many of the white people and feared by them.

A man by the name of Peter Gafney fought a duel with his brother-in-law, whose name was Dr. Ray; the former, who was quite a marksman, was killed by the latter, who was considered a very poor one. This led many who were in favor of Mr. Gafney to feel that there had been foul play by Dr. Ray, the contestant. Mr. Brown, who acted as a second for Mr. Gafney in the fight, felt the loss of his old friend very deeply. A short time after this he sent a challenge to Dr. Ray, stating, "You may either meet me at a certain time, on the spot where you killed P. T. Gafney, for a duel, or I will shoot you on first sight wherever I meet you. Yours, M. Brown."

But Dr. Ray refused in the face of the threat to accept the challenge. Knowing the disposition of Mr. Brown, the people in that county were inflamed with excitement, because the doctor was liable at any moment while riding in the road to be killed. In fear of meeting Mr. Brown, the doctor gave up visiting the most of his sick patients, and almost wholly confined himself to his large plantation. At the same time Mr. Brown was closely watched by his friends to keep him from waylaying the doctor.

A short time after this threat Mr. Brown commenced to drink harder than ever, so that at times he did not know his own family. But the providence of

God was slowly leading Mr. Brown through the unknown paths to a sudden change of life, as we shall soon see.

Mr. Brown's family consisted of a wife, one child, and Aunt Betty, the old colored woman who had brought him up. She was the only mother he knew, for his own mother had died when he was an infant, and her dying request had been that mamma Betty, the old woman, should bring up this boy, who was an only child; and when Mr. Brown got married he took Aunt Betty into his family and told her she need not do any work only what she chose to do, and that he would take care of her the balance of her days. And Mrs. Brown regarded Aunt Betty more as a mother-in-law than as a negress servant. Sometimes when Mr. Brown would not listen to his wife, he would to his mamma Betty, when he was sober enough to know her. One afternoon, while Mr. Brown was in one of those drunken fits, he went into his bedroom and lay down across the bed, talking to himself. His wife went in to speak to him, but as she entered he jumped up and got his loaded double barrelled gun and threatened to shoot her. Frightened at this, she ran out of the room and screamed saying, "O, my God, mamma Betty, please go in and speak to your Massa Manning, for he threatened to shoot me." With that old familiar confidence in one who had often listened to her advice, Aunt Betty went into the house and to the room where she found Mr. Brown lying across the bed, with the gun by his side. On entering the room, as she was advancing toward the bed, she said, " Massa Manning, what is the matter with you ? You naughty boy, what is the matter ?" On saying these words, before she had reached the bed, Mr. Brown rose, with the gun in hand, and discharged the contents of both barrels at the old woman ; she dropped instantly to the floor. Mr. Brown lay across the bed as before, with the gun by his side, talking to himself, and soon dropped to sleep. Mrs. Brown fainted away several times under the excitement.

Aunt Betty lived about an hour. Soon after she had been shot she wanted to see Mr. Brown, but when told that she could not, she said, " O, my Lord, I wanted to see my child before I die, and I know that he would want to see his mamma Betty, too, before she leaves him." During the time she lived she prayed for Mr. Brown, and requested that he would change his course of life, become a Christian, and meet her in heaven. After singing one of her familiar hymns, Aunt Betty said to some one who stood by her bedside, " I want you to tell Massa Manning that he must not feel bad for what he did to me, because I know that if he was in his right mind he would not hurt me any more than he would himself. Tell him that I have prayed to the Lord for him that he may be a good boy, and I want him to promise that he will be a Christian and meet me in heaven." With these words Aunt Betty became speechless, dying a few moments afterwards. The doctor was sent for, but had to come from such a distance that she died before he reached there.

When Mr. Brown awoke from his drunken state in the night, and learned the sad news of Aunt Betty's death, of which he had been the cause, he clasped his hands and cried out, " What ! is it possible that my mamma Betty, the only mother I ever knew, was killed by my hands?" He ran into the room where the corpse was and clasped the remains of the old negress in his arms and cried, " Mamma Betty, mamma Betty, please speak to me as you used to." But that voice was hushed in death.

The doctor, overseer and others tried to quiet him, but they could not. That night Mr. Brown took the train to Columbia, the capital of South Carolina, and gave himself up to the law next day. He was told that it was all right; that the old negress was his slave. But Mr. Brown was dissatisfied; he came back home and invited all the white neighbors and slaves to Aunt Betty's funeral, in which he and his family took part. After the excitement was over the message of Aunt Betty was delivered to Mr. Brown; he was told that her last request had been that he would meet her in heaven. He answered, " I will." Mr. Brown then and there took an oath that he would drink no more strong drinks. He then disposed of his slaves, but how I did not learn. Soon after this he was converted and became one of the ablest preachers in Richland county, S. C. Mr. Brown's conversion freed Dr. Ray from his threat. The doctor was so glad of this that he paid quite a large sum towards Mr. Brown's salary for preaching.

CHAPTER III—MY EXPERIENCE IN THE CIVIL WAR.

My knowledge of the Civil War, extends from the time when the first gun was fired on Fort Sumter in April, 1861, to the close of the War.

While the slaves were not pressed into the Confederate service as soldiers, yet they were used in all the slave-holding states at war points, not only to build fortifications, but also to work on vessels used in the war.

The slaves were gathered in each state, anywhere from 6000 to 8000 or more, from different plantations, carried to some centre and sent to various war points in the state.

It would be impossible to describe the intense excitement which prevailed among the Confederates in their united efforts to raise troops to meet the Union forces. They were loud in their expressions of the certainty of victory.

Many of the poor white men were encouraged by the promise of from three to five negroes to each man who would serve in the Confederate service, when the Confederate government should have gained the victory.

On the other hand, the negroes were threatened with an increase of the galling yoke of slavery. These threats were made with significant expressions, and the strongest assumption that the negro was the direct cause of the war.

HOW SLAVES WERE GATHERED AND CARRIED TO WAR POINTS.

No sooner had the war commenced in the spring

of 1861, than the slaves were gathered from the
various plantations, and shipped by freight cars,
or boats, to some centre, and apportioned out and
sent to work at different war points. I do not know
just how many slaves the Confederate Government
required each master to furnish for its service, but I
know that 15 of the 465 slaves on my master's, Col.
M. R. Singleton's, plantation, were sent to work on
fortifications each year during the war.

The war had been going on two years before my
turn came. In the summer of 1863 with thousands
of other negroes, gathered from the various parts of
the state, I was freighted to the city of Charleston,
South Carolina, and the group in which my lot fell
was sent to Sullivan's Island. We were taken on a
boat from the city of Charleston, and landed in a
little village, situated nearly opposite Fort Sumter,
on this island. Leaving behind us Fort Moultrie,
Fort Beauregard, and several small batteries, we
marched down the white sandy beach of the island,
below Fort Marshall, to the very extreme point, where
a little inlet of water divides Sullivan's from Long
Island, and here we were quartered under Capt.
Charles Haskell.

From this point on the island, turning our faces
northward, with Morris Island northwest of us, and
looking directly north out into the channel, we saw a
number of Union gun boats, like a flock of black
sheep feeding on a plain of grass; while the men
pacing their decks looked like faithful shepherds
watching the flock. While we negroes remained upon
Sullivan's Island, we watched every movement of the
Union fleet, with hearts of joy to think that they were

a part of the means by which the liberty of four and one-half millions of slaves was to be effected in accordance with the emancipation proclamation made the January preceding. We kept such close watch upon them that some one among us, whether it was night or day, would be sure to see the discharge of a shot from the gun boat before the sound of the report was heard. During that summer there was no engagement between the Union fleet and the Confederates at that point in South Carolina. The Union gun boats, however, fired occasional shots over us, six miles, into the city of Charleston. They also fired a few shells into a marsh between Sullivan's Island and Mount Pleasant, but with no damage to us.

WHAT WORK THE NEGROES DID ON THE ISLAND.

After we had reached the island, our company was divided. One part was quartered at one end of the Island, around Fort Moultrie, and we were quartered at the other end, at Fort Marshall. Our work was to repair forts, build batteries, mount guns, and arrange them. While the men were engaged at such work, the boys of my age, namely, thirteen, and some older, waited on officers and carried water for the men at work, and in general acted as messengers between different points on the island.

ENGAGEMENT ON LONG ISLAND.

Though there was no fighting on Sullivan's Island during my stay there, Confederate soldiers at times crossed the inlet from Sullivan's to Long Island, in the night and engaged in skirmishes with Union soldiers, who had entered the upper end of that island

and camped there. Whether these Confederate scouts were ever successful in routing the Union forces on the island or not I have never learned, but I know that they were several times repulsed with considerable loss.

NEGROES ESCAPE.

The way the Confederates came to the knowledge that Union soldiers were on Long Island was that the group of negroes who preceded us on Sullivan's Island had found out that Union soldiers were camping on the upper end of Long Island. So one night quite a number of them escaped by swimming across the inlet that divides Sullivan's Island and Long Island, and succeeded in reaching the Union line.

The next day it was discovered that they had swam across the inlet, and the following night they were pursued by a number of Confederate scouts who crossed in a flat boat. Instead of the capture of the negroes, who would have been victims of the most cruel death, the Confederate scouts were met by soldiers from the Union line, and after a hot engagement they were repulsed, as they usually were.

BUILDING A BATTERY ON LONG ISLAND.

Finally the Confederates took a large number of the group of which I was a member from Sullivan's to the south shore of Long Island and there built a battery, and mounted several small field guns upon it. As they were afraid of being discovered in the daytime we were obliged to work on the battery nights and were taken back to Sullivan's in the morning, until the work was completed.

We were guarded by Confederate soldiers while building the battery, as, without a guard it would have been easy for any of us to have reached the Union line on the north end of Long Island. Sullivan's Island was about five miles long.

A NEGRO SERVANT MURDERED.

One of the most heartless deeds committed while I was on Sullivan's Island, was that of the murder of a negro boy by his master, a Confederate officer to whom the boy had been a body servant. What the rank of this officer was I am not sure, but I think he was a Major, and that he was from the state of Georgia. It was a common thing for southern men to carry dirks, especially during the war. This officer had one, and for something the boy displeased him in, he drew the knife and made a fatal stab between the boy's collar bone and left shoulder. As the victim fell at the brutal master's feet, we negroes who had witnessed the fiendish and cowardly act upon a helpless member of our race, expected an immediate interference from the hand of justice in some form or other. But we looked and waited in vain, for the horrible deed did not seem to have changed the manner of those in authority in the least, but they rather treated it as coolly as though nothing had happened. Finding that the Confederates failed to lay the hand of justice upon the officer, we, with our vague ideas of moral justice, and with our extreme confidence that God would somehow do more for the oppressed negroes than he would ordinarily for any other people, anxiously waited a short time for some token of Divine vengeance, but as we found that no such token as we desired, in the heat of our passion, came, we finally concluded to wait God's way and time, as to how, and when this, as every other wrong act, should be visited with his unfailing justice.

But aside from this case we fared better on these fortifications than we had at home on the plantations. This was the case at least with those of us who were on Sullivan's Island. Our work in general on the fortifications was not hard, we had a great deal of spare time, and although we knew that our work in the Confederate service was against our liberty, yet we were delighted to be in military service.

We felt an exalted pride that, having spent a little time at these war points, we had gained some knowledge which would put us beyond our fellow negroes at home on the plantations, while they would increase our pride by crediting us with far more knowledge than it was possible for us to have gained.

Our daily rations from the Commissary was a quart of rice or hard-tack, and a half pound of salt pork or corn-beef.

The change from the cabins and from the labor on the old plantations so filled our cup of joy that we were sorry when the two months of our stay on the island was ended.

At the end of about two months, I, with the rest of my fellow negroes of that group, was sent back to the plantation again, while others took our places.

MY EXPERIENCE IN FORT SUMTER.

In the summer of 1864, when I was in my fourteenth year, another call was made for negro laborers for the Confederate government, and fifteen from our plantation, including myself, with thousands from other plantations, were sent down to Charleston again.

There the negroes were apportioned in groups to be sent to the different fortifications. My lot fell among the group of three hundred and sixty, who were assigned to Fort Sumter. I shall never forget with what care they had to move in carrying us in a steamer from the government wharf in Charleston to John's island wharf, on account of the network of torpedo mines in Charleston Harbor.

From John's island wharf they carried us in rowboats to Fort Sumter, and, as those boats could not carry many, it took all night to convey us with other freightage to Fort Sumter.

The steamer which carried us from Charleston to John's island wharf had to run at night. Indeed every move the Confederates made about there near the close of the war had to be made at night because the Yankees on gunboats outside the channel and those on Morris island kept so close a watch it was very dangerous to convey us from John's island wharf to Fort Sumter because the oars dipping into the salt water at night made sparks like fire, and thus the Yankees on Morris island were able to see us. Indeed their shots oftentimes took effect.

Many of the negroes were killed. Of the fifteen from our plantation, one boy of about my age was struck by a parrot shell while climbing from the boat into the fort. We were told of the perils we were to meet, both before and after we reached our destination. For one of the most disheartening things was the sad report of the survivors of those whose places we were to fill. As the rowboats left them on John's island wharf and as we were about to embark they told us of the great danger to which we would be exposed,—of the liability of some of us being killed before we reached the fort, which proved true, and of how fast their comrades were killed in Fort Sumter. A number, it was said, died from fright before reaching Sumter.

THE OFFICERS AND QUARTERS.

The officers who were then in command of the fort were Capt. J. C. Mitchell and Major John Johnson. The name of the overseer in charge of the negroes in the fort was Deburgh,—whether that was his right name I can not say.

Deburgh was a foreigner by birth. He was one of the most cruel men I ever knew. As he and his atrocious deeds will come up later in this history, I will say no more of him here.

CONDITION OF THE FORT.

Fort Sumter, which previous to this, had not only been silenced by the Union forces, but also partly demolished, had but one gun mounted on it, on the west side. That cannon we used to call the "Sundown Gun," because it was fired every evening as the sun went down,—as well as at sunrise. On this west side the Confederate officers and soldiers were sheltered in the bomb-proof safe during bombardment. On the east side of the fort, facing Morris island, opposite Fort Wagner, there was another apartment called the " Rat-hole " in which we negroes were quartered.

WHAT THE NEGROES DID IN FORT SUMTER.

Fort Sumter had been so badly damaged by the Union forces in 1863, that unless something had been done upon the top, the continued bombardment which it suffered up to the close of the war, would have rendered it uninhabitable.

The fort was being fired upon every five minutes with mortar and parrot shells by the Yankees from Morris Island.

The principal work of the negroes was to secure the top and other parts against the damage from the Union guns.

Large timbers were put on the rampart of the fort, and boards laid on them, then baskets, without bottoms, about two feet wide, and four feet high, were put close together on the rampart, and filled with sand by the negroes.

The work could only be done at night, because, besides the bombardment from Fort Wagner which was about a mile or little less from us, there were also sharp-shooters there who picked men off whenever they showed their heads on the rampart.

The mortar and parrot shells rained alternately upon Fort Sumter every five minutes, day and night, but the sharp-shooters could only fire by day-light.

The negroes were principally exposed to the bombardment. The only time the few Confederate soldiers were exposed to danger was while they were putting the Chevaldefrise on the parapet at night.

The " Chevaldefrise" is a piece of timber with wooden spikes pointed with iron, and used for defence on fortifications.

In the late war between the Spaniards and the

Americans, the former used barbed wire for the same purpose.

If my readers could have been in Fort Sumter in the summer of 1864 they would have heard the sentinel cry, every five minutes, " Look out ! Mortar !" Then they would have seen the negroes running about in the fort yard in a confused state, seeking places of safety from the missile sure to bring death to one or more of them. Another five minutes, and again the cry of the sentinel, " Look out," means a parrot shell, which is far more deadly than is the mortar because it comes so quickly that one has no chance to seek a place of safety.

The next moment the survivors of us, expecting that it would be our turn next, would be picking up, here and there, parts of the severed bodies of our fellow negroes ; many of those bodies so mutilated as not to be recognizable.

DEBURGH, THE OVERSEER.

Deburgh, the overseer, of whom I have spoken, was a small man, of light complexion, and very light hair.

If my readers could have been in Fort Sumter in July, 1864, they would have seen Deburgh with a small bar of iron or a piece of shell in his hand, forcing the surviving portion of the negroes back into line and adding to these, other negroes kept in the Rat-hole as reserves to fill the places of those who were killed and wounded.

They would also have heard him swearing at the top of his voice, while forcing the negroes to rearrange themselves in line from the base of the fort to the top.

This arrangement of the negroes, enabled them to sling to each other the bags of sand which was put in the baskets on the top of the fort. My readers ask, what was the sand put on the fort for ? It was to smother the fuses of such shells as reached the ramparts before bursting.

After the bombardment of Fort Sumter in 1863, by the Union forces, its top of fourteen or sixteen feet in thickness, built of New Hampshire granite, was left bare. From that time all through 1864, the shells were so aimed as to burst right over the fort; and it was pieces of these shells which flew in every direction that were so destructive.

The fuses of many of these shells fired on Fort Sumter did not burn in time to cause the shells to burst before falling. Now as the shells fell on the rampart of the fort instead of falling and bursting on the stone, they buried themselves harmlessly in the sand, which put out the fuse and also kept them from bursting.

But while the destruction of life was lessened by the sand, it was fully made up by the hand of that brute, the overseer. God only knows how many negroes he killed in Fort Sumter under the shadow of night. Every one he reached, while forcing the slaves back into working position after they had been scattered by the shells, he would strike on the head with the piece of iron he carried in his hand, and, as his victim fell, would cry out to some other negro, " Put that fellow in his box," meaning his coffin.

Whether the superior officers in Fort Sumter knew that Deburgh was killing the negroes off almost as fast as the shells from Fort Wagner, or whether they

did not know, and did not care, I never have learned.
But I have every reason to believe that one of them
at least, namely, Major John Johnson, would not have
allowed such a wholesale slaughter, had he known.
On the other hand I believe that Capt. J. C. Mitchell
was not only mean enough to have allowed it, but
that he was fully as heartless himself.

Whatever became of Deburgh, whether he was
killed in Fort Sumter or not, I never knew.

OUR SUPERIOR OFFICERS.

The two officers in command of Fort Sumter in
July of 1864 were Capt. J. C. Mitchell, and Major
John Johnson.

Major Johnson was as kind, gentle, and humane to
the negroes as could have been expected.

On the other hand, the actions of Capt. Mitchell
were harsh and very cruel. He had a bitter hatred
toward the Yankees, and during the rain of shells on
Fort Sumter, he sought every opportunity to expose
the negroes to as much danger as he dared.

I remember that one night Capt. Mitchell ordered us
outside of Fort Sumter to a projection of the stone-
bed upon which the Fort was built, right in front of
Fort Wagner. At that place we were in far greater
danger from the deadly missiles of the Union forces
than we were exposed to on the inside of Sumter, and
I could see no other reasons for his ordering us outside of the fort that night than that we might be
killed off faster.

It seems that during the incessant firing on Fort
Sumter the officers held a consultation as to whether
it was not best to evacuate the fort. It was at this

time that it was rumored,—a rumor that we had every reason to believe,—that Capt. Mitchell plotted to lock us negroes up in our quarters in Sumter, known as the Rat-hole; and put powder to it and arrange it so that both the negroes and the Yankees should be blown up, when the latter should have taken possession after the evacuation of the fort by the Confederates.

But we learned that Major John Johnson, who has since become an Episcopal minister, in Charleston, S. C., wholly refused to agree with Capt. Mitchell in such a barbarous and cowardly act, and, as though Providence were watching over the innocent and oppressed negroes, and over the Yankees as well, because they were fighting in a righteous cause, Capt. Mitchell's career and further chances of carrying out his cruel intentions were cut short. He was mortally wounded by the sharp-shooters of Fort Wagner, on the 14th of July, 1864, and died four hours afterwards.

OUR RATIONS IN SUMTER.

The working forces of negroes in Sumter with the exception of the boys who carried messages to the different parts of the fort day and night, were locked up days, and turned out nights, to work. We drew our rations of hard-tack and salt pork twice a day; mornings when we ceased work and turned in for the day, and again, between three and four o'clock in the afternoon, so as to have supper eaten in time to go to work at dark.

We often ate our salt pork raw with the hard-tack, as there were no special means of cooking in the negroes' apartment. We were not only in danger, while at work, from the continued rain of shells, but oftentimes when we were put in line to draw our rations some of us were killed or wounded.

I cannot say how they got fresh water in Fort Sumter, as I do not remember seeing any brought there in boats, neither did I notice any conveniences there for the catching of rain water.

The water we negroes used was kept in large hogsheads with coal tar in them ; I do not know what the tar was put in the water for unless it was for our health. The " rat-hole" into which we were locked, was like a sweat box ; it was so hot and close, that, although we were exposed to death by shells when we were turned out to work, we were glad to get into the fresh air.

We had little cups in which they used to give us whiskey mornings when we went in, and again when we were going out to work at night.

I don't know how many of the forty survivors of the three hundred and sixty of us who were carried into the Fort in the summer of 1864 besides myself are still alive. But if there are any with the keen tenderness of a negro, they cannot help joining me in an undying sense of gratitude to Major John Johnson, not only for his kind and gentle dealings with us which meant so much to a negro in the days of slavery, but also for his humane protection, which saved us from some of the danger from shells to which we were exposed in Sumter.

A short time after Capt. J. C. Mitchell had been killed, Major Johnson was dangerously wounded in the head by a piece of shell.

MY LAST NIGHT IN FORT SUMTER AND THE GLORIOUS
END OF THE WAR.

During the time we spent in Fort Sumter we had
not seen a clear day or night. In harmony with the
continual danger by which we were surrounded, the
very atmosphere wore the pall of death ; for it was
always rainy and cloudy. The mutilated bodies of the
negroes, mingled with the black mud and water in
the fort yard, added to the awfulness of the scene.
Pieces of bombshells and other pieces of iron, and
also large southern pine timbers were scattered all over
the yard of the fort. There was also a little lime
house in the middle of the yard, into which we were
warned not to go when seeking places of safety from
the deadly missiles at the cry of the sentinel.

The orders were that we should get as near the
centre of the fort yard as possible and lie down. The
reason for this was that the shells which were fired
upon Sumter were so measured that they would burst
in the air, and the pieces would generally fly toward
the sides of the fort. But the orders were not strictly carried out, because, at the warning cries of the
sentinel, we became confused. That night, at the cry
of the sentinel, I ran and lay down on one of the
large southern pine timbers, and several of my fellow
negroes followed and piled in upon me. Their weight
was so heavy that I cried out as for life. The sense
of that crush I feel at certain times even now.

At the next report of a shell I ran toward the lime
house, but some one tripped me up, and, by the time
I had got to my feet again, twelve or thirteen others
were crowded into it. Another negro and I reached
the doorway, but we were not more than there before

a mortar shell came crushing down upon the little lime house, and all within were so mangled that their bodies were not recognizable.

Only we two were saved. My companion had one of his legs broken, and a piece of shell had wounded me over my right eye and cut open my under lip. At the moment I was wounded I was not unconscious, but I did not know what had hurt me. I became almost blind from the effect of my wounds, but not directly after I was wounded, and I felt no pain for a day or so. With other wounded I was taken to the bombproof in the fort. I shall never forget this first and last visit to the hospital department. To witness the rough handling of the wounded patients, to see them thrown on a table as one would a piece of beef, and to see the doctor use his knife and saw, cutting off a leg, or arm, and sometimes both, with as much indifference as if he were simply cutting up beef, and to hear the doctor say, of almost every other one of these victims, after a leg or an arm was amputated, " Put that fellow in his box," meaning his coffin, was an awful experience. After the surgeon had asked to whom I belonged, he dressed my wounds.

My readers will remember that I stated that no big boat could run to Fort Sumter at that time, on account of the bombardment. We had to be conveyed back to John's Island wharf in rowboats, which was the nearest distance a steamer could go to Fort Sumter.

As one of those rowboats was pushed out to take the dead and wounded from the fort, and as the former were put into the boat, which was generally done before they put in the latter, fortunately, just before the wounded were put in, a Parrott shell was fired into it from Fort Wagner by the Union forces, which sunk both the boat and the coffins, with their remains.

My readers would ask how the Confederates disposed of the negroes who were killed in Fort Sumter. Those who were not too badly mutilated were sent over to the city of Charleston and were buried in a place which was set apart to bury the negroes. But others, who were so badly cut up by shells, were put into boxes, with pieces of iron in them, and carried out a little away from Sumter and thrown overboard.

I was then taken to John's Island wharf, and from there to the city of Charleston in a steamer, and carried to Doctor Rag's hospital, where I stopped until September. Then I was sent back home to my master's plantation. Quoting the exact words of Major John Johnson, a Confederate officer under whom I was a part of the time at the above-named place, I would say : "July 7th, Fort Sumter's third great bombardment, lasting sixty days and nights, with a total of 14,666 rounds fired at the fort, with eighty-one casualties."

WHAT TOOK PLACE AFTER.

I said that after I got well enough to travel I was sent back home to my master's plantation, about a hundred miles from the city of Charleston, in central South Carolina. This was in September of 1864, and I, with the rest of my fellow-negroes on this extensive plantation, and with other slaves all over the South, were held in suspense waiting the final outcome of the emancipation proclamation, issued January, 1863, but as the war continued, it had not taken effect until the spring of 1865.

Here I had less work than before the war, for the nearer the war approached its close the less the slaves had to do, as the masters were at the end of their wits what to do. In the latter part of 1864 Gen. Sherman, with his army of a hundred thousand men and almost as many stragglers, covered the space of about sixty miles in width while marching from Georgia through South Carolina. The army camped around Columbia, the capital of South Carolina, for a short time. Early in the spring of 1865 the commissary building first took fire, which soon spread to such extent that the whole city of Columbia was consumed ; just a few houses on the suburbs were left.

The commissary building was set on fire by one of the two parties, but it was never fully settled whether it was done by Gen. Sherman's men or by the Confederates, who might have, as surmised by some, as they had to evacuate the city, set it on fire to keep Gen. Sherman's men from getting the food. After this Columbia was occupied by a portion of Sherman's men, while the others marched on toward North Carolina.

THE GLORIOUS END.

In closing this brief sketch of my experiences in the war, I would ask my readers to go back of the war a little with me. I want to show them a few of the dark pictures of the slave system. Hark ! I hear the clanking of the ploughman's chains in the fields; I hear the tramping of the feet of the hoe-hands. I

hear the coarse and harsh voice of the negro driver
and the shrill voice of the white overseer swearing at
the slaves. I hear the swash of the lash upon the backs
of the unfortunates; I hear them crying for mercy
from the merciless. Amidst these cruelties I hear the
fathers and mothers pour out their souls in prayer,—
"O, Lord, how long!" and their cries not only awaken
the sympathy of their white brothers and sisters of
the North, but also mightily trouble the slave masters of the South.

The firing on Fort Sumter, in April of 1861,
brought hope to the slaves that the long looked for
year of jubilee was near at hand. And though the
South won victory after victory, and the Union
reeled to and fro like a drunken man, the negroes
never lost hope, but faithfully supported the Union
cause with their prayers.

Thank God, where Christianity exists slavery cannot exist.

At last came freedom. And what joy it brought!
I am now standing, in imagination, on a high place
just outside the city of Columbia, in the spring of
1865. The stars and stripes float in the air. The
sun is just making its appearance from behind the
hills, and throwing its beautiful light upon green
bush and tree. The mocking birds and jay birds sing
this morning more sweetly than ever before. Beneath
the flag of liberty there is congregated a perfect network of the emancipated slaves from the different
plantations, their swarthy faces, from a distance,
looking like the smooth water of a black sea. Their
voices, like distant thunder, rend the air,—

" Old master gone away, and the darkies all at home,
There must be now the kingdom come and the year of
    jubilee."

The old men and women, bent over by reason of age
and servitude, bound from their staves, praising God
for deliverance.

NARRATIVE

OF THE

LIFE OF MOSES GRANDY,

INTRODUCTION.

ABOUT a fortnight ago, the subject of the following brief
Memoir came to me, bearing with him a letter from a dear
friend and distinguished abolitionist in the United States,
from which the following is an extract:—'I seize my pen
in haste to gratify a most worthy colored friend of mine, by
giving him a letter of introduction to you, as he intends
sailing this week (August 8th, 1842) for Liverpool and
London, *via* New Orleans. His name is Moses Grandy.
He knows what it is to have been a slave, and what are
the tender mercies of the southern slave-drivers. His history is not only authentic, but most extraordinary, and full
of thrilling interest. Could it be published, it would make
a deep sensation in every quarter. He was compelled to
buy his freedom *three times over!* He paid for it $1,850.
He has since bought his wife, and one or two of his children; and before going to England will first go to New
Orleans, to purchase some of his other children, if he can
find them, who are still held in captivity. His benevolence,
affection, kindness of heart, and elasticity of spirit, are truly
remarkable. He has a good head, a fine countenance, and
a great spirit, notwithstanding his education has been obtained in the horrible school of slavery. Just get him to
tell you his narrative, and if you happen to have an anti-
slavery meeting, let him tell his tale to a British audience.'
In the letter of another highly esteemed friend, he is spoken
of as ' unsurpassed for faithfulness and perseverance;' in
the letter of a third, as a ' worthy and respectable man.'

On examining a book containing a list of the donations made him by American friends, in aid of his noble design to rescue from the miseries of slavery his relations, I found the names and certificates of persons of the highest respectability. It will be amply sufficient with those who are acquainted with the Abolitionists of the United States, for me to name General Fessenden, and Nathan Winslow, Esq., of Portland, Maine; the Rev. A. A. Phelps, Ellis Gray Loring, and Samuel E. Sewall, Esqs., of Boston, Massachusetts. Being satisfied, by these indubitable vouchers, of Moses Grandy's title to credit, I listened to his artless tale with entire confidence, and with a feeling of interest which all will participate who peruse the following pages. Considering his Narrative calculated to promote a more extensive knowledge of the workings of American slavery, and that its sale might contribute to the object which engages so entirely the mind of Moses, namely, the redemption of those who are in bonds, belonging to his family, I resolved to commit it to the press, as nearly as possible in the language of Moses himself. I have carefully abstained from casting a single reflection or animadversion of my own. I leave the touching story of the self-liberated captive to speak for itself, and the wish of my heart will be gratified, and my humble effort on his behalf be richly rewarded, if this little book is the means of obtaining for my colored brother the assistance which he seeks, or of increasing the zeal of those who are associated for the purpose of ' breaking every yoke and setting the oppressed free.'

GEORGE THOMPSON.

9, *Blandford Place, Regent's Park,*
    October 18*th,* 1842.

NARRATIVE.

My name is Moses Grandy. I was born in Camden county, North Carolina. I believe I am fifty-six years old. Slaves seldom know exactly how old they are; neither they nor their masters set down the time of a birth; the slaves, because they are not allowed to write or read, and the masters, because they only care to know what slaves belong to them.

The master, Billy Grandy, whose slave I was born, was a hard-drinking man; he sold away many slaves. I remember four sisters and four brothers; my mother had more children, but they were dead or sold away before I can remember. I was the youngest. I remember well my mother often hid us all in the woods, to prevent master selling us. When we wanted water, she sought for it in any hole or puddle formed by falling trees or otherwise. It was often full of tadpoles and insects. She strained it, and gave it round to each of us in the hollow of her hand. For food, she gathered berries in the woods, got potatoes, raw corn, &c. After a time, the master would send word to her to come in, promising he would not sell us. But, at length, persons came who agreed

Sell a child from mother

to give the prices he set on us. His wife, with much to be done, prevailed on him not to sell me; but he sold my brother, who was a little boy. My mother, frantic with grief, resisted their taking her child away. She was beaten, and held down; she fainted; and, when she came to herself, her boy was gone. She made much outcry, for which the master tied her up to a peach-tree in the yard, and flogged her.

Another of my brothers was sold to Mr. Tyler, Dewan's Neck, Pasquotank county. This man very much ill treated many colored boys. One very cold day, he sent my brother out, naked and hungry, to find a yoke of steers; the boy returned without finding them, when his master flogged him, and sent him out again. A white lady, who lived near, gave him food, and advised him to try again; he did so, but, it seems, again without success. He piled up a heap of leaves, and laid himself down in them, and died there. He was found through a flock of turkey buzzards hovering over him; these birds had pulled his eyes out.

My young master and I used to play together; there was but two days' difference in our ages. My old master always said he would give me to him. When he died, all the colored people were divided amongst his children, and I fell to young master; his name was James Grandy. I was then about eight years old. When I became old enough to be taken away from my mother and put to field work, I was hired out for the year, by auction, at the court house, every January: this is the common practice with respect to slaves belonging to persons who are under age. This continued till my master and myself were twenty-one years old.

The first who hired me was Mr. Kemp, who used me pretty well; he gave me plenty to eat, and sufficient clothing.

The next was old Jemmy Coates, a severe man. Because I could not learn his way of hilling corn, he flogged me naked with a severe whip, made of a very tough sapling; this lapped round me at each stroke; the point of it at last entered my belly and broke off, leaving an inch and a half outside. I was not aware of it until, on going to work again, it hurt my inside very much, when, on looking down, I saw it sticking out of my body. I pulled it out, and the blood spouted after it. The wound festered, and discharged very much at the time, and hurt me for years after.

In being hired out, sometimes the slave gets a good home, and sometimes a bad one: when he gets a good one, he dreads to see January come; when he has a bad one, the year seems five times as long as it is.

I was next with Mr. Enoch Sawyer, of Camden county. My business was to keep ferry, and do other odd work. It was cruel living. We had not near enough of either victuals or clothes. I was half starved for half my time. I have often ground the husks of Indian corn over again in a hand-mill, for the chance of getting something to eat out of it which the former grinding had left. In severe frosts, I was compelled to go into the fields and woods to work, with my naked feet cracked and bleeding from extreme cold: to warm them, I used to rouse an ox or hog, and stand on the place where it had lain. I was at that place three years, and very long years they seemed to me. The trick by which he kept me so long was this: the court house was but a mile off. At hiring day, he prevented me from going till he went himself and bid for me. On the last occasion, he was detained for a little while by other business; so I ran as quickly as I could, and got hired before he came up.

Mr. George Furley was my next master; he employed me as a car-boy in the Dismal Swamp; I had to drive lumber, &c. I had plenty to eat and plenty of clothes. I was so overjoyed at the change, that I then thought I would not have left the place to go to heaven.

Next year I was hired by Mr. John Micheau, of the same county, who married my young mistress, one of the daughters of Mr. Grandy, and sister of my present owner. This master gave us very few clothes, and but little to eat. I was almost naked. One day he came into the field, and asked why no more work was done. The older people were afraid of him; so I said that the reason was, we were so hungry we could not work. He went home and told the mistress to give us plenty to eat, and at dinner-time we had plenty. We came out shouting for joy, and went to work with delight. From that time we had food enough, and he soon found that he had a great deal more work done. The field was quite alive with people striving who should do most.

He hired me for another year. He was a great gambler. He kept me up five nights together, without sleep night or day, to wait on the gambling table. I was standing in the corner of the room, nodding for want of sleep, when he took up the shovel and beat me with it; he dislocated my shoulder, and sprained my wrist, and broke the shovel over me. I ran away, and got another person to hire me.

This person was Mr. Richard Furley, who, after that, hired me at the court house every year till my master came of age. He gave me a pass to work for myself; so I obtained work by the piece where I could, and paid him out of my earnings what we had agreed on; I maintained myself on the rest, and saved what I could. In this way I was not liable to be flogged and ill used. He paid seventy, eighty, or ninety dollars a year for me, and I paid him twenty or thirty dollars a year more than that.

When my master came of age, he took all his colored people to himself. Seeing that I was industrious and persevering, and had obtained plenty of work, he made me pay him almost twice as much as I had paid Mr. Furley. At that time the English blockaded the Chesapeake, which made it necessary to send merchandise from Norfolk to Elizabeth City by the Grand Canal, so that it might get to sea by Pamlico Sound and Ocracock Inlet. I took some canal boats on shares; Mr. Grice, who married my other young mistress, was the owner of them. I gave him one half of all I received for freight; out of the other half I had to victual and man the boats, and all over that expense was my own profit.

Some time before this, my brother Benjamin returned from the West Indies, where he had been two years with his master's vessel. I was very glad to hear of it, and got leave to go see him. While I was sitting with his wife and him, his wife's master came and asked him to fetch a can of water; he did so, and carried it into the store. While I was waiting for him, and wondering at his being so long away, I heard the heavy blows of a

hammer: after a little while I was alarmed, and
went to see what was going on. I looked into the
store, and saw my brother lying on his back on the
floor, and Mr. Williams, who had bought him, driving staples over his wrists and ankles; an iron bar
was afterwards put across his breast, which was
also held down by staples. I asked what he had
been doing, and was told that he had done nothing
amiss, but that his master had failed, and he was
sold towards paying the debts. He lay in that
state all that night; next day he was taken to jail,
and I never saw him again. This is the usual
treatment under such circumstances. I had to go
by my mother's next morning, but I feared to tell
her what had happened to my brother. I got a boy
to go and tell her. She was blind and very old,
and was living in a little hut, in the woods, after
the usual manner of old, worn-out slaves; she was
unable to go to my brother before he was taken
away, and grieved after him greatly.

It was some time after this that I married a
slave belonging to Mr. Enoch Sawyer, who had
been so hard a master to me. I left her at home,
(that is, at his house,) one Thursday morning,
when we had been married about eight months.
She was well, and seemed likely to be so. We
were nicely getting together our little necessaries.
On the Friday, as I was at work, as usual, with the
boats, I heard a noise behind me, on the road which
ran by the side of the canal. I turned to look, and
saw a gang of slaves coming. When they came
up to me, one of them cried out, ' Moses, my dear ! '
I wondered who among them should know me, and
found it was my wife. She cried out to me, ' I am
gone ! ' I was struck with consternation. Mr. Roger-

son was with them, on his horse, armed with pistols. I said to him, 'For God's sake, have you bought my wife?' He said he had; when I asked him what she had done, he said she had done nothing, but that her master wanted money. He drew out a pistol, and said that, if I went near the wagon on which she was, he would shoot me. I asked for leave to shake hands with her, which he refused, but said I might stand at a distance and talk with her. My heart was so full that I could say very little. I asked leave to give her a dram. He told Mr. Burgess, the man who was with him, to get down and carry it to her. I gave her the little money I had in my pocket, and bade her farewell. I have never seen or heard of her from that day to this. I loved her as I loved my life.

Mr. Grice found that I served him faithfully. He and my young mistress, his wife, advised me, as I was getting money fast, to try to buy myself. By their advice, I asked my master what he would take for me. He wanted $800; and, when I said that was too much, he replied, he could get $1000 for me any minute. Mr. Grice afterwards went with me to him; he said to him that I had already been more profitable to him than any five others of his negroes, and reminded him that we had been playfellows. In this way he got him to consent to take $600 for me. I then went heartily to work, and, whenever I paid him for my time, I paid him something, also, towards my freedom, for which he gave me receipts. When I made him the last payment of the $600 for my freedom, he tore up all the receipts. I told him he ought not to have done so; he replied it did not signify, for, as soon as court day came, he should give me my free papers. On Monday, in court week, I went to him; he was playing at billiards, and would not go with me, but told me to come again the next day; the next day he did the same, and so on daily. I went to his sister, Mrs. Grice, and told her I feared that he did not mean to give them to me; she said she feared so too, and sent for him. He was a very wicked young man; he came, and cursed her, and went out of the house. Mr. Grice was from home; on his return, he went to my master, and told him he ought to give me my free papers; that I had paid for myself, and it was court week, so that there was no excuse. He promised he would; instead of which, he rode away, and kept away till court was over. Before the next court came, he sold me to Mr. Trewitt for $600.

The way in which Mr. Trewitt came to buy me was this: I had left the boats, and had gone with a schooner collecting lumber in Albemarle Sound for the merchants. Coming to Elizabeth City, I found a new store had been opened by Mr. Grice, which Mr. Sutton was keeping: the latter gentleman was glad to see me, and was desirous that I should return to my old employment with the canal boats, as lumber was in great demand at Norfolk. I did so, and sold some cargoes to Mr. Moses Myers, of Norfolk. As I was waiting at the door of his store for settlement, he came up with Mr. Trewitt, whom I did not then know. Mr. Myers said to Mr. Trewitt, 'Here is a captain doing business for you.' Mr. Trewitt then asked me who had chartered the boats, and to whom I belonged. I told him Mr. Sutton had chartered me, and that I had belonged to Mr. James Grandy, but had bought myself. He said he would buy me; on which Mr.

Myers told him he could not, as I had already bought myself, and further said I was one of their old war captains, and had never lost a single thing of the property intrusted to me. Mr. Trewitt said he would buy me, and would see about it as soon as he got to Elizabeth City. I thought no more about it. On my return voyage, I delivered a cargo at Elizabeth City, for Mr. Trewitt. I had been at Mr. Grice's, the owner of the boats; and, on my going away from him to meet Mr. Trewitt for settlement, he said he would go with me, as he wanted money. Opposite the custom house we met Mr. Trewitt, who said, 'Well, captain, I have bought you.' Mr. Grice said, 'Let us have no nonsense; go and settle with him.' Angry words passed between them, one saying he had bought me, and the other denying that he had or could, as I had bought myself already. We all went to Mr. Grice's dwelling house; there Mr. Trewitt settled with me about the freight, and then, jumping up, said, 'Now I will show you, Mr. Grice, whether I am a liar or not.' He fetched the bill of sale; on reading it, Mr. Grice's color changed, and he sent for Mrs. Grice. When she read it, she began to cry; seeing that, I began to cry too. She sent me to her brother, who was at Mr. Wood's boarding house. He was playing at billiards. I said to him, 'Master James, have you sold me?' He said, 'No.' I said he had; when he turned round and went into another room, crying; I followed him. All the gentlemen followed us, saying, 'Captain Grandy, what is the matter?' I told them Master James had sold me again. They asked him why he had done it; he said it was because people had jeered him by saying I had more sense than he had. They would not suffer him to remain in the boarding house, but turned him out, there and then, with all his trunks and boxes. Mrs. Grice, his sister, sued him in my name for my liberty, but he gained the cause. The court maintained that I, and all I could do, belonged to him, and that he had a right to do as he pleased with me and all my earnings, as his own property, until he had taken me to the court house, and given me my free papers, and until, besides that, I had been a year and a day in the Northern States to gain my residence.

So I was forced to go to Mr. Trewitt. He agreed that, if I would pay him the same wages as I paid my late master, and the $600 he gave for me, he would give me my free papers. He bought two canal boats, and, taking me out of Mr. Grice's employment, set me to work them on the same terms as I did for my former master. I was two years and a half in earning $600 to pay for myself the second time. Just when I had completed the payment, he failed. On Christmas eve he gave me a letter to take to Mr. Mews, at Newbegun Creek. I was rather unwilling to take it, wishing to go to my wife; I told him, too, I was going to his office to settle with him. He offered to give me two dollars to take the letter, and said he would settle when I came back : then Mr. Shaw came from another room, and said his vessel was ready loaded, but he had nobody he could trust with his goods; he offered me five dollars to take the vessel down, and deliver the goods to Mr. Knox, who also was at Newbegun Creek. The wind was fair, and the hands on board, so I agreed; it being Christmas eve, I was glad of something to carry to my wife. I ran the vessel down to the mouth of the creek, and anchored; when the moon rose, I went up the river. I reached the wharf, and commenced taking out the goods that night, and delivered them all safely to Mr. Knox next morning. I then took the letter to Mr. Mews, who read it, and, looking up at me, said, 'Well, you belong to me.' I thought he was joking, and said, 'How? What way?' He said, 'Don't you recollect when Trewitt chartered Wilson Sawyer's brig to the West Indies?' I said, I did. He told me Trewitt then came to him to borrow $600, which he would not lend, except he had a mortgage on me : Trewitt was to take it up at a certain time, but never did. I asked him whether he really took the mortgage on me. He replied that he certainly thought Trewitt would have taken up the mortgage, but he had failed, and was not worth a cent, and he, Mews, must have his money. I asked him whether he had not helped me and my young mistress in the court house, when master James fooled me before. He said he did help me all he could, and that he should not have taken a mortgage on me, but that he thought Trewitt would take it up. Trewitt must have received some of the last payments from me, after he had given the mortgage, and knew he should fail; for the mortgage was given two months before this time.

My head seemed to turn round and round; I was quite out of my senses; I went away towards the woods; Mr. Mews sent his waiter after me to persuade me to go back. At first I refused, but afterwards went. He told me he would give me another chance to buy myself, and I certainly should have my freedom that time. He said Mr. Enoch Sawyer wanted to buy me, to be his overseer in the

Swamp. I replied I would never try again to buy myself, and that they had already got $1,200 from me.   My wife* (this was my second wife) belonged to Mr. Sawyer; he told me that her master would not allow me to go to see her, if I would not consent to what he now proposed; for any colored person going on the grounds of a white man, after being warned off, is liable to be flogged, or even shot.   I thus found myself forced to go, although no colored man wishes to live at the house where his wife lives, for he has to endure the continual misery of seeing her flogged and abused, without daring to say a word in her defence.

In the service of Mr. Sawyer, I got into a fair way of buying myself again; for I undertook the lightering of shingles or boards out of the Dismal Swamp, and hired hands to assist me.   But my master had become security for his two sons-in-law at Norfolk, who failed; in consequence of which he sold eighteen colored people, his share of the Swamp, and two plantations.   I was one of the slaves he kept, and after that had to work in the corn-field the same as the rest.   The overseer was a bad one; his name was Brooks.   The horn was blown at sunrise; the colored people had then to march before the overseer to the field, he on horse-

---

* It will be observed that the narrator married a second wife, without having heard of the decease of the first. To explain this fact, it is necessary to state, that the frequent occurrence of cases where husbands and wives, members of Christian societies, were finally separated by sale, led the ministers, some years ago, to deliberate on the subject : they decided that such separation might be considered as the death of the parties to each other, and they therefore agreed to consider subsequent marriages not immoral. The practice is general. It is scarcely necessary to remark, that a more unequivocal and impressive proof of the heinous nature of the system could hardly exist. It breaks up the fondest connections, it tears up the holiest attachments, and induces the ministers of religion, as much as in them lies, to carve the divine law to a fitting with its own infernal exigencies.

back. We had to work, even in long summer days,
till twelve o'clock, before we tasted a morsel, men,
women, and children all being served alike. At
noon the cart appeared with our breakfast. It was
in large trays, and was set on the ground. There
was bread, of which a piece was cut off for each
person; then there was small hominy boiled, that
is, Indian-corn, ground in the hand-mill, and besides this two herrings for each of the men and
women, and one for each of the children. Our
drink was the water in the ditches, whatever might
be its state; if the ditches were dry, water was
brought to us by the boys. The salt fish made us
always thirsty, but no other drink than water was
ever allowed. However thirsty a slave may be, he
is not allowed to leave his employment for a moment to get water; he can only have it when the
hands in working have reached the ditch, at the
end of the rows. The overseer stood with his
watch in his hand, to give us just an hour; when
he said, ' Rise,' we had to rise and go to work again.
The women who had children laid them down by
the hedge-row, and gave them straws and other tri-
fles to play with; here they were in danger from
snakes; I have seen a large snake found coiled
round the neck and face of a child, when its mother
went to suckle it at dinner-time. The hands work
in a line by the side of each other; the overseer
puts the swiftest hands in the fore row, and all must
keep up with them. One black man is kept on purpose to whip the others in the field; if he does not
flog with sufficient severity, he is flogged himself;
he whips severely, to keep the whip from his own
back. If a man have a wife in the same field with
himself, he chooses a row by the side of hers, that,

2

with extreme labor, he may, if possible, help her. But he will not be in the same field if he can help it; for, with his hardest labor, he often cannot save her from being flogged, and he is obliged to stand by and see it; he is always liable to see her taken home at night, stripped naked, and whipped before all the men.   On the estate I am speaking of, those women who had sucking children suffered much from their breasts becoming full of milk, the infants being left at home; they therefore could not keep up with the other hands.   I have seen the overseer beat them with raw hide, so that blood and milk flew mingled from their breasts.   A woman who gives offence in the field, and is large in the family way, is compelled to lie down over a hole made to receive her corpulency, and is flogged with the whip, or beat with a paddle, which has holes in it; at every hole comes a blister.   One of my sisters was so severely punished in this way, that labor was brought on, and the child was born in the field. This very overseer, Mr. Brooks, killed in this manner a girl named Mary; her father and mother were in the field at the time.   He killed, also, a boy about twelve years old.   He had no punishment, or even trial, for either.

There was no dinner till dark, when he gave the order to knock off and go home.   The meal then was the same as in the morning, except that we had meat twice a week.

On very few estates are the colored people provided with any bedding: the best masters give only a blanket; this master gave none; a board, which the slave might pick up any where on the estate, was all he had to lie on.   If he wished to procure bedding, he could only do so by working at nights. For warmth, therefore, the negroes generally sleep near a large fire, whether in the kitchen, or in their log huts; their legs are often in this way blistered and greatly swelled, and sometimes badly burnt: they suffer severely from this cause.

When the water-mill did not supply meal enough, we had to grind with the hand-mill. The night was employed in this work, without any thing being taken from the labor of the day. We had to take turn at it, women as well as men; enough was to be ground to serve for the following day.

I was eight months in the field. My master, Mr. Sawyer, agreed to allow me eight dollars a month, while so employed, towards buying myself; it will be seen he did not give me even that. When I first went to work in the corn-field, I had paid him $230 towards this third buying of my freedom. I told him, one night, I could not stand his field work any longer; he asked, why; I said I was almost starved to death, and had long been unaccustomed to this severe labor. He wanted to know why I could not stand it as well as the rest. I told him he knew well I had not been used to it for a long time; that his overseer was the worst that had ever been on the plantation, and that I could not stand it. He said he would direct Mr. Brooks to give each of us a pint of meal or corn every evening, which we might bake, and which would serve us next morning, till our breakfast came at noon. The black people were much rejoiced that I got this additional allowance for them. But I was not satisfied; I wanted liberty.

On Sunday morning, as master was sitting in his porch, I went to him, and offered to give him the $230 I had already paid him, if, beside them,

he would take for my freedom the $600 he had
given for me. He drove me away, saying I had no
way to get the money. I sat down for a time, and
went to him again. I repeated my offer to procure
the $600, and he again said I could not. He
called his wife out of the room to the porch, and
said to her, ' Don't you think Moses has taken to
getting drunk ? ' She asked me if it was so ; I denied it, when she inquired what was the matter.
Master replied, ' Don't you think he wants me to
sell him ? ' She said, ' Moses, we would not take
any money for you. Captain Cormack put a thousand dollars for you on the supper table last Friday
night, and Mr. Sawyer would not touch it ; he
wants you to be overseer in the Dismal Swamp.'
I replied, ' Captain Cormack never said any thing
to me about buying me ; I would cut my throat
from ear to ear rather than go to him. I know
what made him say so ; he is courting Miss Patsey,
and he did it to make himself look big.' Mistress
laughed and turned away, and slammed to the
door; master shook himself with laughing, and put
the paper he was reading before his face, knowing
that I spoke the truth. Captain Cormack was an
old man who went on crutches. Miss Patsey was
the finest of master's daughters. Master drove me
away from him again.

On Monday morning, Mr. Brooks, the overseer,
blew the horn as usual for all to go to the field. I
refused to go. I went to master, and told him that
if he would give me a paper, I would go and fetch
the $600 ; he then gave me a paper, stating that he
was willing to take that sum for my freedom : so I
hired an old horse and started for Norfolk, fifty
miles off.

When I reached Deep Creek, I went to the house of Captain Edward Minner. He was very glad to see me, for in former days I had done much business for him; he said how sorry he had been to hear that I was at field work. He inquired where I was going. I said, to Norfolk, to get some of the merchants to let me have money to buy myself. He replied, ' What did I always say to you ? Was it not, that I would let you have the money at any time, if you would only tell me when you could be sold ? ' He called Mrs. Minner into the room, and told her I could be sold for my freedom; she was rejoiced to hear it. He said, ' Put up your horse at Mr. Western's tavern, for you need go no farther; I have plenty of old rusty dollars, and no man shall put his hand on your collar again to say you are a slave. Come and stay with me to-night, and in the morning I will get Mr. Garret's horse, and go with you.'

Next morning we set off, and found master at Major Farrence's, at the cross canal, where I knew he was to be that day, to sell his share of the canal. When I saw him, he told me to go forward home, for he would not sell me. I felt sick and sadly disappointed. Captain Minner stepped up to him, and showed him the paper he had given me, saying, ' Mr. Sawyer, is not this your hand-writing ? ' He replied, ' Mistress said, the last word when I came away, I was not to sell him, but send him home again.' Captain Minner said, ' Mind, gentlemen, I do not want him for a slave; I want to buy him for freedom. He will repay me the money, and I shall not charge him a cent of interest for it. I would not have a colored person, to drag me down to hell, for all the money in the world.' A gentleman who was by said it was a shame I should be so treated; I had bought myself so often that Mr. Sawyer ought to let me go. The very worst man as an overseer over the persons employed in digging the canal, Mr. Wiley M'Pherson, was there; he was never known to speak in favor of a colored person; even he said that Mr. Sawyer ought to let me go, as I had been sold so often. At length, Mr. Sawyer consented I should go for $650, and would take no less. I wished Captain Minner to give the extra $50, and not stand about it. I believe it was what M'Pherson said that induced my master to let me go; for he was well known for his great severity to colored people; so that after even he had said so, master could not stand out. The Lord must have opened M'Pherson's heart to say it.

I have said this M'Pherson was an overseer where slaves were employed in cutting canals. The labor there is very severe. The ground is often very boggy; the negroes are up to the middle, or much deeper, in mud and water, cutting away roots and baling out mud; if they can keep their heads above water, they work on. They lodge in huts, or, as they are called, camps, made of shingles or boards. They lie down in the mud which has adhered to them, making a great fire to dry themselves, and keep off the cold. No bedding whatever is allowed them; it is only by work done over his task that any of them can get a blanket. They are paid nothing, except for this overwork. Their masters come once a month to receive the money for their labor; then, perhaps, some few very good masters will give them $2 each, some others $1, some a pound of tobacco, and some nothing at all. The food is more abundant than that of field slaves : indeed, it is the best allowance in America — it consists of a peck of meal and six pounds of pork per week ; the pork is commonly not good ; it is damaged, and is bought, as cheap as possible, at auctions.

M'Pherson gave the same task to each slave ; of course, the weak ones often failed to do it. I have often seen him tie up persons and flog them in the morning, only because they were unable to get the previous day's task done ; after they were flogged, pork or beef brine was put on their bleeding backs to increase the pain ; he sitting by, resting himself, and seeing it done. After being thus flogged and pickled, the sufferers often remained tied up all day, the feet just touching the ground, the legs tied, and pieces of wood put between the legs. All the motion allowed was a slight turn of the neck. Thus exposed and helpless, the yellow flies and musquitoes in great numbers would settle on the bleeding and smarting back, and put the sufferer to extreme torture. This continued all day, for they were not taken down till night. In flogging, he would sometimes tie the slave's shirt over his head, that he might not flinch when the blow was coming ; sometimes he would increase his misery, by blustering, and calling out that he was coming to flog again, which he did or did not, as happened. I have seen him flog them with his own hands till their entrails were visible ; and I have seen the sufferers dead when they were taken down. He never was called to account in any way for it.

It is not uncommon for flies to blow the sores made by flogging ; in that case, we get a strong weed growing in those parts, called the Oak of Jerusalem ; we boil it at night, and wash the sores with the liquor, which is extremely bitter. On this the creepers or maggots come out. To relieve them in some degree, after severe flogging, their fellow-slaves rub their backs with part of their little allowance of fat meat.

For fear the slaves should run away, while unable to work from flogging, he kept them chained till they could work again. This man had from 500 to 700 men under his control. When out of other employment, I sometimes worked under him, and saw his doings. I believe it was the word of this man which gained my freedom. He is dead, but there are yet others like him on public works.

When the great kindness of Captain Minner had set me clear of Mr. Sawyer, I went to my old occupation of working the canal boats. These I took on shares, as before. After a time, I was disabled for a year from following this employment by a severe attack of rheumatism, caught by frequent exposure to severe weather. I was anxious, however, to be earning something towards the repayment of Captain Minner, lest any accident, unforeseen by him or me, should even yet deprive me of the liberty for which I so longed, and for which I had suffered so much. I therefore had myself carried in a lighter up a cross canal in the Dismal Swamp, and to the other side of Drummond's Lake. I was left on the shore, and there I built myself a little hut, and had provisions brought to me as opportunity served. Here, among snakes, bears, and panthers, whenever my strength was sufficient, I cut down a juniper-tree, and converted it into cooper's timber. The camp, like those commonly set up for negroes, was entirely open on one side ; on that side a fire is lighted at night, and a person sleeping puts his feet towards it. One night I was awoke by some animal smelling my face, and snuffing strongly; I felt its cold muzzle. I suddenly thrust out my arms, and shouted with all my might; it was frightened, and made off. I do not know whether it was a bear or a panther; but it seemed as tall as a large calf. I slept, of course, no more that night. I put my trust in the Lord, and continued on the spot; I was never attacked again.

I recovered, and went to the canal boats again; by the end of three years from the time he laid down the money, I entirely repaid my very kind and excellent friend. During this time he made no claim whatever on my services; I was altogether on the footing of a free man, as far as a colored man can there be free.

When, at length, I had repaid Captain Minner, and had got my free papers, so that my freedom was quite secure, my feelings were greatly excited. I felt to myself so light, that I could almost think I could fly; in my sleep I was always dreaming of flying over woods and rivers. My gait was so altered by my gladness, that people often stopped me, saying, 'Grandy, what is the matter?' I excused myself as well as I could; but many perceived the reason, and said, 'O! he is so pleased with having got his freedom.' Slavery will teach any man to be glad when he gets freedom.

My good master, Captain Minner, sent me to Providence, in Rhode Island, to stay a year and a day, in order to gain my residence. But I staid only two months. Mr. Howard's vessel came there laden with corn. I longed much to see my master and mistress, for the kindness they had done me, and so went home in the schooner. On my arrival, I did not stop at my own house, except to ask my wife at the door how she and the children were in health, but went up the town to see Captain and Mrs. Minner.   They were very glad to see me, and consulted with me about my way of getting a living.   I wished to go on board the New York and Philadelphia packets, but feared I should be troubled for my freedom.   Captain Minner thought I might venture, and I therefore engaged myself.   I continued in that employment till his death, which happened about a year after my return from Providence.   Then I returned to Boston ; for, while he lived, I knew I could rely on his protection ; but when I lost my friend, I thought it best to go wholly to the Northern States.

At Boston I went to work at sawing wood, sawing with the whip-saw, laboring in the coal-yards, loading and unloading vessels, &c.   After laboring in this way for a few months, I went a voyage to St. John's, in Porto Rico, with Captain Cobb, in the schooner *New Packet.*   On the return voyage, the vessel got ashore on Cape Cod ; we left her, after doing in vain what we could to right her : she was afterwards recovered.   I went several other voyages, and particularly two to the Mediterranean : the last was to the East Indies, in the ship *James Murray*, Captain Woodbury, owner Mr. Gray.   My entire savings, up to the period of my return from this voyage, amounted to $300 ; I sent it to Virginia, and bought my wife.   She came to me at Boston. I dared not go myself to fetch her, lest I should be again deprived of my liberty, as often happens to free colored people.

At the time, called the time of the Insurrection, about eight years ago, when the whites said the colored people were going to rise, and shot, hanged, and otherwise destroyed many of them, Mrs. Minner thought she saw me in the street, and fainted there. The soldiers were seizing all the blacks they could find, and she knew, if I were there, I should be sure to suffer with the rest. She was mistaken; I was not there.

My son's master, at Norfolk, sent a letter to me at Boston, to say, that if I could raise $450, I might have his freedom; he was then fifteen years old. I had again saved $300. I knew the master was a drinking man, and was therefore very anxious to get my son out of his hands. I went to Norfolk, running the risk of my liberty, and took my $300 with me, to make the best bargain I could. Many gentlemen in Boston, my friends, advised me not to go myself; but I was anxious to get my boy's freedom, and I knew that nobody in Virginia had any cause of complaint against me. So, notwithstanding their advice, I determined to go.

When the vessel arrived there, they said it was against the law for me to go ashore. The mayor of the city said I had been among the cursed Yankees too long; he asked me whether I did not know that it was unlawful for me to land, to which I replied, that I did not know it, for I could neither read nor write. The merchants for whom I had formerly done business came on board, and said they cared for neither the mare (mayor) nor the horse, and insisted that I should go ashore. I told the mayor the business on which I came, and he gave me leave to stay nine days, telling me that if I were not gone in that time, he would sell me for the good of the state.

I offered my boy's master the $300; he counted

the money, but put it back to me, refusing to take less than $450. I went on board to return to Boston. We met with head winds, and put back three times to Norfolk, anchoring each time just opposite the jail. The nine days had expired, and I feared the mayor would find me on board and sell me. I could see the jail, full of colored people, and even the whipping-post, at which they were constantly enduring the lash. While we were lying there by the jail, two vessels came from Eastern Shore, Virginia, laden with cattle and colored people. The cattle were lowing for their calves, and the men and women were crying for their husbands, wives, or children. The cries and groans were terrible, notwithstanding there was a whipper on board each vessel, trying to compel the poor creatures to keep silence. These vessels lay close to ours. I had been a long time away from such scenes; the sight affected me very much, and added greatly to my fears.

One day I saw a boat coming from the shore with white men in it. I thought they were officers coming to take me; and such was my horror of slavery, that I twice ran to the ship's waist to jump overboard into the strong ebb tide then running, to drown myself; but a strong impression on my mind restrained me each time.

Once more we got under way for New York; but, meeting again with head winds, we ran into Maurice's River, in Delaware Bay. New Jersey, in which that place lies, is not a slave state. So I said to the captain, ' Let me have a boat, and set me on the free land once more; then I will travel home over land; for I will not run the risk of going back to Virginia any more. The captain said there was no danger, but I exclaimed, ' No, no! captain, I will not try it; put my feet on free land once again, and I shall be safe.' When I once more touched the free land, the burden of my mind was removed; if two ton weight had been taken off me, the relief would not have seemed so great.

From Maurice's Creek I travelled to Philadelphia, and at that place had a letter written to my wife, at Boston, thanking God that I was on free land again. On arriving at Boston, I borrowed $150 of a friend, and, going to New York, I obtained the help of Mr. John Williams to send the $450 to Norfolk; thus, at length, I bought my son's freedom. I met him at New York, and brought him on to Boston.

Six other of my children, three boys and three girls, were sold to New Orleans. Two of these daughters have bought their own freedom. The eldest of them, Catherine, was sold three times after she was taken away from Virginia; the first time was by auction. Her last master but one was a Frenchman; she worked in his sugar-cane and cotton fields. Another Frenchman inquired for a girl, on whom he could depend, to wait on his wife, who was in a consumption. Her master offered him my daughter; they went into the field to see her, and the bargain was struck. Her new master gave her up to his sick wife, on whom she waited till her death. As she had waited exceedingly well on his wife, her master offered her a chance of buying her freedom. She objected to his terms as too high; for he required her to pay him $4 a week out of her earnings, and $1,200 for her freedom. He said he could get more for her, and told her she might get plenty of washing, at a dollar a

dozen: at last she agreed.   She lived near the
river side, and obtained plenty of work.   So anxious was she to obtain her freedom, that she worked
nearly all her time, days and nights, and Sundays.
She found, however, she gained nothing by working on Sundays, and therefore left it off.   She paid
her master punctually her weekly hire, and also
something towards her freedom, for which he gave
her receipts.   A good stewardess was wanted for
a steamboat on the Mississippi; she was hired for
the place at $30 a month, which is the usual salary;
she also had liberty to sell apples and oranges on
board; and, commonly, the passengers give from
twenty-five cents to a dollar to a stewardess who
attends them well.   Her entire incoming, wages
and all, amounted to about sixty dollars a month.
She remained at this employment till she had paid
the entire sum of $1,200 for her freedom.

As soon as she obtained her free papers, she left
the steamboat, thinking she could find her sister
Charlotte.   Her first two trials were unsuccessful;
but on the third attempt she found her at work in
the cane-field.   She showed her sister's master her
own free papers, and told him how she had bought
herself; he said that, if her sister would pay him
as much as she paid her master, she might go too.
They agreed, and he gave her a pass.   The two
sisters went on board a steamboat, and worked together for the wages of one, till they had saved the
entire $1,200 for the freedom of the second sister.
The husband of Charlotte was dead; her children
were left behind in the cotton and cane-fields;
their master refuses to take less than $2,400 for
them; their names and ages are as follows: Zeno,
about fifteen; Antoinette, about thirteen; Joseph,

about eleven; and Josephine, about ten years old. Of my other children, I only know that one, a girl, named Betsey, is a little way from Norfolk, in Virginia. Her master, Mr. William Dixon, is willing to sell her for $500.

I do not know where any of my other four children are, nor whether they be dead or alive. It will be very difficult to find them out: for the names of slaves are commonly changed with every change of master: they usually bear the name of the master to whom they belong at the time: they have no family name of their own by which they can be traced. Through this circumstance, and their ignorance of reading and writing, to which they are compelled by law, all trace between parents and children, who are separated from them in childhood, is lost in a few years. When, therefore, a child is sold away from its mother, she feels that she is parting from it forever; there is little likelihood of her ever knowing what of good or evil befalls it. The way of finding out a friend or relative who has been sold away for any length of time, or to any great distance, is to trace them, if possible, to one master after another, or if that cannot be done, to inquire about the neighborhood where they are supposed to be, until some one is found who can tell that such or such a person belonged to such or such a master: and the person supposed to be the one sought for, may, perhaps, remember the names of the persons to whom his father and mother belonged: there is little to be learned from his appearance, for so many years may have passed away that he may have grown out of the memory of his parents, or his nearest relations. There are thus no lasting

family ties to bind relations together, not even the
nearest, and this aggravates their distress when
they are sold from each other. I have little hope
of finding my four children again.

I have lived in Boston ever since I bought my
freedom, except during the last year, which I have
spent at Portland, in the state of Maine.

I have yet said nothing of my father. He was
often sold through the failure of his successive
owners. When I was a little boy, he was sold
away from us to a distance : he was then so far off
that he could not come to see us oftener than once
a year. After that, he was sold to go still farther
away, and then he could not come at all. I do not
know what has become of him.

When my mother became old, she was sent to
live in a little lonely log-hut in the woods. Aged
and worn-out slaves, whether men or women, are
commonly so treated. No care is taken of them,
except, perhaps, that a little ground is cleared
about the hut, on which the old slave, if able, may
raise a little corn. As far as the owner is concerned, they live or die, as it happens : it is just the
same thing as turning out an old horse. Their
children, or other near relations, if living in the
neighborhood, take it by turns to go at night with
a supply saved out of their own scanty allowance
of food, as well as to cut wood and fetch water for
them : this is done entirely through the good feelings of the slaves, and not through the masters'
taking care that it is done. On these night-visits,
the aged inmate of the hut is often found crying
on account of sufferings from disease or extreme
weakness, or from want of food or water in the
course of the day : many a time, when I have

drawn near to my mother's hut, I have heard her
grieving and crying on these accounts: she was
old and blind too, and so unable to help herself.
She was not treated worse than others: it is the
general practice. Some few good masters do not
treat their old slaves so: they employ them in
doing light jobs about the house and garden.

My eldest sister is in Elizabeth City. She has
five children, who, of course, are slaves. Her
master is willing to sell her for $100: she is grow-
ing old. One of her children, a young man, cannot
be bought under $900.

My sister Tamar, who belonged to the same
master with myself, had children very fast. Her
husband had hard owners, and lived at a distance.
When a woman who has many children belongs to
an owner who is under age, as ours was, it is customary to put her and the children out yearly to
the person who will maintain them for the least
money, the person taking them having the benefit
of whatever work the woman can do. But my
sister was put to herself in the woods. She had a
bit of ground cleared, and was left to hire herself
out to labor. On the ground she raised corn and
flax; and obtained a peck of corn, some herrings,
or a piece of meat, for a day's work among the
neighboring owners. In this way she brought up
her children. Her husband could help her but
little. As soon as each of the children became big
enough, it was sold away from her.

After parting thus with five, she was sold along
with the sixth, (about a year and a half old,) to the
speculators; these are persons who buy slaves in
Carolina and Virginia, to sell them in Georgia and
New Orleans. After travelling with them more

3

than one hundred miles, she made her escape, but could not obtain her child to take it with her. On her journey homeward she travelled by night, and hid herself in thick woods by day. She was in great danger on the road, but in three weeks reached the woods near us: there she had to keep herself concealed : I, my mother, and her husband, knew where she was : she lived in a den she made for herself. She sometimes ventured down to my mother's hut, where she was hid in a hollow under the floor. Her husband lived ten miles off ; he would sometimes set off after his day's work was done, spend part of the night with her, and get back before next sunrise : sometimes he would spend Sunday with her. We all supplied her with such provisions as we could save. It was necessary to be very careful in visiting her ; we tied pieces of wood or bundles of rags to our feet, that no track might be made.

In the wood she had three children born ; one of them died. She had not recovered from the birth of the youngest when she was discovered and taken to the house of her old master.

She was afterwards sold to Culpepper, who used her very cruelly. He was beating her dreadfully, and the blood was streaming from her head and back one day when I happened to go to his house. I was greatly grieved, and asked his leave to find a person to buy her : instead of answering me, he struck at me with an axe, and I was obliged to get away as fast as I could. Soon after this he failed, and she was offered for sale in Norfolk ; there Mr. Johnson bought her and her two children, out of friendship for me : he treated her exceedingly well, and she served him faithfully ; but it was not long before she was claimed by a person to whom Culpepper had mortgaged her before he sold her to Johnson. This person sold her to Long, of Elizabeth City, where again she was very badly treated. After a time, this person sold her to go to Georgia: she was very ill at the time, and was taken away in a cart. I hear from her sometimes, and am very anxious to purchase her freedom, if ever I should be able. Two of her children are now in North Carolina, and are longing to obtain their freedom. I know nothing of the others, nor am I likely ever to hear of them again.

The treatment of slaves is mildest near the borders, where the free and slave states join: it becomes more severe, the farther we go from the free states. It is more severe in the west and south than where I lived. The sale of slaves most frequently takes place from the milder to the severer parts: there is great traffic in slaves in that direction, which is carried on by the speculators. On the frontier between the slave and free States there is a guard; no colored person can go over a ferry without a pass. By these regulations, and the great numbers of patrols, escape is made next to impossible.

Formerly slaves were allowed to have religious meetings of their own; but after the insurrection which I spoke of before, they were forbidden to meet even for worship. Often they are flogged if they are found singing or praying at home. They may go to the places of worship used by the whites; but they like their own meetings better. My wife's brother Isaac was a colored preacher. A number of slaves went privately into a wood to hold meetings; when they were found out, they

were flogged, and each was forced to tell who else
was there.   Three were shot, two of whom were
killed, and the other was badly wounded.   For
preaching to them, Isaac was flogged, and his back
pickled; when it was nearly well, he was flogged
and pickled again, and so on for some months; then
his back was suffered to get well, and he was sold.
A little while before this, his wife was sold away
with an infant at her breast; and out of six children, four had been sold away by one at a time.
On the way with his buyers he dropped down
dead; his heart was broken.

Having thus narrated what has happened to myself, my relatives and near friends, I will add a few
matters about slaves and colored people in general.

Slaves are under fear in every word they speak.
If, in their master's kitchen, they let slip an expression of discontent, or a wish for freedom, it is often
reported to the master or mistress by the children
of the family who may be playing about: severe
flogging is often the consequence.

I have already said that it is forbidden by law
to teach colored persons to read or write.   A few
well-disposed white young persons, of the families
to which the slaves belonged, have ventured to
teach them, but they dare not let it be known they
have done so.

The proprietors get new land cleared in this way.
They first 'dead' a piece of ground in the woods
adjoining the plantation: by 'deading' is meant
killing the trees, by cutting a nick all round each,
quite through the bark.   Out of this ground each
colored person has a piece as large as he can tend
after his other work is done; the women have
pieces in like manner.   The slave works at night,

cutting down the timber and clearing the ground; after it is cleared, he has it for his own use for two or three years, as may be agreed on. As these new clearings lie between the woods and the old cultivated land, the squirrels and raccoons first come at the crops on them, and thus those on the planter's land are saved from much waste. When the negro has had the land for the specified time, and it has become fit for the plough, the master takes it, and he is removed to another new piece. It is no uncommon thing for the land to be taken from him before the time is out, if it has sooner become fit for the plough. When the crop is gathered, the master comes to see how much there is of it; he then gives the negro an order to sell that quantity; without that order, no storekeeper dare buy it. The slave lays out the money in something tidy to go to meeting in, and something to take to his wife.

The evidence of a black man, or of ever so many black men, stands for nothing against that of one white; in consequence of it the free negroes are liable to great cruelties. They have had their dwellings entered, their bedding and furniture destroyed, and themselves, their wives and children, beaten; some have even been taken, with their wives, into the woods, and tied up, flogged, and left there. There is nothing which a white man may not do against a black one, if he only takes care that no other white man can give evidence against him.

A law has lately been passed in New Orleans prohibiting any free colored person from going there.

The coasting packets of the ports on the Atlantic commonly have colored cooks. When a vessel goes from New York or Boston to a port in the slaveholding states, the black cook is usually put in jail till the vessel sails again.

No colored person can travel without a pass.   If he cannot show it, he may be flogged by any body; in such a case he often is seized and flogged by the patrols.   All through the slave states there are patrols; they are so numerous that they cannot be easily escaped.

The only time when a man can visit his wife, when they are on different estates, is Saturday evening and Sunday.   If they be very near to each other, he may sometimes see her on Wednesday evening.   He must always return to his work by sunrise; if he fail to do so, he is flogged.   When he has got together all the little things he can for his wife and children, and has walked many miles to see them, he may find that they have all been sold away, some in one direction, and some in another.   He gives up all hope of seeing them again, but he dare not utter a word of complaint.

It often happens that, when a slave wishes to visit his wife on another plantation, his own master is busy or from home, and therefore he cannot get a pass.   He ventures without it.   If there be any little spite against his wife or himself, he may be asked for it when he arrives, and, not having it, he may be beaten with thirty-nine stripes, and sent away.   On his return, he may be seized by the patrol, and flogged again for the same reason ; and he will not wonder if he is again seized and beaten for the third time.

If a negro has given offence to the patrol, even by so innocent a matter as dressing tidily to go to a place of worship, he will be seized by one of them, and another will tear up his pass ; while one is

flogging him, the others will look another way ; so
when he or his master makes complaint of his having been beaten without cause, and he points out
the person who did it, the others will swear they
saw no one beat him. His oath, being that of a
black man, would stand for nothing ; but he may
not even be sworn ; and, in such a case, his tor-
mentors are safe, for they were the only whites
present.

In all the slave states there are men who make
a trade of whipping negroes ; they ride about inquiring for jobs of persons who keep no overseer ;
if there is a negro to be whipped, whether man or
woman, this man is employed when he calls, and
does it immediately ; his fee is half a dollar. Wid-
ows and other females, having negroes, get them
whipped in this way. Many mistresses will insist
on the slave who has been flogged begging pardon
for her fault on her knees, and thanking her for the
correction.

A white man, who lived near me in Camden
county, Thomas Evidge, followed this business.
He was also sworn whipper at the court house.
A law was passed that any white man detected in
stealing should be whipped. Mr. Dozier frequently missed hogs, and flogged many of his negroes on
suspicion of stealing them ; when he could not, in
his suspicions, fix on any one in particular, he
flogged them all round, saying that he was sure of
having punished the right one. Being one day
shooting in his woods, he heard the report of
another gun, and shortly after met David Evidge,
the nephew of the whipper, with one of his hogs
on his back, which had just been shot. David was
sent to prison, convicted of the theft, and sen-

tenced to be flogged. His uncle, who vapored about greatly in flogging slaves, and taunted them with unfeeling speeches while he did it, could not bear the thought of flogging his nephew, and hired a man to do it. The person pitched on chanced to be a sailor; he laid it well on the thief; pleased enough were the colored people to see a white back for the first time subjected to the lash.

Another man of the same business, George Wilkins, did no greater credit to the trade. Mr. Carnie, on Western Branch, Virginia, often missed corn from his barn. Wilkins, the whipper, was very officious in pointing out this slave and that, as very likely to be the thief; with nothing against them but his insinuations, some were very severely punished, being flogged by this very Wilkins, and others, at his instigation, were sold away. One night, Mr. Carnie, unknown to his colored people, set a steel trap in the barn; some of the negroes, passing the barn before morning, saw Wilkins standing there, but were not aware he was caught. They called the master, that he might seize the thief before he could escape; he came and teased Wilkins during the night; in the morning, he exposed him to the view of the neighbors, and then set him at liberty without further punishment.

The very severe punishments to which slaves are subjected, for trifling offences, or none at all, their continued liability to all kinds of ill usage, without a chance of redress, and the agonizing feelings they endure at being separated from the dearest connections, drive many of them to desperation, and they abscond. They hide themselves in the woods, where they remain for months, and, in some cases, for years. When caught, they are flogged with extreme severity, their backs are pickled, and the flogging repeated as before described: after months of this torture, the back is allowed to heal, and the slave is sold away. Especially is this done when the slave has attempted to reach a free state.

In violent thunder-storms, when the whites have got between feather-beds to be safe from the lightning, I have often seen negroes, the aged as well as others, go out, and, lifting up their hands, thank God that judgment was coming at last. So cruelly are many of them used, that judgment, they think, would be a happy release from their horrible slavery.

The proprietors, though they live in luxury, generally die in debt: their negroes are so hardly treated that no profit is made by their labor. Many of them are great gamblers. At the death of a proprietor, it commonly happens that his colored people are sold towards paying his debts. So it must and will be with the masters while slavery continues: when freedom is established, I believe they will begin to prosper greatly.

Before I close this Narrative, I ought to express my grateful thanks to the many friends in the Northern States, who have encouraged and assisted me: I shall never forget to speak of their kindness, and to pray for their prosperity. I am delighted in saying, that not only to myself, but to very many other colored persons, they have lent a benevolent and helping hand. Last year, gentlemen whom I know bought no less than ten families from slavery; and this year they are pursuing the same good work. But for these numerous and heavy claims on their means and their kindness, I should have had no need to appeal to the generosity of the British public; they would gladly have helped me to redeem all my children and relations.

When I first went to the Northern States,— which is about ten years ago, — although I was free as to the law, I was made to feel severely the difference between persons of different colors. No black man was admitted to the same seats in churches with the whites, nor to the inside of public conveyances, nor into street coaches or cabs : we had to be content with the decks of steamboats in all weathers, night and day, not even our wives or children being allowed to go below, however it might rain, or snow, or freeze; in various other ways, we were treated as though we were of a race of men below the whites. But the abolitionists boldly stood up for us, and, through them, things are much changed for the better. Now, we may sit in any part of many places of worship, and are even asked into the pews of respectable white families; many public conveyances now make no distinction between white and black. We begin to feel that we are really on the same footing as our fellow-citizens. They see we can and do conduct ourselves with propriety, and they are now admitting us, in many cases, to the same standing with themselves.

During the struggles which have procured for us this justice from our fellow-citizens, we have been in the habit of looking in public places for some well-known abolitionists, and, if none that we knew were there, we addressed any person dressed as a Quaker; these classes always took our part against ill usage, and we have to thank them for many a contest in our behalf.

We were greatly delighted by the zealous efforts and powerful eloquence in our cause of Mr. George

Thompson, who came from our English friends to aid our suffering brethren. He was hated and mobbed by bad men amongst the whites; they put his life in great danger, and threatened destruction to all who sheltered him. We prayed for him, and did all we could to defend him. The Lord preserved him, and thankful were we when he escaped from our country with his life. At that time, and ever since, we have had a host of American friends, who have labored for the cause night and day; they have nobly stood up for the rights and honor of the colored man; but they did so at first in the midst of scorn and danger. Now, thank God, the case is very different. William Lloyd Garrison, who was hunted for his life by a mob in the streets of New York, has lately been chairman of a large meeting in favor of abolition, held in Faneuil Hall, the celebrated public hall of Boston, called the ' Cradle of Liberty.'

I am glad to say also that numbers of my colored brethren now escape from slavery; some by purchasing their freedom, others by quitting, through many dangers and hardships, the land of bondage. The latter suffer many privations in their attempts to reach the free states. They hide themselves, during the day, in the woods and swamps; at night, they travel, crossing rivers by swimming or by boats they may chance to meet with, and passing over hills and meadows which they do not know : in these dangerous journeys they are guided by the north-star, for they only know that the land of freedom is in the north. They subsist only on such wild fruit as they can gather, and as they are often very long on their way, they reach the free states almost like skeletons. On their arrival they have

no friends but such as pity those who have been
in bondage, the number of whom, I am happy to
say, is increasing; but if they can meet with a man
in a broad-brimmed hat and Quaker coat, they
speak to him without fear — relying on him as a
friend.   At each place the escaped slave inquires
for an abolitionist or a Quaker, and these friends of
the colored man help them on their journey north-
wards, until they are out of the reach of danger.

Our untiring friends, the abolitionists, once obtained a law that no colored person should be seized
as a slave within the free states; this law would
have been of great service to us, by ridding us of
all anxiety about our freedom while we remained
there; but I am sorry to say, that it has lately been
repealed, and that now, as before, any colored person who is said to be a slave, may be seized in the
free states and carried away, no matter how long
he may have resided there, as also may his children and their children, although they all may have
been born there.   I hope this law will soon be altered again.   At present many escaped slaves are
forwarded by their friends to Canada, where, under
British rule, they are quite safe.   There is a body
of ten thousand of them in Upper Canada; they
are known for their good order, and loyalty to the
British government; during the late troubles, they
could always be relied on for the defence of the
British possessions against the lawless Americans
who attempted to invade them.

As to the settlement of Liberia, on the coast of
Africa, the free colored people of America do not
willingly go to it.   America is their home: if their
forefathers lived in Africa, they themselves know
nothing of that country.   None but free colored

people are taken there: if they would take slaves, they might have plenty of colonists. Slaves will go any where for freedom.

We look very much to England for help to the cause of the slaves. Whenever we hear of the people of England doing good to black men, we are delighted, and run to tell each other the news. Our kind friends, the abolitionists, are very much encouraged when they hear of meetings and speeches in England in our cause. The first of August, the day when the slaves in the West Indies were made free, is always kept as a day of rejoicing by the American colored free people.

I do hope and believe that the cause of freedom to the blacks is becoming stronger and stronger every day. I pray for the time to come when freedom shall be established all over the world. Then will men love as brethren; they will delight to do good to one another; and they will thankfully worship the Father of All.

And now I have only to repeat my hearty thanks to all who have done any thing towards obtaining liberty for my colored brethren, and especially to express my gratitude to those who have helped me to procure for myself, my wife, and so far of my children, the blessing of freedom — a blessing of which none can know the value, but he who has been a slave. Whatever profit may be obtained by the sale of this book, and all donations with which I may be favored, will be faithfully employed in redeeming my remaining children and relatives from the dreadful condition of slavery.

NOTE.

I have paid the following sums to redeem myself and relatives from slavery, viz :

For my own freedom,	. . .	$1,850
For my wife's "	. . . .	300
For my son's "	. . . . .	450
Grandchild's "	. . . . . .	400
To redeem my kidnapped son,	.	60

———$3,060

I now wish to raise $100 to buy the freedom of my sister Mary, who is a slave at Elizabeth City, N. C. Her master says he will take that sum for her.   M. G.

Boston, Jan. 19, 1844.